MAMOULIAN

MAMOULIAN

LIFE ON STAGE AND SCREEN

David Luhrssen

UNIVERSITY PRESS OF KENTUCKY

Scholarly publisher for the Commonwealth,
serving Bellarmine University, Berea College, Centre
College of Kentucky, Eastern Kentucky University,
The Filson Historical Society, Georgetown College,
Kentucky Historical Society, Kentucky State University,
Morehead State University, Murray State University,
Northern Kentucky University, Transylvania University,
University of Kentucky, University of Louisville,
and Western Kentucky University.

Editorial and Sales Offices: The University Press of Kentucky
663 South Limestone Street, Lexington, Kentucky 40508-4008
www.kentuckypress.com

17 16 15 14 13   5 4 3 2 1

Library of Congress Cataloging-in-Publication Data

Luhrssen, David.
Mamoulian : life on stage and screen / David Luhrssen.
pages cm. — (Screen classics)
Includes bibliographical references and index.
ISBN 978-0-8131-3676-9 (hardcover : alk. paper) —
ISBN 978-0-8131-3686-8 (epub) — ISBN 978-0-8131-4119-0 (pdf)
1. Mamoulian, Rouben. 2. Motion picture producers and directors—United States—Biography. 3. Theatrical producers and directors—United States—Biography. I. Title.
PN1998.3.M3205L84 2012
791.4302'33092—dc23
[B]

2012038978

This book is printed on acid-free paper meeting
the requirements of the American National Standard
for Permanence in Paper for Printed Library Materials.

Manufactured in the United States of America.

Member of the Association
of American University Presses

To Hacheck Chobanian

Contents

Introduction

Forgotten Innovator

Rouben Mamoulian is one of the twentieth century's most important overlooked cultural figures. His bicoastal life as a director in Hollywood and on Broadway was highly unusual and led to a roster of influential accomplishments in film and theater, yet historians in both fields usually mention him only in passing. While several of his films are familiar to fans of classic Hollywood movies from the 1930s through the 1950s, Mamoulian's name is seldom associated in popular memory with *Dr. Jekyll and Mr. Hyde*, *Queen Christina*, and *The Mark of Zorro*. *Porgy and Bess*, *Oklahoma!* and *Carousel* are among the most familiar musicals of the last century, yet Mamoulian's role in bringing them to the stage is seldom understood. Even the important part he played in establishing the grammar of contemporary filmmaking is usually relegated to footnotes. Before Mamoulian, the sound movies that followed *The Jazz Singer* were static, stagy, and often slightly ridiculous. He helped restore motion to motion pictures and eventually endowed them with color, cultivating all the while the idea that film could be artful as well as entertaining.

"To make your life a true work of art is the highest achievement man can aspire to," he wrote, and he strove to remain true to his ambition. Never less than elegant in appearance and erudite in speech, Mamoulian maintained the image and substance of an artist-intellectual, and yet was also a man of practical affairs. One New York reporter caught the essence of Mamoulian after the 1927 premiere of *Porgy*. "He seems spontaneously simple and direct in his conversation, talking about directing and the stage as a banker talks about banking and money; enthusiastically, but with his feet on the ground. His complete lack of affectation indicates a well-balanced mind."[1]

Mamoulian was engaged in a lifelong struggle to maintain the integrity of his artistic vision in the commercial environs of Hollywood and Broadway, but his vision encompassed the importance of finding a popular audience. During auditions for the debut run of *Oklahoma!* he argued with choreographer Agnes de Mille, insisting that only beautiful, leggy dancers need apply. The audience expected no less and without an audience, there would be no show.

Because he considered himself an artist and a humanist, the culture of celebrity held no appeal for Mamoulian. Except for a reported affair with Greta Garbo and occasional sightings in the company of starlets, he was seldom the subject of gossip columnists or show business writers except when he clashed with producers over artistic control or money. His public life was defined by his role as a director, in which capacity he was remembered for his exuberance and intelligence as well as his habit of smoking cigars. Mamoulian was raised in comfort and insisted on living comfortably. His personal life was conducted in private or around the parties of his Hollywood and Broadway colleagues and left little impression on his contemporaries. "He carried with him a sort of unspoken protocol, a grand-ducal dignity and reserve that made his arrival anywhere something of an event," remembered a friend from his early years in the United States before Mamoulian made a name for himself on Broadway. He added, "I don't think I ever heard him give an equivocal judgment, even for the sake of tact and good manners, when the critical values of art were involved."[2]

Mamoulian's arrival in America coincided with a significant inflow of creativity and talent as artists and intellectuals poured from Europe into the New World. He always stressed that he was not a political refugee, but came to Rochester, New York, from London to accept a promising position at the Eastman School of Music. Of course, the full truth is more complicated. Mamoulian and the survivors of his family could not have returned to the nascent Soviet Union without being branded as class enemies. The Mamoulians were wealthy Armenian subjects of the Russian Empire who had lived for generations in Georgia; well educated and part of the region's cultural elite, Mamoulian came to the United States draped in a cosmopolitan aura that served him well in a nation still laboring under a sense of cultural inferiority. His carefully groomed, slightly exotic image was one of his passkeys to success.

Unlike many émigrés of his class and credentials, Mamoulian never looked down on American culture but was fascinated by its vitality. At the same time, he was never blind to the faults of his adopted nation. On the New York stage, where he was welcomed for his ties to Stanislavski, he was among the first American directors to insist on an all-black cast in a major dramatic production, *Porgy* (1927). He continued to push for African or African American themes on Broadway in *Porgy and Bess* (1935), *St. Louis Woman* (1946), and *Lost in the Stars* (1949).

With the advent of talking pictures, successful Broadway directors were much in demand by movie studios. Mamoulian proved more inventive than most of his colleagues, more attuned to the particular possibilities of cinema. With his first film, *Applause* (1929), Mamoulian freed movies from the cumbersome technology of early sound stages. He would be first to employ overlapping dialogue and voice-overs, doing so against the wishes of studio moguls who feared he would confuse audiences. He encouraged the development of multi-track recording, new lenses, and, with *Dr. Jekyll and Mr. Hyde* (1932), special effects. He directed *Becky Sharp* (1935), Hollywood's first nonanimated, three-color Technicolor feature. Mamoulian's earliest movies, especially *Queen Christina* (1933), were thematically daring for their time.

Mamoulian was associated with many of the great names in entertainment and the arts. He collaborated with dancers such as Martha Graham and Fred Astaire and choreographer Hermes Pan. On stage he oversaw Alfred Lunt and Pearl Bailey and such future Hollywood stars as Katharine Hepburn, Bette Davis, Claude Rains, and Sydney Greenstreet. He worked with Kurt Weill on a stage musical and Maurice Chevalier and Jeanette MacDonald on a movie musical. The list of other actors he directed on-screen is impressive and includes Marlene Dietrich, Greta Garbo, Henry Fonda, Gary Cooper, Mickey Rooney, Walter Huston, Agnes Moorehead, Gene Tierney, Tyrone Power, Anthony Quinn, Barbara Stanwyck, Adolphe Menjou, Lee J. Cobb, William Holden, Irene Dunne, Randolph Scott, Walter Brennan, Dorothy Lamour, Ida Lupino, Nigel Bruce, and Fredric March.

Mamoulian was at the center of Hollywood in the 1930s and into the 1940s, attending glittering parties in the company of Charlie

Chaplin, Edward G. Robinson, Dashiell Hammett, and Lillian Hellman. He was one of the studios' highest-paid directors, but was marginalized after being fired from the film noir classic *Laura* (1944) and worked only sporadically in Hollywood afterward. Although he was a seminal director of musicals with *Applause* and *Love Me Tonight* (1932), he was never pegged to the genre. Likewise, he directed one of the great early horror films, *Dr. Jekyll and Mr. Hyde,* but never developed a reputation as a horror director. He also worked frequently in comedy and costume drama and gangster pictures. The early film historians of the 1950s and 1960s tended to privilege directors associated with particular genres, crediting John Ford for his association with westerns, Howard Hawks with screwball comedy and action pictures, and Alfred Hitchcock with thrillers. Eclectic, harder to categorize filmmakers were often overlooked. Film critic and historian Andrew Sarris notoriously dismissed Mamoulian as "an innovator who ran out of innovations."[3]

The assessment is accurate but perhaps unfair. Mamoulian's vocation as a filmmaker was cut short by conflicts with studio management, whose members regarded him as difficult for his insistence on making movies according to his design. He was seldom allowed to fulfill his cinematic ambitions after the mid-1940s. With most of his earlier films shelved under the stricter regime of the Hollywood Production Code after 1934, and reduced after 1944 to completing only a couple of pictures, Mamoulian's fame evaporated. By the time he was given a final chance, at the end of 1959, to direct Elizabeth Taylor in *Cleopatra,* his troublesome reputation as a stickler for detail and an artist unwilling to compromise undermined his position. He was fired for the last time from a movie that became, in the hands of his replacement, one of Hollywood's greatest financial disasters. A more recent assessment than Sarris's is more to the point. "Mamoulian is out of fashion now," wrote critic and historian David Thompson, "his reputation dwarfed by people remarkable for their coarseness."[4]

The development of Hollywood narrative filmmaking, however, cannot be understood apart from Mamoulian. Although the director has been honored with a star on the Hollywood Walk of Fame, he is among the least recognized among the important filmmakers from the era of Hollywood's studio system. His little-understood career on Broadway and in Hollywood opens a fascinating portal into the worlds of American theater and cinema from the 1920s through the 1950s. Mamoulian left behind a body of work that was both commercial and infused with artistic integrity. Despite interference from studio bosses, Mamoulian balanced head with heart, intellect with emotion, and box office success with critical respect. The aspirations Mamoulian brought to all his movies and his struggle for artistic control remain valid concerns for filmmakers and film audiences in the twenty-first century.

Chapter 1

Caucasian Youth

Rouben Mamoulian was born at the edge of the earth, in the heart of Eurasia at the seam where continents meet. His birthplace, Tiflis, was a cosmopolitan outpost on the lawless frontier between East and West. Mamoulian grew up in a city where men and women wearing the latest European fashions mingled in the outdoor markets with mountain folk clad in kaftans, where fruit vendors sang couplets as they made their rounds and musicians with wooden flutes serenaded passersby on the streets. On any given day Tiflis welcomed merchants from Paris and Constantinople, commercial agents from Calcutta and Madras, and traders from across the vast Russian Empire. Many languages were spoken. The great political and cultural ideas of the day were eagerly entertained in the city's cafes and salons.

At the time of Mamoulian's birth on October 8, 1897, Tiflis was the seat of the Russian governor-general of Transcaucasia, a dominion incorporating the present-day republics of Georgia, Armenia, and Azerbaijan. Tiflis, now called Tbilisi, has since become Georgia's capital.

Mamoulian, however, was not Georgian. Like more than one-third of the capital's inhabitants he was Armenian, an ethnic minority whose business interests dominated the city's political life through the local duma, or town council.[1] The diverse population of Tiflis is unsurprising given the history of the Caucasus and the long relationship between Georgians and Armenians. The Orthodox churches of both peoples shared similar myths of origin and architectural traditions. The Bible had been translated from Armenian to Georgian in the fifth century, many Armenian words entered the Georgian language, and the thirty-eight characters of Georgia's alphabet bear close similarity to Armenia's distinctive letters.

The spiritual capital of Armenians was in Armenia proper, at Etchmiadzin, the sanctuary of the supreme patriarch, but by the late nineteenth century Tiflis had become "the intellectual, cultural, and financial center" of the Russian Empire's Armenian subjects.[2] Mamoulian was born to a family well situated in all three respects. Rouben's father, Zacharie (1866–1966), had been a colonel in the Russian army. His mother, Virginie Kalantarian (1876–1972), was related to General M.T. Loris-Melikov, an Armenian in the tsar's service who defeated the Turks at Kars (1877–78). Virginie's father was a wealthy banker and landowner who made his son-in-law a director of the Second Mutual Credit Bank.

Virginie's greatest love, apart from her son, was the theater. She became enraptured from the age of twelve when a neighbor woman brought her to see *Vartan Mamigonian*, a play about a fifth-century warrior saint who led the Armenians in a struggle of conscience and national religious identity against the Persians. Braving her father's traditional disapproval of the theater as a den of illusion and immorality, she often appeared onstage, was president of the Tiflis Dramatic Society, and cofounded a drama company called the People's House. By her own account, she acted in three Georgian films early in the Soviet period, shortly before she emigrated to the West.[3]

Tiflis had been a center for Transcaucasian theater since 1836 when the Armenian merchant and dramatist Galust Shermazanian turned the ground floor of his townhouse into a playhouse for satires on bureaucracy and other social ills. By the 1860s, formally organized Armenian theater companies existed in Tiflis, many of them vaudevilles spoofing the local bourgeoisie. One playwright of enduring significance emerged from the period in Tiflis, Gabriel Sundukian. His dramas explored "the effects of incipient capitalism and modernism on urban life in the tradition of Gogol and Ostrovsky." Like much of the work Mamoulian would later direct, Sundukian's plays expressed the defiance of little men against corrupt magnets and strong women against an unresponsive patriarchy. Sundukian has also been compared to Ibsen, although he handled his subjects with a bittersweet, lighter touch than his dour Scandinavian contemporary.[4]

Virginie's career as actress and impresario coincided with a remarkable expansion of Russian provincial theaters beginning in the 1880s, which afforded new opportunities for women who aspired to autonomy and creative expression.[5] Willful and talented, Virginie lived beyond the conventional expectations for a woman of her class and time, eagerly probing the boundaries of a world with limited sympathy for ambitious women. Coded and in various costumes, the image of his mother would be impressed upon the female characters in most of Mamoulian's films. The tension in his parents' marriage between Zacharie, a sensualist and inveterate womanizer, and Virginie, an artist who cultivated platonic affairs with men of the theater, would be replayed in his movies as the pull between the selfish and the divine in human nature.

The proliferation of Armenian-language theater in Tiflis was part of a national, political, and cultural renaissance of Armenians under the protection of the Romanovs.[6] Rouben was born in a crossroads town at a fertile moment for his own people, yet his formative cultural experience was never insular or exclusionary. In the environs of Tiflis, with its maze of narrow alleys opening onto cobbled courtyards hung with fancifully carved balconies and verandas, the revival of Armenian and Georgian national cultures was celebrated even as the cafes hummed with conversation over the wider world. Newspapers and magazines thrived in many languages, as did academies, dramatic societies, and orchestras. In his youth Rouben learned at least five languages, including Armenian, Georgian, Russian, French, and possibly some English.

In the years preceding World War I, many important Armenian cultural figures emerged from Tiflis in playwriting, poetry, and literature. None played as widely on the world stage as composer Aram Khachaturian, born seven years after Mamoulian. The author of *Sabre Dance* and other music resonant of the Caucasus recalled Tiflis as "a surprising city of sounds . . . saturated with music."[7] Aram's brother Suren became a director at the Moscow Art Theatre, which Rouben would attend.

Not all was well in the city of his birth as discontent simmered in the outlying districts. Like other cities of the Russian Empire in the late nineteenth century, Tiflis experienced the growth of an urban proletariat as rural populations migrated to cities in search of factory work. Armenians owned many of Tiflis's industries. Working conditions were often poor, encouraging militant groups by the example of the ills of capitalism. A young Bolshevik called Joseph Djugashvili, later known to the world as Stalin, embraced Marxism after his expulsion from the Tiflis Orthodox Seminary in 1899 and completed his education by borrowing the works of Marx and Darwin from a local lending library.

Mamoulian was reticent about his early life and preferred, once he had established himself in the United States, to cultivate an image of exotic Old World cosmopolitanism. In public he neither alluded to the genocide that killed many hundreds of thousands of Armenians in the neighboring Ottoman Empire nor to the Bolshevik Revolution, whose reverberations drove the Mamoulians from the comfort of Tiflis and into the unknown. He avoided speaking of his younger sister, Svetlana, who married a British soldier stationed in Tiflis during the international military intervention against the Bolsheviks in 1918 and died in poverty in London in the early 1920s. Rouben also made for London and from there to America, where his parents eventually followed.

The years before his permanent exile from the Caucasus cannot be reconstructed with precision, given the brief and contradictory accounts from Mamoulian and the sketchy and subjective memoirs of his mother, handwritten in the 1960s and discovered among Mamoulian's papers after his death. What can be gathered is that the Mamoulian house was a salon for Tiflis's Armenian intelligentsia and for visiting actors and artists. The Mamoulian family often went to the theater. Rouben's maternal family possessed a sprawling dacha in the country, surrounded by gardens, greenhouses, and stables. He recalled with great fondness his paternal grandmother, Kato Babo. "People gathered in large groups in the evening to sit at the feet of my grandmother and listen to one of her marvelous stories. . . . Later you find yourself pondering the point she made, and, like a seed, it seemed to grow with you and give you help, courage and a lift when you most needed it." Mamoulian also remembered mystical intimations in childhood, the experience of "living in two worlds, the visible and the hidden—the hidden being the strongest."[8]

The memory of a physics lesson in his Tiflis gymnasium would influence the rhythm of the performances he would direct on stage and screen. His teacher asserted that a marching company of soldiers crossing a stone bridge "is always ordered to break step, because if it walked in step, the power of its rhythmic vibration would destroy the bridge," Mamoulian recalled. "It stuck in my mind that rhythm can have a great power."[9]

The childhood memories he bestowed on interviewers often referenced points of inspiration for his filmmaking. For example, the rhythmic progression of images in the unforgettable closing scene of *Queen Christina,* with the camera moving in for a tight close-up of Greta Garbo's enigmatic face, was stimulated by memories of a magic lantern given him by his parents for Christmas. "I thought of that long glass slide on which there were four separate pictures that could be projected on a white sheet or a wall by gradually moving the glass slide in front of the lens," Mamoulian said.[10]

He was exposed to ideas about America at a young age through literature. "As a child I read all of Mark Twain and Bret Harte and O. Henry, in Russian," Mamoulian recalled. His exposure to American and British authors was not unlikely given the wealth of foreign literature available in translation during the Russian Empire's cultural "Silver Age," which corresponded to Mamoulian's childhood and youth. During this time the lurid, thrilling undertones of fin de siècle literature and art nouveau continued to persist in the Russian Empire. "By the time I was seventeen I had subscribed to the slogan *ars gratia ars*—art for art's sake," Mamoulian said, repeating the aesthetic motto promoted by James McNeil Whistler and Oscar Wilde. "Well, by the time I got to be twenty I had outgrown this silly notion."[11] By the time he turned twenty the collapse of the Russian Empire and the Bolshevik Revolution (1917) left Mamoulian with little time for silly ideas as he scrambled to find footing in a world where certainty had crumbled.

The Mamoulian family had already experienced exile. They may have fled unrest in Georgia once before, if under circumstances less dangerous and of shorter duration than the events following the Bolshevik Revolution. An extended visit in Paris, a customary port of refuge for Russians escaping the politics of their homeland, apparently ended in 1906 when the Mamoulians returned home to Georgia. The length of their stay was given as two years in Virginie's account; the reason for their return was explained as the death of her father. Later in life Rouben consistently claimed a sojourn lasting six years, during which he attended the prestigious Lycée Montaigne in the same class as René Clair, but this is unlikely.[12] A *lycée* is a secondary school and Rouben was most likely only nine years old when he returned to Tiflis. While Rouben and Virginie agree on 1905 as the beginning of their stay in Paris, the end date of their sojourn is in dispute. Mamoulian may have exaggerated his time in Paris in order to burnish the polished, cosmopolitan image he always cultivated.

Both Rouben and Virginie left behind incomplete accounts. Although she complained in her memoir that Russian authorities were persecuting "foreigners," Virginie explained that a European tour with her Armenian theater troupe brought her to Paris in 1905. The explanation is probably correct in part, but fails to account for the presence of her otherwise employed husband and their two children throughout the time in Paris. While Virginie may have performed in Europe, and she may have received a message of gratitude from President Theodore Roosevelt for organizing a Paris benefit for the victims of the San Francisco earthquake (April 1906), as Mamoulian sometimes claimed, he contradicted himself: "People are always talking about the starving Armenians. To me this is a strange thing because one of my earliest recollections, as a child in Tiflis, is seeing my mother raise money for the starving Americans of the San Francisco earthquake."[13] The Mamoulians' departure from Tiflis was most likely connected to a violent upheaval called the "Armenian Church Crisis."

From 1903 through 1905 the Russian governor-general of Transcaucasia, Prince Grigorii Golitsyn, launched a repressive policy of Russification against his Armenian subjects. The centerpiece of his scheme was the confiscation of Armenian Church property, including its schools, and the imposition of a Russian curriculum in a campaign of forced assimilation. The Armenian Revolutionary Federation, an ethnic-based socialist party whose primary aim had been the liberation of Armenians in the Ottoman Empire, turned its guns and bombs on the Russian administration, wounding Golitsyn and killing hundreds of officials. The Armenian Church organized mass protests, and even Armenian Marxists rallied to the defense of the church, historically the unifying symbol of Armenian culture and national aspiration. By the end of 1905 the tsar rescinded the oppressive policy, recalled Golitsyn, and appointed a conciliatory viceroy in his stead.[14] One of the deposed governor-general's relatives, Alexander Golitsyn, would begin his Hollywood career as an art director as a set illustrator for Mamoulian's *Queen Christina*.

In addition to the Church Crisis, the Caucasus was shaken by the failed October 1905 revolution in St. Petersburg. Public order was not restored in Georgia until the end of January 1906. In the aftermath the

Caucasus settled down to a low simmer, although the region's ethnic and social tensions remained unresolved. The year 1906, after hostilities in Tiflis had settled down, corresponds to Virginie's chronology for the conclusion of the Mamoulians' Paris sojourn. The family resumed its normal pace of life after returning to Tiflis, with Virginie acting as hostess for cultural gatherings in their home. Rouben attended gymnasium and was fond of recalling the day he played violin for the tsar.[15]

If the performance ever occurred, it most likely happened in 1914. With the outbreak of World War I, Nicholas II toured the Caucasus preparing Armenian political and religious leaders for the coming campaign against the Ottoman Turks. Tiflis's Armenian mayor, Aleksandr Khatisian, was given money from the tsarist regime to organize volunteer brigades under the slogan "The war to final victory and everything for the war." Armenians responded enthusiastically, seeing the world crisis as an opportunity to liberate their brethren across the border from Turkish rule.

Zacharie was recalled to the army. As Transcaucasia became a military frontline, Rouben was sent away, sitting out the darkening war years as a law student at Moscow University. In his recollection both parents tried to dissuade him from a theatrical career because the profession was too unstable. Since he showed talent in geometry and mathematics, they urged him to study engineering. The Mamoulians compromised with law.[16] Perhaps Zacharie tried to force his son, already in love with the stage, to prepare for a legal or civil service career in preference to the financial uncertainty of the theater. However, a liberal arts education through the study of jurisprudence was common among Russia's gentry and upper bourgeoisie. Mamoulian may have embroidered the story of struggle between an artistic son and his worried parents when recalling his early life. In his adult life he was always a practical man of the world as well as an artist, and in his youth, he may already have understood the value of a career to fall back on if the performing arts failed to provide him with a living.

While enrolled at the university, Rouben pursued his artistic inclinations in amateur drama clubs and several months of night classes at one of the world's most important theaters in the early years of the last century, Konstantin Stanislavski's famed Moscow Art Theatre. The experience would exert an enduring influence on his directing. "You have to put the truth on the screen—the whole truth, not a fraction of the truth," Mamoulian insisted decades later in an echo of Stanislavski.[17] The Moscow Art Theatre's quest for revelation of the internal spiritual and psychological nature of its characters and its revulsion against a declamatory style of acting were part of the general movement away from copybook versions of Western European art forms during the Russian Silver Age. Unlike the solipsism that often accompanied Stanislavski's American offshoot, the method acting characteristic of Hollywood during the years of Mamoulian's decline, the 1950s, the Russian students of Stanislavski Mamoulian encountered were not focused on psychological self-absorption but reflected the Eastern Orthodox ethos of Russian culture, as redefined by Dostoyevsky and Tolstoy, in a self-emptying that allowed actors to live through their roles to access their inner meaning.

Mamoulian met the master, although probably only in passing. "A marvelous man with lucid blue eyes," he recalled of Stanislavski many years later. However, he rejected "the complete realism" of Stanislavski and studied acting under Evgeny Vakhtangov in the Art Theatre's Third Studio. The scion of a wealthy Armenian merchant family, Vakhtangov was an important theater director in his own right who continued to work into the Bolshevik period. Vakhtangov became an innovator within the Stanislavski system, revising and editing according to his own devices and emphasizing theatricality over realism. "Let the audience not forget for even a second that it is in a theater. Let it constantly realize that the actor is an expert playing a role," Vakhtangov taught. The importance of stylization in acting and design would never be lost on Mamoulian. "Naturalism doesn't really satisfy me," he said. "It's very strange. But when you stylize something properly, its impact is more real than if you played it naturalistically."[18]

Mamoulian's life was never murkier than in the period after 1917 when the Russian Empire descended into a civil war involving not only Reds against Whites but Bolshevik versus Menshevik Communists, anarchists and nationalists, and a dozen foreign armies marching at cross-purposes. Mamoulian said that he returned to Tiflis after the disorder of the Bolshevik Revolution by walking, hopping trains, and begging for rides. Flush with the excitement and insights he had gained in Moscow, he wrote theater criticism for a local newspaper and, following his mother's path, founded a theater company and appeared in the production of Gogol's *The Inspector General*.[19]

According to the account found in his mother's memoirs, Virginie fled Tiflis in the wake of revolutionary turmoil with both her children. The Mamoulians feared the growing power of the Mensheviks, who dominated the workers soviets that rose up in Tiflis after the tsar's abdication in October 1917 and gained ascendance over the newly independent Democratic Republic of Georgia. Zacharie was apparently absent at this time, still in the military or unable to return home in the chaos. Virginie, Svetlana, and Rouben wandered between opposing armies, heads down during the shooting; robbed by bandits, they sustained themselves through impromptu performances employing the family's thespian talents. After the British army occupied Tiflis on December 25, 1918, the Mamoulians slipped back into the city. Svetlana then married below her class to a common soldier, a mechanic by trade, and left with him for London when the British pulled out during the first half of 1919.

Virginie's reminiscences reflect the unstable and Byzantine politics of the Caucasus in the interregnum between the empire and the Soviet Union. The Georgian Mensheviks were eager to dispossess wealthy Armenians and distrusted the Armenian Revolutionary Federation, suspected of working in a cryptic alliance with the Bolsheviks because of Moscow's professed pro-Armenian line. The Mensheviks were not above playing to the resentment of Georgians, especially the industrial proletariat of Tiflis, over the prominent role of Armenians in Georgian politics, commerce, and culture.[20] When the Mensheviks returned, Rouben went to live in London with his sister, Virginie wrote.

Leaving Georgia for good in 1920, Mamoulian would not see his birthplace again until a half century later, when he visited Tbilisi as a guest of the Soviet government. By his account he stayed briefly in Paris among exiled Russian actors before moving on to London, where he enjoyed the first success of his long exile.

Zacharie and Virginie apparently found the Bolshevik regime congenial after it was forcibly installed in Tiflis on February 26, 1921. In a distant corner of the nascent Soviet Union, in the years before the full implications of Soviet policy became apparent, Bolshevik rule may have seemed a respite from chaos. According to Virginie's memoirs, Zacharie decided to visit Svetlana again in 1924. The final Menshevik uprising in rural Georgia, which took thousands of lives, may have spurred the trip. From London, Zacharie instructed Virginie to sell their house and possessions and follow him. By the time she arrived her daughter had succumbed to tuberculosis in the dampness and poverty of lower-class London. Rouben was already gone, having departed in 1923 for a new life in the New World.

Chapter 2

From West End to Rochester

With the Russian civil war and the Bolshevik victory, many Russian subjects, including intellectuals and artists of all sorts, found themselves in exile from their homeland. Some were stranded in Manchuria; others established flourishing communities in Prague, Paris, and Berlin. With his sister already living in London, one of the world's great centers for theater, the British capital was an obvious choice for a young man of his ambitions, yet he claimed no political or professional motives. "I did not flee. I simply went to visit my sister," he later insisted.[1]

By the time he arrived on New Year's Eve, 1920, Russian refugees were already active in London theater, especially ballet, which Russian dancers and choreographers lifted to new heights before World War I, but also in opera and other fields. Mamoulian might have already met some of these émigrés in Paris, including Theodore Komisarjevsky, an important director and stage designer from the Stanislavski milieu who presented groundbreaking performances in opera in London and would be acclaimed for introducing British audiences to Chekhov. Fifteen years older than Mamoulian, Komisarjevsky expounded many of the ideas already familiar to the young hopeful. When he founded an acting studio in Moscow in 1910, Komisarjevsky promised, "the naturalistic ideas of the theatre of Stanislavski will be completely unknown. It is to be a theatre purely esthetic and theatrical," a harmony of color and form, scenery and costumes, music and light. In his stage work Mamoulian would mirror many of Komisarjevsky's imaginative visual concepts, including the older man's ingenious use of a fine meshed gauze screen stretched across the proscenium, an illusion that pushed the actors into the distance without diminishing their size.[2]

Meanwhile, Mamoulian addressed himself to mastering English, "the last of my eight languages," and lived comfortably for a short time on a monthly allowance from his father until the worsening situation in Georgia made the stipend impossible. Mamoulian claimed he was reduced to lodging in an unheated room, although he always maintained a polished appearance and might have embroidered his starving artist tale for the sake of good storytelling. He always found money to attend the theater. Mamoulian later recalled his excitement on learning that Sarah Bernhardt and Eleonora Duse, rivals as the most famous actresses in the world, were both scheduled to perform at the London Pavilion in October 1922. "I took a pencil and dedicated the next half hour to some complicated calculations," he said. "At the end of that time I had the hard facts in front of me: Bernhardt and Duse would cost me five dinners, three breakfasts, two movies, a quarter of a pound of smoking tobacco, and two and a half haircuts! There it was in a nutshell—take it or leave it. And I took it, of course."[3]

Mamoulian's entry into the London theater came through a fellow refugee from the Russian Empire, Grigori Macaroff, formerly of the Imperial Opera in St. Petersburg. Macaroff was rehearsing a Russian variety show, featuring song and dance along with dramatic and comical sketches, in the former Russian embassy on Belgrave Square. Mamoulian was desperate for a chance to direct. "Why don't you let me try?" he begged Macaroff. "Don't pay me. Let me rehearse for a few weeks and then see if you like it. If it's no good, you can always fire me." Macaroff was generous with the young aspirant, paying him a salary of 30 shillings a week plus 10 for directing rehearsals.[4]

Members of the Macaroff Theatre had been engaged to sing musical interludes in the upcoming premiere of a three-act play on the Russian Revolution, Austin Page's *The Beating on the Door.* During Mamoulian's rehearsals at the old Russian embassy, a cast member of the variety show invited Page and Alexander Nethersole, manager of London's St. James's Theatre, to watch.[5] The eagerness of British theater veterans to seek out the émigrés is no surprise given the Western vogue for Russian culture that began before World War I with Diaghilev and Stravinski, whose primeval-modern, Euro-Asian aesthetic was pleasantly alien yet strangely familiar to Western eyes and ears.

Although only twenty-five and unknown outside Tiflis, Mamoulian was asked to codirect *The Beating on the Door.* Nethersole and Page were probably happy to find a talented young Russian director, even if he was Armenian, familiar not only with the play's critique of Bolshevism but the aesthetics of contemporary Russian theater. It was a remarkable turn of events, even if Mamoulian always enhanced the story by claiming he was only twenty-three at the time. "To direct a professional production in London at that early age was unprecedented," Mamoulian said. "The management put into my contract that whenever asked, in public or in print, as to how old I was, my answer should be: 'Around thirty.'"[6] The obliqueness of such an answer, and the fuller story it obscured, would be echoed throughout Mamoulian's life. Although warm and personable, he crafted the persona of a slightly ambiguous figure of uncertain provenance. Standing over six feet, with jet-black hair and a dark complexion, Mamoulian cut a suave, exotic figure on the London streets. He rarely spoke of his family or background and kept his private life a mystery.

With *The Beating on the Door,* Mamoulian began his long career of wrestling with authority figures over his artistic vision by clashing with his elderly British codirector and cast of familiar names from the London stage, including Athole Stewart and Mary Jerrold. "The first three days of rehearsal were the worst of my life. They were terribly polite, but their very politeness was like a dagger," he recalled. On the fourth day, Mamoulian quit. "I realized that my conception of the production was drastically different from that of my distinguished colleague who was more than twice my age," he explained. "It was a matter of honesty." Mamoulian fought for the integrity of his ideas, even when it spelled lost opportunities. Although "I badly needed both the money and the break," Mamoulian stood firm. His defiance paid off when Neversole and Page offered him the sole directorship.[7]

While directing *The Beating on the Door,* Mamoulian was still sorting through his influences. "I was totally under the influence of the Stanislavski method of the Moscow Art Theatre," he said. "You know, utter realism—chopping wood, real wood, naturalistic action and all that." It would be the last production he would direct in that manner.

"I discovered I had no affinity for naturalism on the stage. In my subsequent work, my aim was always rhythm and poetic stylization." Such were the goals of several of Stanislvaski's pupils, including Mamoulian's teacher Vakhtangov, and Mamoulian never wholly rejected Stanislavski, calling him "the greatest man in the theatre."[8]

The Beating on the Door opened on November 6 and enjoyed only a modest run of fifteen performances. The play was negatively reviewed for its script and the acting, with no mention made of Mamoulian's role. The venue, however, was notable. *The Beating on the Door* played at St. James's Theatre, a prestigious twelve-hundred-seat house in London's West End that had witnessed the premiere of Oscar Wilde's *The Importance of Being Earnest* and became the springboard to Hollywood for Laurence Olivier, Vivien Leigh, and Claude Rains.[9]

Although *The Beating on the Door* could not be mistaken for a success, the production became Mamoulian's gateway to America. Apparently, the little-known young director caught the eye of Russian impresario and tenor Vladimir Rosing, a successful opera producer in London who had just accepted management of the new Rochester American Opera Company, an outgrowth of the lavishly endowed Eastman School of Music founded in 1922 by the American camera tycoon George Eastman. The inventor of roll film, who brought photography into everyday life and made motion pictures possible, was a septuagenarian bachelor from an old American family; passionate about music, Eastman retained a classical quartet to serenade him at breakfast. An eclectic array of world-famous artists performed at the magnificently endowed Eastman Theatre near the Eastman Kodak offices in Rochester, New York, including Paderewski, Pavlova, and Toscanini along with Nellie Melba, Isadora Duncan, Jascha Heifetz, Paul Whiteman, and the Russian Ballet. The industrial city near Lake Ontario boasted a wealthy class ensconced in mansions behind deep lawns, yet Rochester would have been an unlikely center for such cultural activity if not for Eastman's philanthropy. Although he saw his mission as bringing music to the American public, Eastman largely staffed his music school with Europeans for their aura of sophistication.[10]

According to Eastman student Paul Horgan, who became a prize-winning novelist after leaving the school, Rosing convinced the camera tycoon that "the superb establishment in Rochester should be the seat of America's first modern opera company, whose taste would overcome the dramatically ridiculous conventions of the traditional opera, and whose members should be young, handsome, plausible figures of drama."[11] Although Mamoulian had enjoyed music lessons in Tiflis and dabbled in directing music for the Macaroff Theatre, his appointment to a rising opera company in a foreign land was a leap of good fortune.

Mamoulian always maintained that he turned down another offer after *The Beating on the Door*, a position at Jacques Herbertot's Theatre des Champs-Elysées in Paris alongside the peripatetic Komisarjevsky and renowned French actor Louis Jouvet, who in later years directed premiers by Sartre and Gide. Herbertot tried to engage Mamoulian's intellect through "four or five days of Socratic dialogue." Eastman proved more persuasive by accessing Mamoulian's imagination. The young man was impressed by the tycoon's three hundred-word telegram, a lengthy and expensive message to send across the transatlantic cable in those years, and was intrigued by America. "As a boy at school in Paris I'd adored *Les Aventures de Buffalo Bill;* I remembered my mother's letter from Teddy Roosevelt; and anyway, I'd never seen such a long telegram."[12]

Eastman was not alone among the American elite in his admiration for Europe and eagerness to raise the country's cultural level with an infusion of European artists. As an outgrowth of the Eastman School of Music, the new opera company was expected to uphold European standards in an American context. Despite producing great works of literature in the nineteenth century that were embraced by the world, most Americans continued to labor under the mark of inferiority as a cultural colony of Europe. The Russian Revolution was only the first in a series of epoch-shattering events whose refugees differed significantly from the huddled masses that came to America in earlier years. Russia was soon followed by other nations in experiencing a massive hemorrhaging of talent through political upheaval. American institutions, in Hollywood as well as more established fields, were financially able to indulge their voracious appetite for all things European. "I was certain that this must be a wealthy country," Mamoulian observed on landing in New York in the middle of 1923.[13] Along with his fascination with America and the promise of a substantial salary from Eastman, Mamoulian was eager to try his hand at the *Gesamtkunstwerk* of opera, which allowed him to stage a complete work of performance in accord with the theories he had learned in Moscow.

Mamoulian cut an elegantly Old World figure upon arriving in America. Tall, slender, and black haired, with a pince-nez perched on his prominent nose, he wore beautifully tailored Savile Row suits and spats and carried a gold-headed black walking stick. He began teaching at the Eastman School in the fall semester of 1923, determined to give his students a broad education in the performing arts. Fifty years later Paul Horgan wrote a warmly remembered memoir of an instructor who taught with authority, sympathy, and humor. "His English was at that time thoughtful and cultivated," but not yet fluent. "You felt that he was always just ahead of his sentences, consciously selecting and arranging his words." If Rosing and Eastman intended to hire an artist whose scope was broad and erudition profound, they were not disappointed. In Horgan's classes Mamoulian referred to painting, sculpture, literature, and philosophy "in order to shed light from all possible quarters upon the musical and theatrical problems at hand."[14]

Mamoulian employed Stanislavski's "circles of attention" for class exercises, awing students with his own powers of concentration. Horgan recalls Mamoulian telling his class that "if at every second and with every gesture I concentrate wholly upon my own dramatic problem, you will see everything and you will believe everything, though I will use no props, no speech, no co-actors, and no program notes."[15] Mamoulian was among the first directors in America to employ the ideas of Stanislavski, teaching them to his students just as fellow alumni from the Moscow Art Theatre, Richard Boleslavski and Maria Ouspenskaya, formed the American Laboratory Theater School in New York, the institution that would drill Lee Strasberg and Stella Adler in method acting.

The Kodak tycoon George Eastman watched Mamoulian's performances on opening night from his reserved seat in the mezzanine of his marbled theater, a black skullcap pulled over his white hair. "Eastman, of course, was only interested in the musical aspects," Mamoulian said. "I was already seeking a truly dramatic theatre, a theatre that would combine all the elements of movement, dancing, acting, music, singing, décor, lighting, colour and so on." He was fearless in disagreeing with his patron's ideas on directing theater and was one of the few people who openly disagreed with the camera baron. Some of their arguments ended in shouting matches. "He could have had an easier and earlier popularity if he had permitted himself flattery now and then," Horgan said. Despite their arguments, Eastman showed respect and even fondness for Mamoulian. When the director announced that he reached "the end of my street" at the school and wanted to move on to New York, Eastman granted Mamoulian a two-month leave of absence. Mamoulian returned to Rochester at the end of his leave. "No one wanted me," he said dejectedly.[16]

No one could fault Mamoulian for lack of energy or commitment. For the Rochester American Opera's debut, the third act of Verdi's *Rigoletto,* Mamoulian supervised three separate student casts in an arrangement that provided each student with a full set of experiences. Eastman insisted on English in all American Opera performances, contending that to lift the language barrier was to open opera to a wider audience.[17]

The artifice of opera, and early cinema, was ideal for Mamoulian's developing sensibility. "Style is actually your point of view on life—on the world," he explained. "In other words, any play or film has to have the elements of life's truth in it. . . . But the outward expression of it can be highly stylized and by stylizing it you are intensifying it and the emotion." He added that the actor must not only portray the world he knows but also "imply and suggest the world as you would like it to be." Without that dimension of imagination, a play or film "lacks inspiration and it really doesn't stay with you. You'll find in analyzing every work of art, whether it is literature, drama, music, painting—you see the world and you also see the other world. The one we're longing for."[18]

The American Opera's second production, Charles Gounod's *Faust,* opened on December 17, less than a month after *Rigoletto*'s last night. Mamoulian's ambitious production involved a cast of seventy, including chorus and ballet on a stage whose width was "magnificently ample for opera, but which in its depth was barely able to take a vaudeville act." The local press praised Mamoulian for his imaginative interpretation of the prison scene in act 4. Using a scrim, Mamoulian made it appear that Faust and Mephistopheles were outside the prison as the curtain rose until, as if by magic, they materialized inside the locked cell with Marguerite. The black-clad Mephisto was "a figure of monstrously shadowy significance. . . . The means by which this suggestion is achieved are simple, chiefly light effects."[19] The shadows created by the lighting accented the rhythm of the actors and became extensions of the characters as they cascaded across the backdrop and stage floor. Mamoulian mastered the still-recent application of electricity to the theater, which allowed a modulation of light, through dimmers on a switchboard, that had never been possible in the age of candles, kerosene, and gaslight.

Eastman rewarded Mamoulian's success with more work, and despite his patrician bearing, the director shouldered his responsibility with an immigrant's characteristic sweat and determination. The Eastman Theatre presented multimedia programs featuring a pit orchestra, student performances, newsreels, and screenings of Hollywood silent films. Mamoulian occasionally directed the student performances, unifying them thematically with the films and music.

The assembly line of classes and productions gave Mamoulian ample opportunity to hone his skills as well as his aesthetics, which would remain consistent in Hollywood and on Broadway. Little was left to chance. "I believe in overall design," Mamoulian said, reflecting on his career in his twilight years. "It's quite fashionable, I hear it so frequently, the fellow says, 'Oh, I go on the set and I improvise.' That's ridiculous. Improvising is for the birds and for amateurs."[20]

From January through November 1924, Mamoulian directed eight productions for the American Opera Company, usually excerpts of operas booked for one-week runs, beginning with Rossini's *The Barber of Seville* on January 13. For act 3 of *Tannhauser,* opening on March 2, Mamoulian told the local press that Wagner's aesthetic "is fundamentally the same that we are trying to put into life . . . that is, to produce operas as music-dramas, to have music, singing, dramatic action and scenery blended into a perfect rhythmical harmony." The production was praised for its staging: "the scene emerges out of darkness: the foreground is backed by curtains, with a drop on which is indicated the castle on the height: the idea is simple and by lighting is made effective."[21]

Mamoulian filled the Eastman stage through the end of the year with excerpts from Gounod's *Romeo and Juliet,* Tchaikovsky's *The Queen of Spades,* Charles Wakefield Cadman's *Shanewis,* Gilbert and Sullivan's *H.M.S. Pinafore,* and Mussorgsky's *Boris Godunov.* Most of the repertoire was familiar to any cultivated European, but with one exception. *Shanewis* was Mamoulian's first encounter with distinctly American material in its story of a Native American woman's tragic love for an Anglo-American man.

Mamoulian was busier than ever during the summer of 1924. He was named artistic director of a Rochester community theater, one of many such civic cultural organizations that sprang up across America in those years. He announced a search for plays by local writers, but never saw one through to production. Mamoulian's demand for artistic control caused friction with the theater's board; he resigned by the end of summer.[22]

Inspired by the success of *Faust* act 4, Mamoulian began 1925 by mounting the opera in its entirety. The production was praised for its lack of "ponderousness," the "simplicity about the whole thing which made both the story and the music come with an entirely new face." Mamoulian was probably pleased when one critic noticed that the well-drilled chorus was "really a part of the story and of the various scenes in which they appeared."[23] With *Faust,* he had achieved a true Gesamtkunstwerk, a performance embracing all the arts, visual and musical as well as theatrical.

Mamoulian triumphed again two months later with a full version of Bizet's *Carmen.* Once again, he managed to cast an older standard in a modern light. One critic raved that the direction "assumed a striving actuality" and was "a remarkably successful study in the psychology of color."[24]

Nearly a year later Mamoulian reached his peak at Rochester with *Sister Beatrice,* Paul Horgan's English translation of Maurice Maeterlinck's *Soeur Beatrice,* performed on January 15 and 16, 1926. Mamoulian likely felt an affinity with the poet-philosopher-playwright Maeterlinck for his leading role in the symbolist movement, which sought to loosen the grip of realism and naturalism in the arts by suggesting the mystery of existence and the power of the unconscious. For the Belgian playwright, dramatic confrontation was less important than the atmospherics of tension. Symbolism was influential on Russian culture during Mamoulian's formative years, encouraging a synthesis of the visual and auditory, the spiritual and the material. When Vsevolod Meyerhold staged *Soeur Beatrice* in Moscow in 1906, he deployed the actors and chorus as a kind of living bas-relief in the mystic medieval tale of an unfaithful nun. The Moscow Art Theatre also mounted productions of Maeterlinck, belying its reputation for rigid realism. "Like Edgar Allan Poe, Stanislavski asserted a certain reality within the fantasy."[25]

Mamoulian explained that he strove to "integrate all the elements—pedestrian, every-day action and dance, dialogue with song, and rhythm in all the movements." He assigned Eastman's organist Otto Luening to produce a score echoing the cadence of Gregorian chant. Martha

Graham, only months before becoming a sensation in New York City, choreographed the dance movement. According to the program notes, "The Music completes the action and is being used throughout the whole play, not as an incidental accompaniment. The Spoken Word is treated not as the main element in the drama but as additional to theatrical action. Scenery, Costumes, and Light are used in the same way of Music and Word, supplementing theatrical movement and joining with it to form an artistic unit." Using rhythm as the metronome, actors moved between song, dance, and recitation as lights changed and scenery moved into place.[26]

Mamoulian spent much of his remaining months at Eastman presenting scenes from *Carmen,* Saint-Saëns's *Sampson and Delilah,* and Beethoven's *Fidelio* on February 12 and 13 and excerpts from Franz Lehar's *The Count of Luxembourg* for one week beginning March 21.

The art of motion was important in Mamoulian's concept of total theater, and in that spirit he pushed for a new program in Rochester, the Eastman School of Dance and Dramatic Action. Horgan explained the name by recalling that the eccentric George Eastman "did not much like the sound of the word *acting,* or the word *theater,* or *theater art.*"[27]

In an oft-told story, Mamoulian faced down the skeptical tycoon. "You have fifteen minutes, Mamoulian," Eastman said brusquely, marking the seconds on his pocket watch as the director protested. "You have thirteen minutes left," he soon added, and as Mamoulian continued to press for a dance program, he snarled, "Are you arguing with me, Mamoulian?" When the director held his ground with a resounding "Yes!" the tycoon finally relented.[28]

Mamoulian drew on classical aesthetics to explain the new program. "In Greek thought . . . Dance and dramatic action were thought of as twin arts." He added, "The whole body was to become a graceful instrument at the service of the mind." Students of the School of Dance and Dramatic Action, which fast became a magnet for young performers interested in modern dance, remember that Mamoulian played an active role, even auditioning applicants and approving scholarships. Mamoulian hired two instructors, Esther Gustafson, a dancer in the fin de siècle Isadora Duncan mode, and Martha Graham, working toward a modernist style whose movements were abstracted from the conventional representation of dance. Mamoulian chose her after witnessing her concerts in Rochester with the Denishawn Dancers. Impressed by his remark,

"Dance is the foundation of the theatre," Graham accepted his invitation to teach three days a week beginning in the fall of 1925. After shocking some students by wearing a clinging red kimono with slits up each leg to class, she explained to Mamoulian, "Well, they needed it."[29] Mamoulian provided her with a studio as well as students, enabling her to "begin to create a dance style that was exclusively her own."

Despite the opportunities offered in Rochester, Graham felt constrained by the relentless burden of teaching and choreographing dances for the multimedia shows at the Eastman Theatre. Three of her Rochester students, Thelma Biracree, Evelyn Sabin, and Betty MacDonald, left with her to form the nucleus of her own company at its New York City debut on April 18, 1926. Mamoulian was in the audience, and her break from Eastman might have rekindled his own ambition to move on. Three months later he announced his resignation to accept a position with the Theater Guild School in New York City, but he always fondly remembered his years in Rochester. "At the risk of using a cliché, it was at Eastman that I 'found myself,' professionally speaking."[30]

Chapter 3

Young Lion of Broadway

The Armory Show of 1913 had an incalculable effect on all the arts in the United States, but nowhere more than in New York City. The first significant American exhibition of postimpressionist painters such as Picasso, Duchamp, and Matisse stimulated the imagination of intellectuals and artists who were fascinated by the emergence of modernism in Europe. They were excited by the prospect of spreading the new art in America, a provincial backwater to those who defined culture exclusively in the terms of fine arts. "Little magazines" sprang up to promote modern aesthetics in poetry and prose and "little theaters" mounted work by George Bernard Shaw, August Strindberg, and Henrik Ibsen. Inspired by reports of the Moscow Art Theatre and the Abbey Theatre in Dublin, the Washington Square Players began to coalesce in New York the year after the Armory Show. They were the toast of Greenwich Village for staging challenging, socially critical plays in contrast to the conventional melodrama and comedy of Broadway. In 1919 the Washington Square Players reorganized as the Theatre Guild and became one of the most important producers of contemporary theater in the world.

The remarkable growth of the Theatre Guild, from its debut in the six-hundred-seat Garrick Theatre on West Thirty-fifth Street through the time Mamoulian left for Hollywood, was proof that a large American audience was hungry for Shaw's *Heartbreak House,* Ibsen's *Peer Gynt,* A. A. Milne's *Mr. Pim Passes By,* Ferenc Molnar's *The Guardsman,* Karel Capek's *R.U.R.,* and Ernest Vadja's *Fata Morgana.* Many of its actors would become famous on Broadway or in Hollywood, especially Alfred Lunt and Lynn Fontanne, Fredric March, Edward G. Robinson, and Claude Rains. By 1929 the Guild had designed its own hall on West

Fifty-second Street with a unique fifty-foot-deep stage and leased two additional theaters to accommodate thirty thousand season subscribers in New York. The Guild also ran subscription series in six other American cities and mounted tours to the Pacific coast and London. The antithesis of theater as escapism and entertainment, the company produced plays with a sharp intellectual appeal. Like the Pre-Raphaelites and the Bauhaus, it looked to the craft guilds of medieval Europe as an antecedent. Paradoxically, the Theatre Guild strove to sustain itself through ticket sales while remaining noncommercial, and it sought American themes while sticking in the early years to a European repertoire.

The six men and women of the Guild's original board of managers compared themselves to a faculty debating society. Five had graduated from prestigious East Coast schools where America's first theater programs had coalesced in the early years of the twentieth century. Although the board took pride in being a collective, complete with "managers' rehearsals" that could assume virtual codirectorship over a play, the sixth member, Lawrence Langner, a British patent attorney and financier in New York, gained special prominence. It was Langner who engineered the transformation of the semi-amateur Washington Square Players into the prestigious Theatre Guild. Dapper in bow tie and spats, he would be instrumental in the next step of Mamoulian's career.[1]

In 1926, when the Guild brought the American Opera Company to New York for a short run, Langner met Mamoulian, whom he recognized as a "gifted individual." Eager to play on a bigger stage, Mamoulian "begged us to visit him" in Rochester. Langner was impressed by his abilities as a teacher as well as his "striking personality and enthusiasm for the theater." According to Langner, Mamoulian "walked my legs off pacing the streets of Rochester, telling me all he planned to do in theatre if I would only bring him to New York." Mamoulian pressed for directing a play, but instead was given an instructorship at the newly formed Guild School with the promise the position could be a rung on the way to directing the Guild's subscriber productions.[2]

Mamoulian mounted three student productions at the Theatre Guild School in Scarsborough, New York, after returning from a short European trip in September of 1926.[3] His first plays for the Guild School included *Clarence* by popular American novelist Booth Tarkington, Gilda Varesi Archibald and Dorothea Donn Byrnes's Broadway comedy *Enter Madame,* and Leonid Andreyev's experimental "realistic fantasy"

He Who Gets Slapped (which had earlier received its professional American debut at the Guild). In Langner's good-natured recollection, Mamoulian "began to pester the Guild directors in a most efficiently irritating manner" to see his work. Finally, in May 1927, the board agreed to look in on his production at the Garrick of the popular crime drama *The Seven Keys to Baldpate* by Earl Derr Biggers, who would soon become better known as the creator of Charlie Chan. Mamoulian presented *Seven Keys* in his characteristic stylized, rhythmic manner. Although the board agreed out of courtesy to watch for only a few minutes, Langner and his colleagues found that the play "was so well directed by Mamoulian and so well acted by his pupils, that the Guild directors stayed to the unbitter end." The board's previous lack of attention to Mamoulian's schoolwork was probably no reflection on him. The Guild School would be disbanded shortly after Mamoulian's departure as instructor because the board "could not give it the personal attention and interest they felt a school bearing their name required," according to the Guild's official chronicler, Walter Prichard Eaton.[4]

After Langner met novelist DuBose Heyward and his wife, Dorothy, at a party, he convinced the Guild to produce a play the couple had written based on DuBose's novel *Porgy*. The story of a handicapped black beggar called Porgy and his fatally flawed lover, Bess, was set in the tenements of Catfish Row in Charleston, South Carolina. A member of the city's faded white patrician class, DuBose was progressive in his views on race; a modern poet who vividly evoked the South and its people, he was an active participant in the white Southern Renaissance in writing and letters of the 1920s. "I grew to see the primitive Negro as neither a professional comedian, nor an object for sentimental charity, but a racially self-conscious human being, living out his destiny beside us, and guided by a code," he explained. A real person, one of the "Gullah Negroes" from the Sea Islands of South Carolina who spoke a patois rooted in West Africa, inspired the protagonist, Porgy. DuBose was familiar with the Gullahs, who worked as stevedores on the Charleston cotton wharfs. Published in 1925, *Porgy* was daring in its depiction of sex, drugs, and violence, as well as its intimation that human dignity could reside in the most squalid circumstances. Published at a time when the Ku Klux Klan was not only resurgent in the South but active in many northern states, *Porgy* entered the best-seller lists as an affirmation of the essential humanity of African Americans. At the time, "*Porgy* was the only major work by a white writer to delve deeply into the southern black experience." Dorothy, a Yankee and an award-winning playwright whom DuBose met at the MacDowell Colony artists' retreat in New Hampshire, secretly transformed *Porgy* into a play, showing it to her husband only after completing a first draft.[5]

The Guild approached several veteran directors with *Porgy,* but even in the New York theater community, race prejudice was deep dyed. As Eaton put it, "The play was a distinct challenge to the resources and imagination of the American theatre." According to Langner, no one wanted to work with "an all-colored cast"; he suggested Mamoulian "and the rest of the Guild, in despair, accepted him." Although Mamoulian had already staged work by American authors, he worried that the Guild typecast him as suited only for the European avant-garde. He was determined to prove them wrong.[6]

Although Mamoulian admitted, "The only black man I had ever known was the bootblack at the St. James Theatre in London," he was a cosmopolitan aesthete; as an Armenian, he was acutely aware of the precarious position of ethnic minorities and unlike many immigrants, he did not adopt the prejudices of the New World. He embraced a play about African Americans with a black cast in the spirit of curiosity and sympathy. The Gullahs, who preserved their unique culture under pressure from the majority society surrounding them, might have reminded Mamoulian of the Armenian experience. "I loved the story of *Porgy* and every single character in it," he said. "I loved its changing moods . . . and all the emotional richness of the Negro soul expressed in it." Accompanied by set designer Cleon Throckmorton, Mamoulian traveled by train to Charleston to absorb the setting. "Charleston is typically southern in much the same way that Tiflis is: in its music and its hospitality," he told a local reporter during his visit. "Both cities have a link with the past." A friend of DuBose, author and folklorist John Bennett, showed Mamoulian and Throckmorton around Charleston. Bennett was pleased to bring the director to "the most picturesque and disreputable sections of the city," showing him "much richness, scenery and personality—boys gambling under the fig-trees, Negro men loafing in indescribable purlieus, and women in costumes that soothed [Mamoulian's] soul." Like Dvorak preparing to compose the New World Symphony, Mamoulian was inspired by the soulfulness of black spirituals and intended to key his production to their rhythm.[7]

African Americans were known on Broadway before *Porgy* through several popular musical revues, especially Eubie Blake's *Shuffle Along* (1921), which introduced the characteristic dance of the Jazz Age, the Charleston. Off-Broadway, all-black casts performed as early as 1917. The African American actor Charles Gilpin starred in a small production of Eugene O'Neill's *The Emperor Jones* (1920), and Mary Hoyt Wiborg's *Taboo* (1921) introduced a major talent to the stage, Paul Robeson, who returned a year later in a revival of *The Emperor Jones.* The "little theater" movement had spread to Harlem, but the half dozen companies that existed during the early 1920s enjoyed only an ephemeral existence.[8]

Despite the florescence of African American literature, painting, and poetry during the Harlem Renaissance of the 1920s, relatively few dramas were produced because of the expense of mounting professional theater. The success of *Porgy* encouraged the growth of black theater in Harlem and set a precedent for the 1930s African American productions by the Federal Theatre Project, especially Orson Welles's all-black staging of *Macbeth.* The presence of African Americans in a serious Broadway production was unusual when Mamoulian accepted *Porgy.* The only real precedent was *In Abraham's Bosom* by white North Carolina playwright Paul Green, which had run at the Garrick the previous year.

Mamoulian began work on the project with a fifteen-page memo to the Heywards, insisting they rewrite the text, a demand the couple accepted. The story of Porgy's love for Bess, his unpremeditated murder of her former boyfriend Crown when he returned to reclaim her, Bess being drawn by Sportin' Life with the lure of his "happy powder," and Porgy's brief jail sentence for running from the police were drawn to more suspenseful climaxes. The characters were given more action, less contemplation, yet Porgy retained a spiritual significance as a kind of holy fool who disdains the materialism of the world and values the beauty of life. "To me he's a Charleston, South Carolina, version of Don Quixote," Mamoulian said. "In his way he's a deeply religious man of great faith. He's naïve, but he's capable of tremendous love and devotion . . . and courage." In one respect Mamoulian's sensibility would harmonize with the producers he would soon encounter in Hollywood; possessed by a positive spirit, he appreciated happy endings and changed *Porgy*'s dour conclusion to a more hopeful, if ambiguous, note. Bess leaves for New York with Porgy tagging behind in his goat cart. Realizing that the Gullah patois of the novel and Dorothy's adaptation would be incomprehensible to New York ears, Mamoulian convinced the authors to "blur the dialect into the atmosphere."[9]

Casting *Porgy* was a challenge. Some members of the Guild plotted "to supply Alfred Lunt and his wife, Lynne Fontanne, with burnt cork, to give them the roles of Porgy and Bess." Neither Mamoulian nor the Heywards could accept a blackface version of *Porgy*, which would only serve to erase the play's depiction of the inherent dignity of black folk. While in Charleston, Mamoulian even toyed with the idea of bringing Gullahs to Broadway to play themselves. "Southern Negroes, like southern peoples everywhere, possess such vitality," he said, comparing Armenians and Georgians with the Gullahs he encountered. He added that they would "make an ideal human tapestry for the background of *Porgy*." While his idea proved too ambitious to execute, Mamoulian did hire the famous brass band of the Jenkins Orphanage, whose members had marched in hand-me-down uniforms at the inauguration of Theodore Roosevelt and other presidents, to lead a procession in act 2 to the tune of "Sons and Daughters of Repent Ye Saith the Lord."[10]

Mamoulian and his assistant stage manager Cheryl Crawford, who later joined the influential Group Theatre, received little help from talent agencies, which represented black dancers and singers but not black dramatic actors, and were forced to comb the vaudeville houses and cabarets of Harlem for their cast. According to legend, Mamoulian even approached prospects on the street, asking if they wanted to be in a Broadway play.[11]

Four of the thirty-five black actors eventually cast for *Porgy*, Frank Wilson (Porgy), Rose McClendon (Serena), Richard J. Huey (Mingo), and Melville Green (Scipio), had played together in *In Abraham's Bosom*. Evelyn Ellis (Bess) and Percy Verwayne (Sportin' Life) were recruited from a Harlem musical show. In the aftermath of their success together, they were "almost like a repertory company" on Broadway. As *New York Times* theater critic Brooks Atkinson recalled, "Whenever Negro parts were available they were there." Elegant as usual in his tailored suits, Mamoulian began rehearsals from the rear of the orchestra seats, shouting through a megaphone, "Everybody into his own house!" The cast then took their places on the platforms and steps representing Catfish Row and the play began with a depiction of the sound and motion of everyday life in the impoverished neighborhood. Using a metronome and a conductor's baton, he controlled the shifting rhythm of the production, including the "Symphony of Noises," where actors and technicians vocalized the sounds of Catfish Row. Audible were the boom of the street gangs repairing the roads, the women sweeping their stair steps, the harsh edge of knives being sharpened in 4/4, 2/4, and 6/8 beats, syncopated and orchestrated like a jazz orchestra whose rhythms regulated dialogue, movement, and lighting. "I think I came close to being fired for trying out some of my pet theories," Mamoulian said. "Only later could they [the Guild] appreciate a stage full of actors snoring, hammering and making other homely noises. We had to work up to the sound of a whole community busy at living and working."[12] Spotlights concealed in the footlights threw up gigantic, expressionist shadows.

Leigh Whipper (who played the Crab Man) recalled that Mamoulian was open to being coached by his black cast. "I said, 'I see you trying to do the church scene, the wake for Robbins . . . do you want to see the scene unrehearsed?'" Whipper then brought the director to a black church on 136th Street, where they sat in one of the rear pews and observed the handclapping, the fervent "Amens," the testifying. Mamoulian admitted having problems connecting the actors to their roles, saying the cast "had no conception, at first, of the significance of their work." DuBose agreed, telling his mother, "The Negroes got rattled and left out important lines. When they remembered them they said them woodenly like school children reciting." Many of the actors had never had the opportunity for dramatic roles and, given the racial caste system of America in those years, were conditioned to conceal deeper feelings from white eyes. Confidence came only after many rehearsals. "We have all worked like galley slaves this week," DuBose wrote his mother only days before the October 11 opening night. "Yesterday they rehearsed from 10 AM to 12 midnight. How they can stand it I do not know. . . . Mamoulian has been superhuman."[13]

The realism of *Porgy* was not a slice of life but highly stylized, transforming the setting and its characters into something grander and more pointed than everyday reality. It was the apotheosis of the Gesamtkunstwerk the director had been working toward since his arrival in America. *New York Times* theater critic Brooks Atkinson complained in his opening night review that the book was better and the adaptation "only spasmodically vivid," but within a few days he reversed himself and warmed to the production, calling it "an illuminating chronicle of

American folklore." Most critics were amazed by what they saw. Alexander Woollcott declared *Porgy* "the finest performance of a play I have ever seen from a Negro troupe." The *Saturday Review of Literature* praised the black cast as unspoiled, unself-conscious primitives.[14]

The "vicarious interest in blacks among New York socialites of the 1920s" accounted for the first wave of interest, but the high level of the production, from the dilapidated grandeur of the set design to the glimpse it provided the audience of an alien America, drew crowds. By October 20 *Porgy* was playing to standing room only. It ran for 217 performances in New York and departed for a road tour, returning to Broadway in April 1928 for an additional 137 performances. Any lingering skepticism over Mamoulian's risk-taking vision was swept away by the applause. Guild board member Thomas Helburn praised the director for "his startling and beautiful staging" of *Porgy*.[15]

Mamoulian's next production, the premiere of Eugene O'Neill's *Marco Millions* (January 9, 1928), was also a milestone on Broadway. Relations between O'Neill and the Theatre Guild had been frosty and Mamoulian helped break the ice with his staging of *Marco Millions*. After watching a performance of *Porgy*, O'Neill decided that Mamoulian could be the right director for the large cast and ambitious settings of his play. Offers began to come in for Mamoulian with the success of his adaptation of the Heywards' play, but O'Neill's invitation was "the plum of Mamoulian's offerings."[16]

In a production more elaborate than *Porgy*, twenty-one actors played thirty-two characters arrayed on ten different sets filled with Eastern pomp and color by designer Lee Simonson. An Orientalist fantasy that satirized contemporary American society, especially the thoughtless materialism of middle-class Babbitts, *Marco Millions* starred Alfred Lunt in one of his only plays apart from his wife, Lynn Fontanne, as a soulless Marco Polo in far Cathay, animated only by acquisitive instincts. Mamoulian was described as an imposing but patient presence at rehearsals. "To demonstrate a point he frequently stalks about the stage, elaborating and extemporizing, indicating the positions and desired movements."[17]

As with *Porgy*, Mamoulian found that the text for *Marco Millions* could benefit from "judicious cutting." The Guild's board laughed. "They told me that O'Neill doesn't cut. You have to do it exactly as it is," he recalled. In keeping with his self-confident assertion of artistic integrity, Mamoulian visited America's most important living playwright in his room at the Wentworth Hotel with revisions in mind. "I explained to him that although he surely knows his play better than anyone else, it would be improved on the stage by a sharp transformation from a literary to a theatrical point of view," Mamoulian said, convincing the normally aloof writer to join "in the spirit of the process." Crossing out lines with a blue pencil, they worked together to trim dialogue, condense scenes, and sort out transitions that would be possible in a filmmaker's editing room but not on-stage. O'Neill was apparently satisfied with the process and turned up only occasionally at rehearsals to view the results.[18]

Familiar with the colorful yet solemn religious pageantry of Armenian Orthodoxy, Mamoulian transformed many scenes into majestic processionals that overspilled the Guild Theatre's proscenium arch, much as the rites of the Eastern churches spread from the altar into the entire sanctuary in glorious raiment, otherworldly chanting, tinkling bells, and clouds of incense. An eighteen-piece orchestra performed the music from backstage because an apron had been placed over the orchestra pit to accommodate the breadth of the production. Drawing from Near Eastern and Indian influences, Emerson Whitmore composed original music for *Marco Millions* that opened and closed scenes and marked transitions in Marco's journey. The 1923 "Chinese Suite" by Czech-born composer Rudolf Friml, already known for his operettas and Broadway show music before moving to Hollywood, was also woven into the play. A slightly flummoxed New York critic commented on the "bizarre opulence" of the play's staging, especially its "Tartar incantations . . . the pealing of thousands of little church bells big and little, from near and far," while another praised "the wealth of rhythmic variety, of skill in the handling of grouped players." Mamoulian clashed bitterly with Lee Simonson, a Guild board member, over the lighting. "I told them that although Simonson was one of their own number, his lighting was not my kind of lighting. . . . Either I light the show, or I would bow out." Once again, Mamoulian's brave if heedless defense of his aesthetic principles won the day. The show was lit according to his concept, with chiaroscuro and sudden bursts of light, but at the price of making an enemy.[19]

Unlike *Porgy,* where casting carried the weight of social conscience, Mamoulian felt no compunction to find ethnically appropriate actors in *Marco Millions.* In keeping with long-standing theatrical convention, whites played the Oriental roles, including the popular Margalo Gillmore as Princess Kukachin and a supporting cast including such then unknowns as future songwriter Johnny Mercer, playwright Clifford Odets, film director Vincent Sherman, and screen actor Albert Dekker. Although *Marco Millions* received mixed reviews, most of the criticism was directed against the dramaturgy, not the direction. Woollcott lauded Mamoulian for adding "beauty to a play which runs dry through its long course" and the *Times* praised him for finding the satire in "this obvious, occasionally monotonous play."[20] The production was a success nevertheless, running for 102 performances.

Mamoulian was indefatigable in the aftermath of *Marco Millions,* albeit not every production was a success with audiences or critics. In 1928 he directed a pair of pre-Broadway tryouts for the Theatre Guild that apparently ran for one night only, William Dubois's *Café Tomaza* at the Cort Theatre in Jamaica, New York (April 20) and Edith and Edward Ellis's *Women* at Philadelphia's Adelphi Theatre (September 10). Because of bylaws forbidding Theatre Guild members to produce their own plays under the Guild's imprimatur, Mamoulian staged his mentor Lawrence Langner's Shavian comedy *These Modern Women* outside the company, at the Eltinge Theatre, for twenty-four performances (opening February 13). He brought one Guild production, Robert Nichols and Maurice Browne's *Wings over Europe,* to Broadway for thirty-three performances at the Martin Beck Theatre (opening December 10). In addition, he directed his biggest hit of the year, *Congai,* for 137 nights at the Sam H. Harris Theatre (beginning November 27).

In 1929, the year he made his first film, *Applause,* Mamoulian found time to direct French playwright Romain Rolland's *The Game of Love and Death,* a drama about the French Revolution, for forty-eight performances at the Guild Theatre (opening November 25). In 1930, the year before Mamoulian moved to Hollywood, he directed Arnold Schoenberg's *Die glückliche Hand* at the Metropolitan Opera House (April 22) and four plays for the Theatre Guild: Karel Capek's *R.U.R. (Rossum's Universal Robots)* for sixteen performances at the Martin Beck (opening February 17), the U.S. premiere of Ivan Turgenev's *A Month in the Country* at Washington, D.C.'s National Theatre (March 10) followed by seventy-two nights at the Guild Theatre (beginning March 17), Lawrence Stalling's *A Farewell to Arms* for twenty-four performances at New York's National Theatre (opening September 22), and

Lewton Campbell's *Solid South* for twenty-three nights at New York's Lyceum (opening October 14).[21]

Although occupied with his many professional obligations, Mamoulian moved his parents from England to Manhattan in 1929. According to census records, Zacharie, Virginie, and Rouben lived at the same address; Zacharie was listed as "head of family" but gave his occupation as "none." Only Rouben was employed.[22]

Among the many lights of the theater world in attendance at *Porgy* was impresario Sam Harris, a friendly colleague of the Theatre Guild, who offered Mamoulian another opportunity to direct a lavish production set in the Far East, *Congai*. According to Mamoulian, the deal was cinched with a handshake over dinner.[23] Another exercise in Orientalism as a critique of Western society, *Congai* was set in Vietnam in the opening decades of the twentieth century. The protagonist, Thi Linh (played by well-known Broadway star Helen Menken), a Eurasian beauty abandoned by her French father, loves a boy from her village but becomes mistress to a series of French colonial officials in Saigon. The victim of sexism, racism, and colonialism, Thi Linh watches in horror as her son is conscripted to fight in the senseless slaughter of World War I. She was a third world heroine familiar to theatergoers of the day, the cousin to *Madama Butterfly*'s Cio Cio San and *White Cargo*'s Tondelayo, unfairly used by the men of the white empires and an object of sympathy to audiences who might not otherwise question the ethics of empire building.

Working with Cleon Throckmorton, Mamoulian created another enveloping sensory field not unlike *Marco Millions*. Incense burned from pots onstage and throughout the theater; *Congai* might have been the first time a sitar was heard on a Broadway stage. Mamoulian "makes the piece a symphony of whining pipes and menacing drums and fantastic shadows arising from the mists of the rice fields."[24] In one scene, Thi Linh wears tights colored in her skin tones; with her back to the audience, she appeared nude from the waist up.

Harris was not above employing the sort of salacious advertising tags already familiar in Hollywood. "Thi Linh is but with one talent: men" declared one ad. Typical of the critical response was the *New York Evening Post* reviewer who chastised *Congai* for squandering the opportunity "to present a genuinely tragic situation . . . through leering whispers, smutty jokes, and offensive scenes, with all eyes, you may be sure, focused hopefully on the box office."[25] With all of the above in mind,

Congai proved critic proof for audiences seeking an evening of the exotic and forbidden.

Wings over Europe was a harder sell for theatergoers and for Mamoulian. The theme of a catastrophic atomic war was prescient, yet the director found the wordy, largely static play "preposterous nonsense" and "a bloody bore that, as written, would have put the audience to sleep in five minutes." In the original text, the scientist-poet-political activist Francis Lightfoot presents his atomic bomb to his uncle, the British prime minister, at a cabinet meeting. Horrified by the politicians' xenophobia, Lightfoot decides to trigger a nuclear explosion but is run over by a truck upon exiting Downing Street and dies on the cabinet room table, where he pronounces his last words. "The play was flawed by a cancer at the very core of its construction," Mamoulian said. "To have the entire crisis resolved by a lorry hitting the guy is a total bankruptcy. I refused even to rehearse such a Deus-ex-machina ending."[26]

In Mamoulian's reconception, Lightfoot warns the cabinet members that they have only fifteen minutes to accept his demand that the atom bomb be shared with the League of Nations. A clock (actually a loud metronome) ticks from the mantelpiece in a forecast of the digital countdowns of twenty-first-century Hollywood thrillers. Mamoulian asked his actors "silently to question each other about how to dispose" of Lightfoot and to look for "the answer in each other's eyes" as they paced in turn. Finally, the prime minister produces a gold cigarette case, removes a cigarette, and shuts the case with a loud click, suggesting finality. His nephew must die. "I felt we should scale down the action to the lowest possible dramatic level, so that the slightest gesture would be a shock, as though a figure in a wax museum had suddenly winked at you," Mamoulian said. Despite his work to adapt the unwieldy play to the stage, *Wings over Europe* was not one of the Theatre Guild's great successes at the box office.[27]

In 1922 the Guild staged Czech author Karel Capek's *R.U.R.*, the play that introduced the word *robot* to the world's vocabulary one year after its European debut, but critics preferred Mamoulian's rendition. Brooks Atkinson appreciated his treatment of Capek's science fiction theme of dehumanization and automatons turning on their makers because it "shows a lighter touch, with its accent on irony and its flavor of satire." Mamoulian responded well to the play's expressionist exploration of moral responsibility. Eventually the robots, designed as cheap, uncomplaining laborers, were programmed with souls, which endowed them with free will and the ability to make decisions for good or evil. Lee Simonson designed the futuristic sets and Mamoulian employed electronic music to amplify the Machine Age setting. The musicians' union was alarmed, foreseeing a future Broadway using "mechanical theme songs, instead of hiring live musicians."[28]

The cast of *R.U.R.* included such Guild favorites as character actors Sydney Greenstreet, Albert Dekker, and Henry Travers several years before their migration to Hollywood. The ensemble was critically acclaimed as a group of "solid professionals who contributed to a balanced production in which no performance overshadows the work of one's fellow actor." Even more dramatically than in previous productions, Mamoulian was determined to breach the wall between performers and spectators in *R.U.R.* "When the Robots began to destroy people and objects, I had them walking in through doorways and windows, advancing towards the audience. As they stepped through the proscenium arch the lights went suddenly out."[29]

The Moscow Art Theatre had performed Turgenev's *A Month in the Country* in 1910 and Mamoulian copied the costumes and set for its American premiere, starring the flamboyant Russian-born actress of the stage and silent screen, Alla Nazimova. A restrained chamber drama in contrast to such elaborately mounted productions as *Porgy, Congai, R.U.R.,* and even *Wings over Europe, A Month in the Country* was a modest effort well received. According to the *New York Post,* "Mamoulian's direction makes the routine country atmosphere come vividly to life." In one of her earliest Broadway roles, an eager and unknown Katharine Hepburn, who failed her audition with Mamoulian for a lead role, played a maid.[30]

Mamoulian's final significant production before leaving New York was not on Broadway but in the Metropolitan Opera House, Schoenberg's 1913 atonal, expressionist opera *Die glückliche Hand.* The music was daringly new, representing the unattainable in a dense, tangled, and dissonant sound. Mamoulian was drawn to the libretto, which consisted in large part of directions for lighting and staging with sung allegories concerning an artistic dreamer struggling to reconcile worldly fulfillment with a vision of the ineffable.

Mamoulian's success led to his elevation to the Guild's board of managers along with director Herbert Biberman, who would be blacklisted in Hollywood during the McCarthy era. According to Langner, Biberman's recent visit to the USSR left him with a fondness for the Soviet style of "agitprop," which brought him into arguments with Mamoulian. Langner also claimed that Mamoulian became upset with the Guild when Biberman was assigned the Russian play *Roar China* and "after making a dignified speech about minority rights, oppressed directors and his prior claim to direct anything of Russian origin, retired gracefully to Hollywood, much to my regret and consequent loss to the Guild."[31]

Regardless of any argument over *Roar China,* the founders of the Theatre Guild did not share Mamoulian's enthusiasm for the newest of the lively arts. Eaton complained that motion pictures "were increasing the competition in mediocrity" and Langner wrote that with the coming of talking pictures, "Hollywood became, overnight, a Mecca for the second-raters and a graveyard for some of the first-raters" of Broadway. Unlike the Anglo-Saxon elites of the Guild who cultivated an exclusive attitude toward the arts, Mamoulian, imbued with the spirit of the Moscow Art Theatre, was enthusiastic about reaching the masses. "A great play or a good play or a great film must find an audience," he said. "If it doesn't, there's something wrong with it. Audience is an integral part of the theatre arts."[32]

Although Mamoulian was named among America's great theater directors by the time he left for Hollywood in 1930,[33] the stage, which he would always love, was not wide enough to contain his artistic ambition. Only in film could his ideal of the Gesamtkunstwerk be entirely fulfilled.

Chapter 4

The Sound of Applause

By the time Mamoulian immigrated to the West, movies were no longer the flickering, largely stage-bound productions of cinema's earliest years. The grammar of filmmaking was largely in place by then through the innovations of D. W. Griffith and other directors who had mastered multiple camera positions, parallel editing, continuity cutting, and special effects to create a new medium of entertainment—perhaps even a new art form—that represented the world in ways impossible for literature, theater, and the plastic arts. By 1920 the silent film had achieved a sophistication of expression that would soon be threatened by the advent of sound with *The Jazz Singer* (1927).

Some critics complained that the "talking pictures," or "audible pictures" as they were sometimes called, stunted the evolution of the cinema by reducing what had been a largely visual medium to dependence on dialogue. Film's capacity to conjure another dimension of reality, a kingdom of shadows, was jeopardized by the naturalism of human speech.[1] On a more practical level, filmmaking suffered from the clumsiness of the new technology behind the talkies and films regressed to their infancy in terms of visual storytelling. Sound cameras were bulky and mounted inside soundproof glass-paneled booths to prevent the electric whir of their motors from penetrating the soundtrack. Cameras imprisoned in those enclosures could neither tilt nor track. As Mamoulian said, "It was like walking around with a bungalow on your back."[2] The primitive use of microphones limited the ways sound could be recorded and films had to be made indoors to maintain the precarious sound level. As a result of so many curbs, movies no longer moved freely.

The Hollywood studios were skeptical at first of talking pictures, in part because of the capital investment demanded by the new technology, but the mass audience embraced the talkies and wanted to hear the stars speak. "The public, intoxicated with sound by the radio, was coming to feel that noise was now inseparable from entertainment," complained a contemporary critic.[3] Although Japan and the Soviet Union were slow to adopt sound, and Charlie Chaplin fought a rearguard action on behalf of silent film in Hollywood, there was no turning back. The movies would talk and Mamoulian eagerly embraced the creative challenge of the new medium in his debut movie, *Applause* (1929).

In the wake of *The Jazz Singer*'s success, Hollywood rushed to recruit talent of all sorts from the theater, including directors, with no other thought than to produce photographed stage plays. Mamoulian insisted on an entirely different approach. "Talking pictures up to now have been merely substitutions, stage imitation, mirrors of acted plays—and that is not their purpose," he remarked during the making of *Applause*. "They should be motion pictures always using the old motion picture technique, but substituting dialogue for subtitles."[4] Mamoulian had not been a particular fan of most of the movies he had seen until that time but admired the German expressionism of F. W. Murnau's *The Last Laugh*.[5] The influence of German cinema as well as a carryover from Mamoulian's work with the Theatre Guild can be discerned in *Applause*.

Given his success on Broadway, Mamoulian was approached by Paramount, one of Hollywood's top five Hollywood studios as measured in box office success. By his account, he was offered a seven-year deal with the first two years to be spent directing only dialogue before being allowed to make a film of his own. "But, I was in a lucky position. I didn't need films. I was doing well enough on Broadway," Mamoulian said, explaining his refusal.[6] It was a transitional moment as the studios moved from silence to sound, and Mamoulian's profile on Broadway was high enough for Paramount moguls Jesse Lasky and Walter Wanger to agree to the demands of a man who had never set foot on a sound stage. With such respected directors as Josef von Sternberg and Ernst Lubitsch on its roster, Paramount took pride in "prestige pictures," even if such projects represented only a small percentage of output. Unlike at other studios, "the high-cost, high-risk pictures involved the least amount of executive control or front-office interference." It was an ideal environment for the headstrong Mamoulian to begin his career in filmmaking. For its part, Paramount hoped the director would enhance their upmarket reputation. According to a studio press release, "To New York theater-goers, the name Rouben Mamoulian in connection with a stage production is a guarantee of splendid and universal entertainment. In the future, it will have the same significance to motion picture patrons."[7]

Although its main studio was in Hollywood, Paramount maintained a soundstage in Astoria on Long Island for easy access to Broadway. To teach himself the craft of filmmaking, Mamoulian audited the sets of two movies in progress, *A Kiss for Cinderella* by Herbert Brenon, who had directed handsome silent adaptations of *Peter Pan* and *Beau Geste,* and visiting Frenchman Jean de Limur's *Jealousy;* he watched the cumbersome process of recording a talking picture with keen curiosity and imagination. He showed remarkable powers of observation and the ability to assimilate new material. "I must say that what I learned there was mostly, as the Latin language would put it, *ad adversus.* In other words, I really learned what I didn't want to do," Mamoulian said. He insisted that there "is no great mystery to the mechanics of motion picture making, I think you can familiarize yourself with all of it in five weeks." He recalled long conversations with cinematographer George Folsey and asking many "silly questions in the cutting room." Mamoulian's story was supported by the recollection of Marx Brothers' director Robert Florey (*The Cocoanuts*). "Within a few days, the camera had no secrets from Mamoulian."[8]

Mamoulian rejected the plays Paramount offered him, choosing instead a novel recently purchased by the studio, Beth Brown's *Applause.* Distrusting the theater as a source for movies, Mamoulian favored original concepts or ideas taken from novels. "Then you can start out by structuring the whole edifice of our script in graphic terms," he explained. "I do believe that even though we have talking pictures, the main force of the cinema is in imagery, not in words."[9] Backstage musicals were popular in the early days of talking pictures, and *Applause* was a step toward such better-remembered classics as *42nd Street* (1933).

Much of *Applause* would be told visually or through "natural" sound rather than dialogue. The movie opens with the camera pulling back from a rundown storefront with a wavering motion suggesting the handheld cameras of independent film later in the twentieth century. Thrown-away paper litters the soundstage slum neighborhood; the camera quickly focuses on a poster of the story's tragic protagonist, "Kitty

Darling: Queen of Hearts." The editing is fluid and the camera glides with ease across the gritty urban setting.

Applause is a post-Victorian melodrama filmed from expressionist angles, its visual images amplified with sophisticated contrapuntal sound. Kitty, a fading burlesque queen, clings to a manipulative and much younger man whose shadow looms ominously over several scenes. Early in the film, news of Kitty's impending single motherhood is conveyed kinetically. "Kitty's got a baby!" the chorus girls whisper excitedly to one another, the message passed down the line of disheveled hoofers as they prance onstage in a low-class theater. Dialogue was frank in this pre–Hollywood Production Code picture. Fearful of exposing her daughter, April, to the "Johns hanging around at night," Kitty sends the girl to a Roman Catholic convent school in faraway Wisconsin. A vivid contrast is established between the Ave Maria calm of that setting and the clamorous racket of Manhattan. *Applause* might have been the first film to effectively employ sound without a visual source, allowing it to emerge from beyond the frame of the screen; Mamoulian shifted the audio track from foreground to background within the same scenes and explored sound from the psychological perception of his characters.

Years pass in a single cut. A letter from April in Kitty's room ("Mummy, dear, it's been three years since I've seen you") lies open as Kitty sings the bluesy lyric "What wouldn't I do for that man?" That man, her young cad, wants Kitty to cut off April's tuition and bring the teenage girl back to New York to work in the show. He will, soon enough, make sexual advances on April. Although she is well paid, Kitty's status is precarious as a woman dependent on the good graces of men and she can only press her complaints so far.

One of *Applause*'s technical achievements, the use of two microphones to record overlapping dialogue and sounds within a single scene, was prompted by the rhythm of contrast Mamoulian maintained through the film. As a neon light from across the street winks balefully into the darkened bedroom, Kitty sings a burlesque-style lullaby to April, sleepless and confused upon her arrival in New York, while the girl whispers a bedtime prayer. The technicians told Mamoulian that what he wanted was impossible, but he insisted on placing two microphones on the set, one for Kitty and the other under April's pillow. "Get two channels. Record it on two channels," he demanded. In Mamoulian's recollection, his crew refused to carry out his instructions until the studio's management intervened. "Mr. Mamoulian is directing this film. You do what he says." Mamoulian lit many of the scenes himself for the chiaroscuro effect he was known for on Broadway. Placing wheels under the camera booth and marking the floor for each focus change, Mamoulian employed ten men to move the heavy box for tracking shots. With *Applause,* the director achieved a talking picture that not only moved but also used sound creatively.[10]

Shortly after completing work on the film, he joked about a scene "photographed with mobile camera [that] ran for 500 feet," causing studio executives to worry that he was "engulfed in a morass of revolutionary ideas." Simple as his ideas would seem in later years, they were indeed revolutionary at that moment. "The point is, when you get an insane idea, if you can theoretically justify it, do it. Don't back out. Do it!" he insisted. The camera "should not be treated as a witness of things happening but . . . should be the main actor in the picture," he explained while the film was in production. "The camera is the person telling the story."[11]

The touching scene in April's bedroom set standards for camera movement as well as sound. Although nearly five minutes long, it never feels tedious in the manner of most static early talking pictures. The setup position is a medium long shot; the camera rolls into the room for close-ups of mother singing and daughter praying, withdraws to a medium shot of the pair, then pulls back to the medium long position where the scene began without making a single cut.

While the bird's-eye views of chorus girls unfolding like flowers onstage and the choreographed rush of performers toward the footlights were foretastes of the musicals of Busby Berkeley, Mamoulian's attitude to show business was distinctly realistic. The music halls where Kitty performs are filled with leering, lecherous faces of men shot in sharp close-ups; she inhabits a grimy place of dirt and grease paint; the sexuality is claustrophobic. Mamoulian visited burlesque houses for inspiration, finding that "audiences were ugly. The girls were bored. The whole thing was tawdry, shoddy, unworthy of a human being, woman or man," he said. "At the same time, I wanted to show that even in a garbage dump a beautiful flower can grow, because I believe that nothing is all black or all evil." *Applause* was his impression of New York "in all its beauty and its ugliness." To better capture the city, Mamoulian shot several scenes with his cast on location in Pennsylvania Station, on the Brooklyn Bridge, and at the top of a skyscraper.[12]

Despite the tragedy of her mother's life and climactic death by suicide, April falls in love with a young sailor with whom she plans a better life. The sad-happy ending represented the hopeful but realistic view of human possibility at the heart of Mamoulian's worldview. "I believe that the young don't have to succumb to the environment. They can transcend it," he insisted.[13]

The popular Broadway star and torch singer Helen Morgan, cast in the starring role as Kitty, played on Broadway in the hit musical *Show Boat* at night while shooting *Applause* in Astoria by day. Mamoulian had trouble convincing Paramount's wardrobe department to dress her realistically. "They kept wanting to pretty up everything—glamour, you know," he complained. To play April and her sailor, Mamoulian auditioned a pair of unknowns, Joan Peers and Henry Wadsworth. "I wanted two innocent, young, naïve people . . . in certain cases, it is advisable to get somebody who is not yet an actor." He coaxed superbly empathetic performances from the leading members of a cast that, like him, had little or no experience in movies. Morgan had played only a small part in a part-talking, part-silent rendition of *Show Boat* filmed earlier that year. "The actor or actress must like what you are suggesting," he said of the psychology of directing. "Good performances can only come if the cast is both excited and challenged by their roles." Already, Mamoulian had mastered the knack of smiling tenderly at cast members who fell short of his idea, gently encouraging them to try and try again.[14]

With its racy atmosphere and adult content, *Applause* drew the attention of censors. In a successful effort to ward off federal standards for the content of films, the movie industry, through its trade group, the Motion Picture Producers and Distributors Association, operated a self-censorship agency (usually called the Hays Office after its director, Will H. Hays) whose stamp of approval was necessary for the public screening of any movie. Although the Hollywood Production Code would not be strictly enforced until 1934, the office demanded several changes before *Applause* could be shown. Because the Roman Catholic Church exerted a strong influence over the censors, the office deleted a reference to "Catholic girls" in the chorus line. They also cut dialogue between Kitty and her boyfriend "in which she urges him to marry her because of the return of her daughter" in an effort to keep the nature of their relationship vague.[15]

Applause opened at New York's Criterion Theatre on October 8, 1929, and ran for many weeks.[16] Although Mamoulian often referred in later years to how well the film was reviewed in the press, critics did not universally laud his cinematic debut.[17] According to the *New York Times*' Mordaunt Hall, "Mr. Mamoulian commits the unpardonable sin of being far too extravagant," and Dwight Macdonald berated "the trashy emotionalism of the story, which a more honest director would have restrained." Macdonald, however, revealed his white Anglo-Saxon prejudice by adding a reference to Mamoulian's "Oriental greasiness." A false and misleading advertising campaign for *Applause* might have hurt the film at the box office. Helen Morgan was portrayed in newspaper ads as a glamorous performer, "the most vivid personality on the talking screen, in a startling story of wild, jazz-mad nights."[18] Before long the crash of Wall Street cast a shadow on the country and the popular mood turned toward escapism, not social problems.

For the bookkeepers at Paramount, *Applause* was a failure, but studio executives were cognizant of the film's technical achievements and, if they were in no immediate hurry to resume work with the assertive director, they kept him in mind for the future. According to a trade paper, "Rouben Mamoulian is very much the big shot over at Paramount these days." Mamoulian would spend 1930 working in New York theater, but was nonetheless won over by the new medium and what he had managed to accomplish. Shortly before *Applause*'s release, Mamoulian spoke enthusiastically of the artistic potential he found in film. "It can do what the stage can never do because it is not limited by space, by time or by people."[19]

Chapter 5

Hollywood

The Breakthrough Years

Mamoulian could have continued working without interruption on Broadway for many years if he had so chosen. No less an authority than the *New York Times* dubbed him "part of the Theatre Guild's collection of Very Bright Young Men." However, his fascination with filmmaking had been kindled and Paramount was willing to give him another chance. As early as August, the *Times* announced that Mamoulian "will supervise another production for Paramount in the fall. Claudette Colbert will probably have the leading role."[1] As it happened, the director did not depart New York for Los Angeles until late that year, however, and his leading actress would not be Colbert but a face little known to moviegoers, Sylvia Sidney. The film was finally announced as a gangster picture, *City Streets* (1931).

"Took them a whole year," Mamoulian groused years later about Paramount's slowness in getting back to him, "and the whole rigmarole started anew." Once again, the studio wanted to tie him to its usual seven-year contract and he refused. Instead, he signed for a single film.[2]

City Streets was Paramount's answer to the wave of gangster movies inspired by the shocking headlines generated by the St. Valentine's Day Massacre of 1929. The most popular picture was the Warner Brothers' movie based on a fictionalized account of that gangland slaying, *Little Caesar* (1931), with Edward G. Robinson as a character based on Al Capone, the Chicago mobster who made a fortune defying Prohibition. Likewise, the underworld of alcohol trafficking would provide Mamoulian's film with its milieu.

Rouben Mamoulian shortly after his arrival in Hollywood.

City Streets had a hybrid origin. Although originally conceived as a remake of the Clara Bow hit *Ladies of the Mob* (1928), it was based on an original story outline by hardboiled detective writer Dashiell Hammett, whose novels *The Maltese Falcon* and *The Glass Key* would be filmed several times in Hollywood and provide one of the wellsprings for film noir. Producer David O. Selznik had brought Hammett to Paramount, hoping the author would conceive something "new and startlingly original."[3]

Mamoulian claimed that Hammett "gave me a synopsis on two yellow pages and from that we worked the script out. I thought I'd take something familiar and stylize it." Hammett's biographers prefer a different version of events, with the novelist producing a seven-page plot treatment for the film under various working titles before he even met Mamoulian.[4] It was Hammett's sole screen credit for Paramount, but it marked the beginning of a long, successful career as a Hollywood screenwriter, including collaborating with Billy Wilder on the screenplay for *Double Indemnity*.

Clara Bow, one of the sex symbols of silent Hollywood, was originally cast in the picture along with rising star Gary Cooper. Paramount's publicity department claimed she withdrew after suffering a "nervous breakdown." "I thought of Sylvia Sidney, who I knew in New York at the Theatre Guild," Mamoulian said of Bow's replacement. Waiflike but intense, Sidney had appeared in a few small movie parts, while the slim, almost preternaturally handsome Cooper was already a marquee attraction for his star turn in a popular talking western, *The Virginian* (1929). A natural actor who made little fuss over his craft, Cooper adapted easily to his role in *City Streets* as the Kid, a cowboy turned gangster turned good guy. The hurly-burly of the Hollywood studio system is illustrated by his memory of making the movie. "One day I was up in the mountains saving Lily Damita from the Indians. . . . Then I jumped in my car and made it to Hollywood, a hundred miles away, for my scenes with Sylvia Sidney in *City Streets*." By day he was shooting *I Take This Woman* opposite Carol Lombard. At night he starred in *City Streets*. "In those days the average working day was 16 hours," Mamoulian recalled. "I remember doing a scene at midnight with Cooper and Sidney; and they fell asleep *during the take*." [5] Although his professorial bearing could suggest remote superiority, Mamoulian's dark eyes shown brilliantly and his face lit up with a warm smile. He was approachable on the set. Seated in a folding chair dressed for business in suit and tie, Mamoulian often directed with a pet cat perched on his lap.

Much of *City Streets*, with its story of a sympathetic gangster made good by the love of a racketeer's innocent daughter, is set at night or in places of little sunlight, and the nocturnal movie can be seen as a precursor of film noir. One scene in particular, where Sidney's heroine Nan is questioned by a blunt-faced police inspector shot from a low angle with a cage of shadows on the wall behind him, could easily be transposed to any crime thriller from a decade later. *City Streets* shows an affinity with Soviet films of the 1930s in its attention to the industrial aspect of beer bootlegging, the wheels and belts of the bottling assembly line that helped slake America's thirst during Prohibition and funded the rise of murderous organized crime gangs like the mob in Hammett's story. The unusual close-ups of spinning tires on the bootleggers' truck convoys and the foamy head on glasses of beer are visually striking elements.

City Streets is a love story as well as a crime story. The Kid works at a carnival shooting gallery and is in love with Nan. We meet them at the arcade as he escorts her in a tracking shot through the crowd for a hot-dog lunch. The film cuts to a beach where the couple is joined in an embrace. Though fully clothed, the Kid and Nan appear as happily intimate as newlyweds. However, they soon begin to argue over their future. The Kid is an idealist clinging to rugged frontier values while Nan aspires to wealth and luxury. "We can't even afford to get married," she complains, urging him to join the mob just like her foster father, Pop Cooley. "I wouldn't like that kind of work," the Kid replies laconically. After Nan is imprisoned as an accessory to a murder committed by Pop, a moral reversal occurs. The Kid becomes a mobster and Nan turns against the criminal life.

Although the manipulative, jovial Pop thinks nothing of committing murder, he frets over the health of his canary. Casting the role against type, Mamoulian "brought Guy Kibbee from New York because he looks like a benevolent, benign grandfather—like a Santa Claus," he explained. "Contrast makes the character more interesting. Furthermore, it is very true to life. You have people who could be terribly fond of a dog and kill somebody very easily."[6]

Mamoulian had fewer problems overcoming naysayers on the set of *City Streets* than with *Applause*. The biggest argument concerned his innovative use of a voice-over in a silent close-up of Nan to reveal her thoughts and memories. "The magic of sound recording enabled one to achieve effects that would be impossible and unnatural on the stage or in real life, yet meaningful and eloquent on the screen," Mamoulian explained. "No one thought audiences would be able to accept this kind of audible inner monologues and reminiscences combined with a silent face. [But] the audience understood and accepted it quite easily."[7]

Steeped as it was in the subculture of Prohibition-era gangsters, the violence of *City Streets* was implied, not depicted. "It was the gangster era, machine gunning people, bodies being thrown out of cars," Mamoulian said. "I never show a single one of the seven murders except obliquely." He claimed the studio wanted to see bullets flying and bodies falling. "But I had faith in the audiences," Mamoulian explained. "You know, usually, a lot of people underestimate the audience. They very seldom disappoint you."[8]

City Streets received mixed reviews upon its release, though, as with *Applause,* film historians would laud the picture for its technical innovations and balance between stylization and gritty realism. Tom Milne compared *City Streets* to a sonnet in his 1969 study of Mamoulian's films, "in which one main idea is fleshed out through a rigorous system of rhymes and remains incomplete until the last line." At the time of its release, however, *New York Times'* film critic Mordaunt Hall disapproved. "It is all melodrama and incredible," he wrote, adding, "Mr. Cooper gives a satisfactory showing as the Kid. Sylvia Sidney is excellent as Nan."[9]

City Streets was not a hit but performed well enough at box offices during the nadir of the Great Depression.[10] The Hays Office found no objection to the film upon its release on April 19, 1931, but denied a 1936 request from Paramount to reissue the film. In a sign of the tightening enforcement of the Hollywood Production Code, the Hays Office objected to *City Streets* because of its "total lack of any indication that the forces of law and order are capable of coping with the illegal activities of its characters."[11]

While *Applause* and *City Streets* were little seen after their initial theatrical run, Mamoulian's next film would be familiar to future generations. *Dr. Jekyll and Mr. Hyde* was based on a familiar literary work and had the advantage of belonging to the horror genre, whose popularity would grow exponentially later in the twentieth century. For Mamoulian, Hyde represented "the primeval man." His morally complex interpretation of Robert Louis Stevenson's classic story did not involve the usual theme of "evil versus good, but the primitive, the animalistic versus the spiritual because that's in all of us, including the saints," Mamoulian said. He spoke of Hyde as "an animal" that "knows no evil. . . . But you see, just as Jekyll gets gradually corrupted as he continues his experiment, so does Mr. Hyde get more and more corrupted. With each stage he becomes worse." For Mamoulian, "what interested me in *Dr. Jekyll and Mr. Hyde* is the built-in tragedy of man—man who fights the establishment . . . a man who embarks on a dangerous adventure, whose purpose is to benefit mankind."[12]

Stevenson's novella had been adapted for the stage in an 1888 run at London's Lyceum cut short by accusations that it encouraged a series of gruesome murders by the killer known as Jack the Ripper. Several silent movies drew on the story, including a 1910 film that introduced the fast dissolve as a special effect allowing Jekyll's transformation into Hyde, and a 1920 movie with the great John Barrymore in the title roles. Mamoulian's version influenced most future productions by emphasizing something absent from the book, the contrasting characters of two leading women, Hyde's promiscuous music hall singer Ivy and Jekyll's upper-class fiancée Muriel. The director recast the archetypes of whore and virgin in the gaslight setting of Victorian London, but his sympathy extends to both roles, as it does to Jekyll and Hyde. Paramount's decision to produce *Dr. Jekyll and Mr. Hyde* was in response to the enormous success of *Dracula* (1931), starring Bela Lugosi. "With *Dracula* making money at the box office for Universal, other studios are looking for horror titles—but very squeamishly," *Variety* reported.[13]

Paramount wanted middle-aged character actor Irving Pichel to star, but Mamoulian "thought the idea was atrocious, and I said I wouldn't be interested in doing the film with him." Although he agreed with the studio that Pichel would make a wonderful Hyde, he wanted "Jekyll to be young and handsome." Mamoulian pursued a reluctant Fredric March, then a matinee idol, for the parts of Jekyll and Hyde. The idea of playing a monster, or even an animal in Mamoulian's term, was not immediately appealing to the star. Paramount also objected to March, who had generally played in light comedies, as a "crazy idea." Once again, Mamoulian refused to budge. Grudgingly, the studio backed down again.[14] As a leading man, March had always played admirable characters. It was brilliant casting, causing contemporary viewers to sympathize with Jekyll even as he crosses into destruction.

Miriam Hopkins, still a newcomer in Hollywood, wanted to play the safe character, Muriel, but Mamoulian convinced her that the role was "dull," insisting, "You want to play the little cockney streetwalker." She received an Oscar nomination for Ivy and never regretted the decision. "I admire that man," she said of Mamoulian decades afterward, "the things he did stylistically, and because he is so way ahead of his time. Even today we can still appreciate the fact that the way he used the camera, in the way he cut and tracked along, in his approach to actors and actresses, in his whole style—it is so way out!"[15]

The part of Muriel went to another newcomer, Rose Hobart. "I loved working with Freddie and Mamoulian . . . [who] knew exactly what he wanted in every scene," she recalled. "I didn't always agree with him as I felt he was crossing his T's and dotting his I's a little too much and did not leave enough to the audience's imagination, only to realize now that it was that technique for which he was known." Hobart recounted a scene where March and Hopkins played to a camera on the music hall set, unaware that Mamoulian was actually filming them from behind a curtain.[16]

Paramount was confident enough to grant Mamoulian seven weeks of shooting time and a budget of $500,000, twice the cost of most A pictures. Art director Hans Dreier had begun his career with Germany's UFA studio and brought a German expressionist aesthetic of menace to the streets and interiors of London in sets constructed to allow the greatest variety of camera angles and control over lighting, rain, and fog. While shooting the film, Mamoulian explained that camera angles "must be used to match the dramatic angle of the scene, never for their own sake" and added that the angle "definitely enters the realm of the psychological. It can convey the underlying significance of a scene as nothing else can." He illustrated his point with the scene in which Jekyll is forced to seek help from his disapproving friend, Lanyon. "Jekyll is always photographed from above, looking up at the camera—an abject supplicant. Lanyon is always photographed from below, looking down at the camera—a stern and uncompromising Judge."[17]

In the film's remarkable opening scene, the camera shows the world through the eyes of the protagonist, Jekyll, whom we first see when he studies himself in the mirror. The most memorable technical achievement was Jekyll's transformation into Hyde. Mamoulian and cinematographer Karl Struss (who had won an Oscar for his work on F. W. Murnau's *Sunrise*) accomplished the special effect without cuts or dissolves by covering March's face with specially toned makeup, exposed in stages to colored lights and filters to reveal the beastly aspect of Hyde. Also concerned with the sound and rhythm of the transformation scenes, Mamoulian maintained a tense pulse by recording the sound of his own heartbeat and reversing the reverberations of a gong for eerie accompaniment, a remarkable achievement in the era before recording tape. "I wanted to make the transformations a real vicarious experience, more than just a trick. So I used the camera in the first person. The entire opening reel is shot as if through the eyes of Jekyll. . . . The audience does not see him—they *are* him—until he looks into a mirror."[18]

The shambling image of Neanderthal man was Mamoulian's model for Hyde's appearance, complete with protruding false teeth and hairy hands. Pieces of surgical cotton were used to force open his eyes, drooping the lower lids to suggest an animalistic leer. March called Hyde his most "unpleasant" role ever because of the makeup. "I had to get up every morning at five o'clock to be at the studio at six. [Makeup artist] Wally Westmore would start work immediately on my eyes." For March, the psychology of the role was more important than the makeup. "I tried to show the devastating results in Jekyll as well," he explained. "To me, those repeated appearances of the beast within were more than just a mental strain on Jekyll—they crushed him physically as well."[19]

Although *Photoplay* magazine worried that *Dr. Jekyll* was "not good fare for children or even adults who are easily unnerved," moviegoers were fascinated and Fredric March earned an Oscar for Best Actor at the 1932 Academy Awards. "The dreaded night when a love became a madman!" as the film's advertising campaign put it, turned to gold on Oscar night.[20] Struss was nominated for Best Cinematography and Percy Heath and Samuel Hoffenstein for Best Adapted Screenplay. The movie was awarded first prize at the first annual Venice Film Festival.

The Hays Office praised the film upon its release on December 31, 1931, as "magnificently done" and passed it without cuts.[21] Hyde's sexually predatory nature and an early scene in which Ivy seduces Jekyll finally alarmed the office in 1935 during a crackdown on movies released before the Production Code was rigidly enforced. Cuts were made to the master camera negative of many important films, including *Dr. Jekyll, All Quiet on the Western Front, Animal Crackers,* and *Dracula.*

Afterward, the Mamoulian movie disappeared for many years. In 1941 when Metro-Goldwyn-Mayer remade *Dr. Jekyll and Mr. Hyde* with Spencer Tracy and Ingrid Bergman, MGM purchased the rights to Mamoulian's version from Paramount and kept it from circulation to avoid competition. Film preservationist Raymond Rohauer found a print in the MGM vaults in time for the Mamoulian tribute at New York's Gallery of Modern Art in October 1967. Unfortunately, several scenes were missing.[22]

Although a fully restored print was not available until 1992, the legend of Mamoulian's film grew, starting with memories of the effect it had on audiences upon its first release. The *New York Times*' usually skeptical Mordaunt Hall had praised it as "a far more tense and shuddering affair" than John Barrymore's silent picture and horror film buffs of the 1960s were intrigued by rumors of amazing special effects and still photographs of Mr. Hyde circulated in fanzines.[23]

While establishing himself in Hollywood, Mamoulian moved his parents with him to Los Angeles, where they lived together in the same house until the director's marriage in 1945. Zacharie reportedly sold real estate and Virginie organized theater performances and charity benefits for the Armenian Orthodox church in Glendale, which already boasted a sizable Armenian community. Mamoulian seldom spoke of his own relations with California's Armenian community, but he was friends with author William Saroyan. After Saroyan came to Hollywood in 1936 as a screenwriter, he was a frequent guest on the sets of Mamoulian's films, though the two Armenian Americans never collaborated.[24]

Mamoulian's living arrangements were unusual for Hollywood in those years; however, Broadway producer John F. Wharton spoke of Mamoulian's "charm for women" and "rumors of a list of romantic attachments that included such beauties as Greta Garbo and Marlene Dietrich." He added, "No full-blooded male could look at a man with such a reputation without a feeling of deep awe." Traces of his personal life can be found in the always-suspect reporting of the Hollywood gossip columnists. Mamoulian and Hopkins were photographed together in *Photoplay,* smiling and in evening wear. The caption called them "a new nightly combine around town." Hopkins regarded Mamoulian as "one of the warmest, most intelligent and enchanting people," but little is known about their relationship. Myrna Loy called Mamoulian "one of my beaus. We weren't involved in anything important, but we were good friends and used to date once in a while." Kay Francis enjoyed a brief affair with the director and "commented favorably on Mamolian's lovemaking skills."[25]

Mamoulian received many columns of media attention for his alleged affair with the sexually ambiguous (if not ambivalent) Greta Garbo. They often dined together during and after work on *Queen Christina* and took a pair of aborted vacations together, along with Garbo's chauffeur and maid. "Garbo is spending her days on the tennis courts and just playing—with Mamoulian," ran a typical notice in the gossip columns. Reporters and curiosity seekers hounded them as they attempted to hike around the Grand Canyon; they were asked to leave a California dude ranch after only one night because their presence disrupted the routine of their fellow guests. Small crowds of fans along the way often met the couple, and registering in separate hotel rooms as Mary Jones and Robert Bonji did nothing to mask their journey. It is possible that Paramount's publicists fanned media interest in these vacations to maintain the increasingly impossible image of Garbo as a heterosexual screen goddess. However, Mamoulian fed the idea of a romance, telling screenwriter Mary Anita Loos that Garbo's jealous friend Mercedes de Acosta maintained an angry vigil outside the actress's home when he was present. When Mamoulian and Garbo traveled together, the media fanned rumors of an elopement. "All this fuss and stir was for nothing. We were not married and we have no plans whatever for marriage," he told the press. Even his mother was interviewed about his marriage plans. "My son has not made up his mind yet," Virginie said.[26]

Paramount's Joseph Youngerman, who worked as prop man and assistant director for Mamoulian in the 1930s, described him as "a really nice guy, and he was great to play tricks on. . . . He had a hell of a sense of humor." Other than his love of cats, an animal that appeared in most of his films, few other observations on his private life have been recorded other than his presence at many Hollywood parties and his role as host during Sergei Prokofiev's 1938 visit to Hollywood.[27] Mamoulian was remembered for his immaculate wardrobe and ever-present cigar, and as a tireless, inspiring, demanding, and exuberant figure on the sound stage.

When Broadway songwriters Richard Rodgers and Lorenz Hart went to Hollywood in November 1931 with a one-picture deal for Paramount, they expected to start work on a George Cukor musical, *Love Me Tonight.* A week after their arrival, Rodgers was "surprised to learn that Cukor was out and that Rouben Mamoulian had been tapped to succeed him." Dismayed at first to be writing a musical with the director of *Dr. Jekyll and Mr. Hyde,* Rodgers soon conceded, "Mamoulian had a concept of filming that was almost exactly what we had in mind." To maintain aesthetic unity, the director asked Rodgers to compose all of the film's incidental music, an unusual decision at a time when songwriting and music direction were separate departments in Hollywood.[28]

Paramount devised *Love Me Tonight* as a vehicle for Maurice Chevalier, the talented French actor and singer, and Jeanette MacDonald, the rising star of musicals. Mamoulian became interested after he conceived the film as a fully integrated spectacle of music and dance, acting, décor, and lighting, with the songs keeping the movie in motion. Myrna Loy described *Love Me Tonight* as a "musical spoof of Lubitsch" for its gently ironic take on Hollywood song, dance, and romance.[29] She was referring to Ernst Lubitsch, the German émigré director whose unconventional wit, European sophistication, and flair for bedroom farce in *The Love Parade* (1929) and *Monte Carlo* (1930) set the precedent for *Love Me Tonight.* Mamoulian, however, seemed amused by the genre even as he excelled in transforming its operetta conventions into cinema. His approach was entirely opposite from the way musicals were normally developed. First came the songs composed by Rodgers and Hart; only afterward were screenwriters allowed to fill the space between songs with dialogue.

Hollywood musicals usually included a string of numbers shot within individual settings. Breaking from that format and anticipating the music video by four decades, Mamoulian staged musical sequences that, in Rodgers's words, were "performed uninterrupted while the action took the story to whatever locations the director wanted." "Isn't It Romantic," which soon became a standard for pop and jazz performers, began with the tailor Maurice Courtelin (Chevalier) singing in his shop. A humming, singing customer carries the melody out of the store; a passing cab driver begins to whistle the tune, which is picked up by his passenger, a composer on his way to the train station. Cut to the railroad car, where the composer pens words for the melody, overheard by a squad of soldiers who continue singing the song in march tempo while on maneuvers. The camera pans to a Gypsy boy who picks up the tune on his fiddle. Finally, Princess Jeanette (MacDonald) overhears the song through the window of her nearby chateau. The loop is completed. Maurice and Jeanette will be united in love and music. "The whole of *Love Me Tonight* is a poem, from beginning to end," Mamoulian said. "Everything is rhythm, counter point, stylization, slow motion, fast motion, split screen, double exposure, two scenes played at the same time on a split screen."[30]

As always, Mamoulian pushed the crew past the usual limits into innovation. "On *Love Me Tonight* Mamoulian wanted puffs of smoke to come out of the smokestacks in rhythm with the music during the opening scene," said Youngerman, speaking of the symphony of Paris sounds that echoed the opening of *Porgy.* "They had these two special effects men set it up, and they tried for a week, but they couldn't make it work." Youngerman finally figured out how to achieve the effect Mamoulian wanted. When a photo lab technician showed Mamoulian a new kind of camera lens, the director spontaneously employed it in one shot. It might have been the first time the zoom lens was used in place of a dolly.[31]

The mood on the set was tense at first. Mamoulian was exhausted from *Dr. Jekyll* and in an unusually humorless mood, even telling Chevalier that he "hadn't wanted this picture and was only doing it as a favor to Mr. Zukor, and would consider it a very special favor if he could get me taken off of it." The crew responded with passive aggression, dropping lamps and sneezing during takes. Plucky as the characters she portrayed, MacDonald took matters into her own hands. "Rouben, we are supposed to be making a comedy, a gay picture full of laughter," she recalled saying. "But it's almost impossible in the funereal atmosphere you're creating. There you have it. Now don't hold it against me for letting truth be known." With those words the mood lightened, even after Mamoulian exploded at MacDonald's boyfriend, Bob Ritchie, for coaching from the sidelines and banned him from the set.[32]

For Myrna Loy, however, previously cast as vamps, the film changed her career. *Love Me Tonight* opened new roles for her in a lighter vein, including her breakthrough role as Nora Charles in *The Thin Man.* "Rouben Mamoulian rescued me," she insisted. Loy described how

Mamoulian made *Love Me Tonight* according to his lights, not by his usual method of confrontation but through stealth. "'Now listen, Myrna,' he said, 'this is what's happening. Paramount's adamant about eliminating the role of Countess Valentine, but she's very important to my concept for the film. I know what I plan to do with her, but she won't be in the script. I'll send you the lines separately until they see it my way.'" Seeing Loy in the rushes, the management relented.[33]

Mamoulian was put off at first by Chevalier, but they became lifelong friends. "I had never worked with anyone quite like him before," the director said, describing the actor's sulking attitude, sour expression, and pessimistic disposition. "Then the camera started rolling and he underwent a complete transformation. He became happy and jovial, full of life. . . . Then I shouted 'Cut!' and he went back to his corner, looking just as miserable as before." Mamoulian praised Chevalier's performances as "spiritually uplifting to young and old" decades later in the foreword to a book on the actor. "He radiated optimism, good will, and above all the *joie de vivre* that every human being longs for."[34]

Although *Love Me Tonight* was acceptable to the Hays Office upon release in August 1932, the censors withdrew the film from circulation in 1937, "as it apparently contains a great deal of suggestive dialogue."[35]

Song of Songs, Mamoulian's next film, was born amid the sort of Hollywood intrigue that kept gossip columnists at their typewriters. Based on German author Herman Sudermann's 1908 novel *Das Hohe Lied*, *The Song of Songs* had been adapted for the stage by American playwright Edward Sheldon and filmed twice by Paramount during the silent era. Paramount wanted to redo it as *Song of Songs* with Tallulah Bankhead in the lead role of Lily. Screenwriting had been under way in fits and starts for years before the studio opted for Marlene Dietrich as Lily, a country girl lured into debauchery by her cruel aristocratic husband and abandoned to a life of prostitution. Mamoulian recalled that when Zukor asked him to direct the picture, he wondered why it had not been assigned to Dietrich's usual director, Josef von Sternberg. Mamoulian decided to ask Sternberg, who told him, "The only director Marlene and I would accept is you." Mamoulian complained to all parties that the story as scripted was a stereotype, "But they begged me to do it and they said she wouldn't do the picture unless I did it," he added, referring to Dietrich, the movie's temperamental star.[36]

Dietrich's biographer Steven Bach believed that Sternberg secretly supported Paramount's move to keep him out of *Song of Songs* to quell the idea that he exerted undue influence over Dietrich as well as to give him time to pursue other opportunities, including work in Germany for the UFA studio. He also reasoned that if *Song of Songs* failed in another director's hands, it would only reinforce his role in Dietrich's career. "Paramount tried several times to separate us, but since my contract stipulated that 'I could choose my own director,' they gave in," Dietrich recalled. Finally, Sternberg "permitted me to make *Song of Songs* with another director. The film, of course, was a flop." Although she did not care for the picture, she added, enigmatically, "Rouben Mamoulian was a very good friend and took me as I was."[37]

Song of Songs' eight-week schedule was delayed by Dietrich's petulance over being separated from Sternberg. She was supposed to be on the set on December 22, 1932, but her lawyer announced she would not appear without Sternberg. She also threatened to return to Germany in February when her Paramount contract expired. On January 2 the studio filed for breach of contract in federal court and the judge issued an injunction barring her from working anywhere but Paramount. On January 9 she joined Mamoulian for lunch in the studio commissary to begin work on *Song of Songs*.[38] Recollections differ over whether Mamoulian and Dietrich got along well during the production. Brian Aherne, who had made a few films in Britain before becoming a star on the New York stage, had been lured to Hollywood to play the sculptor who was Lily's true love, only to "put down the script of *The Song of Songs* in blank despair." Complaints over the threadbare screenplay were heard across the set. When Mamoulian discovered that the final scene had not been written, he called the production office, which at first had no idea who was still responsible for the project after twelve writers had toiled on the script. Mamoulian was forced to quickly write the ending himself.[39]

Once again, the Hays Office weighed in, objecting to sexual suggestiveness, especially concerning allusions to the demimonde, and to the nude plaster statue of Dietrich's character that played a central role in the plot. Mamoulian wrote a persuasive letter to the Hays Office, convincing it, at least initially, to release the film with few cuts. In a masterful bid for sympathy, the director decried those who think all censors "are many-headed dragons, destroying anything that is in any way unconventional" and insisted, as he would throughout his career, "that I have always tried, to the best of my knowledge, to adhere to honesty and good taste in anything I have ever done either for the theatre or for the screen." As for the nude statue, whose Italian artist Scarpitta was best known for an equestrian sculpture of Mussolini, he considered it no different than statues on display in museums and other public buildings. "It is not for nothing that through many centuries of development the human race, in its search for beauty and its desire to express it in a concrete visual form, has always chosen for its medium the form of the human body."[40] Mamoulian's honeyed words bought the film temporary reprieve until 1935, when censorship tightened, and *Song of Songs* was withdrawn from circulation and largely forgotten. The director would learn that the Hays Office could indeed prove a many-headed dragon when he prepared the final cut of his next film, *Queen Christina*.

Chapter 6

Queen Garbo

Mamoulian's work with Marlene Dietrich in *Song of Songs* led to his next assignment, directing Greta Garbo in *Queen Christina*. Dietrich and Garbo were probably among the most whispered-about stars in Hollywood's European expatriate colony. Both were thought to enjoy sophisticated vices unsuspected by the American public. Both tended toward trousers and masculine garb at a time when clothing was strictly segregated by gender. Suspected of enjoying the intimate company of both men and women, Dietrich and Garbo forced the studio publicists to work overtime to deflect rumors in an era when homosexuality was considered criminal and career ending.

Dietrich's daughter Maria Riva described Mamoulian's appeal to her mother and perhaps to Garbo. "Rouben Mamoulian was not a Hollywood-type director," she wrote. "No von Stroheim boots and riding crop, not even Cecil B. DeMille pomposity . . . he was quiet. Mamoulian wasn't just calm, he seemed becalmed."[1]

Garbo, one of Hollywood's biggest box office stars in 1932, signed an unusual contract with MGM before leaving the United States for a six-month sojourn in her native Sweden. The studio granted her control over production dates and approval of directors and costars, and before departing, she agreed to star in a historical drama based on Christina, Sweden's seventeenth-century monarch.[2] Her friend Salka Viertel immediately launched into a screenplay. Viertel was pleased when producer Irving Thalberg referenced the lesbian-themed German film *Mädchen im Uniform* during an early script conference, telling her that "handled with taste it would give up very interesting themes."[3]

As was common in Hollywood, then and now, the original treatment passed through many hands on the way to production. Viertel complained that other screenwriters filled the script "with so-called 'Lubitsch touches' and the drama turned into a comedy." One of the script doctors, British writer H. M. Harwood, decided that Christina should be depicted "as the prototype of a modern woman who resents any of the feminine functions that tend to remind her of her dependence." Finally, playwright S. N. Behrman, who had written Broadway hits for Lynn Fontanne and Alfred Lunt, was brought in to complete the job. Aware of the lacuna in the historical record of Christina, his main concern was "Does the characterization emerge as a warm, living human being?"[4]

Like Elizabeth I, England's "Virgin Queen," Christina of Sweden reigned in a man's world. She was deliberately raised as a boy by tutors who hoped she would grow into the father and defender of the nation. Intellectually curious, she corresponded with Europe's leading philosophers and was something of a reformer who sided with the commoners against the nobility. As Viertel said, her "masculine education and complicated sexuality made her an almost contemporary character."[5] Christina's refusal to marry and her fascination with a Roman Catholic world far removed spiritually and geographically from her own country's frigid Lutheranism led her to abdicate and depart from Sweden for Rome.

Christina's life had been popularized by a pair of biographies in the 1920s, Faith Compton Mackenzie's *The Sibyl of the North* and Margaret Goldsmith's *Christina of Sweden: A Psychological Biography.* As early as 1927, MGM envisioned Garbo as the ideal Christina, but the vogue for historical biography pictures that began with Alexander Korda's *The Private Life of Henry VIII* was the impetus for finally turning the concept into cinema. Along with her ethnicity and androgyny, Garbo shared Christina's solitary spirit of independence, her aura of mystery, and her sense of being caged in a gilded prison. Like the character she would portray, Garbo eventually renounced her position for a private life. Her sullen lack of interest in stardom had long made her invulnerable to studio threats. By 1932 she already acted as if she would rather disappear from Hollywood than continue to work on projects beneath her contempt.

Mamoulian was never bound to a long-term contract with Paramount, and Paramount executive Walter Wanger, with whom he had worked, was now a producer at MGM. Mamoulian was not MGM's first choice. The studio cabled Garbo as she sailed back to America in March 1933 with suggested directors. She replied that Edmund Goulding and Ernst Lubitsch were acceptable, but neither proved available for *Queen Christina*. Afterward Mamoulian's name, probably at Wanger's suggestion, appeared on the short list of studio head Louis B. Mayer. On May 17 Mamoulian was approved as director after Garbo had been invited to Paramount studio to view a rough cut of *Song of Songs*.[6] Despite that film's patchwork plot, Garbo recognized from the direction of Dietrich that Mamoulian was a man with whom she could enjoy collaborating.

MGM prospered throughout the Great Depression. The studio's characteristic high-key lighting, fantastic opulence, and Middle American cultural values seemed at odds with Mamoulian's aesthetic. He was concerned about MGM's reputation as a studio where the producer, not the director, had final say. "I said to Mr. Mayer, 'I can't work that way. At Paramount I was producer-director; I never had any interference. I had the final say.'" He signed with Mayer on the condition that Wanger produce the film because "he knew how I worked and I knew that I would have no interference from him."[7] The continually fulminating Mayer probably agreed to Mamoulian's demands because Fredric March had just won an Academy Award for *Dr. Jekyll and Mr. Hyde* under his direction.

Mamoulian began by casting the part of Christina's lover, the Spanish envoy Don Antonio, who stood in for the real monarch's fascination with Roman Catholic southern Europe and deflected attention away from the character's ambiguous sexuality. "I was thinking of having John Barrymore do the part . . . and then on second thought it seemed that he would be a little too old," Mamoulian said. Supposedly Leslie Howard turned down the offer; everyone from Fredric March to Franchot Tone and Ronald Coleman were reportedly considered at one moment or another. "Everyone in Hollywood of any importance has been tested for the part, with no one measuring up to the requirements," claimed the *Hollywood Reporter*. "And then I had this crazy idea—there was a young Englishman on the lot who had never done anything to my knowledge," said Mamoulian of Laurence Olivier, overlooking three forgettable films the actor had already made in Hollywood. With Garbo's approval, the director shot a test of the two together. "I looked at the screen and the fellow wasn't there. He was young and callow, you see," Mamoulian explained.[8]

Intimidated, Olivier agreed, admitting, "I was too nervous and scared of my leading lady." The part of Don Antonio finally went to John Gilbert over the furious objections of Mayer, who despised the faded silent-era star and conspired to ruin his career. Gilbert was once engaged to Garbo, until she failed to show up for the wedding, and had not seen her in several years. Wanger tricked Gilbert into the film, informing him of casting problems and inviting him to visit the set to "help Garbo relax." Gilbert thought he was playacting a scene with his former lover, not realizing that it was a screen test. Mindful of the generous help Gilbert had given her when she was new to Hollywood, Garbo "marched into Louis B. Mayer's office and said it would be Gilbert or nobody," recalled actress Colleen Moore. "Mayer screamed and ranted, and Garbo, as always, said nothing until he was finished. Mayer knew it was useless to argue with her." The working relations between Gilbert and Garbo were tense, at first, and became good grist for gossip. "Jack Gilbert is back at work after being out of the studio for a couple of days again with a bad case of nerves or something," the *Hollywood Reporter* snipped, calling him "highly-strung."[9]

Principal photography for *Queen Christina* began on August 17, 1933, in a palace constructed on MGM's soundstage by the celebrated art director Cedric Gibbons. Mamoulian had heard that Garbo could be difficult, even insisting "that everyone except the cameraman—including the director—must leave the set when she was playing an intimate scene. I couldn't have that, of course." Garbo refused to rehearse and insisted that her first take was always best, but Mamoulian persuaded her otherwise. "She is an intuitive artist with very good and correct instincts," he said. Mamoulian's job was to gently guide those instincts according to his vision. "If she doesn't have respect for you, if she doesn't think what you are suggesting is better than what she wants to do, then it's impossible," he added. "But if you make contact then she is absolutely a gift from heaven."[10]

Among Mamoulian's striking accomplishments was coaxing the usually stoic Garbo to laugh. "She herself told me she couldn't do it," he recalled. He first elicited her laughter in the scene where Christina comes across Don Antonio's carriage stuck in the snow by having Gilbert and Akim Tamiroff (who played Don Antonio's retainer) stand outside the camera frame making crazy faces at her. Mamoulian had easier going with melancholy moods. "I would say to her, 'This mood is like the purple sunset when the leaves turn their shadows, and now and then a yellow leaf falls down.' She would say, 'Oh, I know.'"[11]

With the passage of time, *Queen Christina* has come to stand as Garbo's most memorable film. Mamoulian showed an intuitive understanding of Garbo's unique talent; rather than surround her with bustle, he allowed her to simply exist as the film's center of gravity. Critic Kenneth Tynan's description of Garbo's mystique, as "the ecstasy of existing . . . most actresses in action live only to look at men, but Garbo looks at flowers, clouds and furniture with the same admiring compassion, like Eve on the morning of creation," mirrors Mamoulian's objectives in *Queen Christina*.[12] "The scene in the inn bedroom," said Mamoulian, recalling the site of the snowbound erotic encounter between Christina and Don Antonio, "where she walks all round the room, touching everything, caressing everything, storing the whole place in memory—to my mind it's a sonnet. It was done to a metronome. I explained to her: 'This has to be sheer poetry in feeling. The movement must be like a dance. Treat it the way you would do it to music.'" To put his idea another way, it was Stanislavski in rhythm. Mamoulian added, "Of course, I had Miss Garbo. Not many actresses could do this scene with such grace."[13]

Although the bedroom scene, in which Christina and Antonio spend the night together, received the most attention in the censorious 1930s, it was *Queen Christina*'s climactic moments that became one of the most memorable scenes in film history. Christina, her kingdom gone and her lover dead, stands motionless on the deck of a ship bound for an uncertain future. The camera moves toward her until her face fills the screen with an unanswerable enigma.

Mayer first demanded the script be changed because the ending was too depressing. Don Antonio must be kept alive, he insisted. "Well, we couldn't do that, of course," said Mamoulian, staring down the mogul, "but it was true that we had in some way to make the ending uplifting, exhilarating." Elsewhere, Mamoulian recalled saying, "Mr. Mayer, I don't believe in depressing people any more than you do . . . the purpose

Rouben Mamoulian directing Greta Garbo in the famous closing scene of *Queen Christina*, 1933. (Getty Images)

of the theatre and its function is to excite, to stir, to stimulate, to uplift a person. The greatest uplift comes from a tragedy. A tragedy is not cheerful, but when you leave a tragedy you feel marvelous." Subject to audience response at a preview, Mayer granted Mamoulian the opportunity to shoot the scene his way in a purely visual climax unburdened by the falsity of words. When Garbo asked him how she should play the scene, Mamoulian said, "You do nothing. You don't act. You don't have a thought nor a feeling. In fact, try not to blink your eyes. Just hold them open. Make your face into a mask." It worked, turning Garbo into a tabula rasa for the audience. "Let them write: sadness, inspiration, courage, whatever they choose, whatever they prefer."[14]

When Mayer and other MGM executives were shown the results in a projection room, "Nary a one of them mentioned depression; in fact, they were all exhilarated," Mamoulian said. "My trump card in this was the final close-up of Garbo's face, which began with a long view and ended with an enormous close-up that ran for eighty-five feet." Once again, the technicians called Mamoulian's idea impossible. To progressively modify the degrees of diffusion as the camera came within inches of her face seemed beyond filmmaking technology at the time. It was thought no camera lens could encompass the entire scene in one long, uninterrupted take. "Suddenly, an early childhood memory popped into my mind," Mamoulian recalled. A magic lantern with a glass slide that moved a succession of pictures across the lens became the inspiration for a "new gadget" that the studio laboratory quickly cobbled together. "This is one of the regrettable things about the passing of the big studios; they had the most marvelous technical departments for whom nothing seemed impossible," Mamoulian said. "We had the whole M.G.M. laboratory go to work on my magic lantern gadget. It took a whole day but they made it. We fastened it to the front of the camera lens."[15]

As usual, Mamoulian continued to rewrite the script in the interest of rhythm and visualization even as the production rolled toward completion. Viertel resented the many evenings spent "with the indefatigable and painstaking Mamoulian who, after a hard day's work on the set and in the projection room, rushed through dinner to come to my house and go over new problems, prodding, correcting again and again, saying *no* to every suggestion, sure that only he himself could find the solution."[16]

The film was wrapped by the end of October 1933, but Mamoulian called Garbo and Gilbert back for retakes in November. "If only those who dream about Hollywood knew how difficult it all is," Garbo lamented. "The end result seems to be the only thing that counts. I long to get away." Reviewing *Queen Christina* at its gala premiere at New York's Astor Theatre in December, the *Times* called it "a skillful blend of history and fiction." The print had been cut just in time for the screening by order of New York censors and was released without the Production Code seal.[17]

It was not the film's first brush with censors, nor would concessions to New York's relatively liberal censorship board mark the end of it. James Wingate of the Hays Office's Studio Relations Committee had warned MGM to "be careful to avoid anything which might be construed as lesbianism." The bedroom scene had already aroused concern at Hays during production. "It seems to us that the explicit portrayal of any such liaison between these two characters is inadmissible under the Code and likely to endanger the story from a censorship standpoint,"

Wingate warned, referring to state and local censors who, as he anticipated, cut and spliced the film according to their local standards. MGM was told, "Miss Garbo should be kept away from the bed entirely." Memos on the subject multiplied at an alarming rate. "Col. Joy and I conferred with Walter Wanger on a forthcoming production, *Christina*. Col. Joy advised him to shoot several ways and let us take a look at the resulting shots, to which he agreed." As the film was about to go into wide release in January 1934, Joseph I. Breen took charge of the Hays Office and was annoyed that MGM had done little to follow his predecessors' instructions. Breen was incensed when the Producers Appeals Board overruled his cuts. Consisting of three Hollywood producers, the board was the court of final authority over decisions by the Hays Office. As a result, Breen decided to go over Hollywood's head to the American public via the Roman Catholic Legion of Decency and similar organizations as well as a news media hungry for sensationalism. "I can scold and argue and coax and threaten *but I have no real authority* to stop the dirty pictures," he wrote FitzGeorge Dinneen, a Catholic priest who coauthored the Production Code adapted by Hollywood. One of Dinneen's collaborators on the code, Martin Quigley, condemned the bedroom scene for registering "with voluminous and unnecessary detail the fact of a sex affair . . . thereby assuming a pornographic character."[18]

Queen Christina was the most prominent in a rash of movies whose content turned Breen and outside morals groups apoplectic. By the summer of 1934 Hollywood was forced by pressure groups into a stricter regimen. From then on, a $25,000 fine would be levied against any producer who released a film without the seal of the Production Code Authority, as the Hays Office was now officially called. The Producers Appeals Board was abolished.

Queen Christina had another unanticipated consequence in its effect on Garbo's career. According to biographer Karen Swenson, the film left "Garbo's heterosexual male audience . . . perplexed," as were small-town audiences in the South and Midwest.[19] Her legend was assured but her career was in decline.

Mamoulian's next film was conceived as a prestige picture and marketed with high hopes at the box office. Hollywood mogul Samuel Goldwyn was determined to produce a top-drawer period drama from that classiest of sources, the Russian novel. In pursuit of his ambition, he cast the luminously beautiful actress Anna Sten, a onetime student of Stanislavski, opposite one of America's leading men, Fredric March. Goldwyn had discovered Sten in Berlin, where the Russian refugee appeared in a movie adaptation of Dostoyevsky, and was determined to make her the next Garbo or Dietrich. What better director for the project than the "Russian" Mamoulian, who had already directed Goldwyn's role models for his latest discovery? Goldwyn also hired the admired cinematographer Gregg Toland, who would film *Citizen Kane* alongside Orson Welles seven years later. Alfred Newman, whose collaboration with Mamoulian would continue on three more movies, wrote the score, and Russian set designer Sergei Sudeikin, a set designer at the premiere of Stravinsky's *The Rite of Spring*, was snagged for art direction.

Goldwyn spared no expense employing a team of screenwriters to trim Tolstoy's bulky polemic *Resurrection* into an eighty-five-minute feature called *We Live Again*, squeezing an epic of political metaphysics into the star-crossed love story of the young peasant Katusha (Sten) in love with the lord of her manor, Prince Dmitri (March). *Resurrection* was a popular novel written in the twilight of Tolstoy's life; its love story between prince and peasant attracted American moviemakers as early as D. W. Griffith's 1909 short, followed by a 1927 silent feature with Dolores Del Rio and Rod La Rocque, with a forgotten talking rendition appearing four years later. The script bedeviled the new production from the start; none of the writers were able to maintain a sufficiently Hollywood tone while preserving the integrity of a novel advocating pacifism, mystic Christianity, and—worse still for American audiences—the abolition of private property. The distinguished playwright Maxwell Anderson (*Both Your Houses*) rewrote the first draft by Willard Mack. Preston Sturges worked on it, before Goldwyn hired playwright Leonard Praskins to blend the styles of his predecessors and craft dialogue specific to the actors. Finally, Mamoulian's associates from Broadway, Paul Green and Thornton Wilder, were brought in for final polish.[20]

As usual in these situations, it was difficult to recall who contributed what to the screenplay. Sturges claimed that Goldwyn went to "my friend Rouben Mamoulian, who had asked for me as a writer, and [would] say eagerly, 'When can we get rid of this fellow Sturgeon?'" Mamoulian claimed the final script was mostly Sturges, save a love scene by Thornton Wilder, but Sturges's biographer Donald Spoto maintains that Goldwyn finally dismissed Sturges and virtually nothing from his draft was filmed.[21]

Mamoulian was keen to defend Sturges for the unusual fabric of his imagination, saying, "So when you meet someone like Preston who's cut from a totally different pattern, it's a great joy."[22] Meanwhile the censors debated the merits of *We Live Again*. A proposal was vetted to cut all references to Katusha's illegitimate child, but Breen, who respected great literature, refused, grasping the spiritual significance of Tolstoy's novel. "We feel that this picture could . . . serve as a model for the proper treatment of the element of illicit sex in pictures," he wrote.[23]

At first Fredric March turned down the part of Prince Dmitri, worried that Anna Sten, after her poor showing opposite Gary Cooper in the box office failure *Nana*, would poison his career. However, the prospect of working with Mamoulian and, more important, Goldwyn's offer to double his normal salary convinced him to don the uniform of a dashing tsarist officer.[24] March's intuition about Sten's unsuccessful career proved correct, but his role in *We Live Again* prepared him to play Count Vronsky in the more commercially successful *Anna Karenina*.

We Live Again opens with a Soviet-style montage whose low-angled shots of the countryside convey viewers into the vast expanse of Mother Russia. The cinematic peak comes early, during the Russian Orthodox Easter liturgy, where candlelit midnight processions symbolically reenact the discovery that Christ had risen from the dead, pointing the way to human regeneration. Mamoulian understood this from similar ceremonies in the Armenian Church and almost certainly observed the Russian rites as a student in Moscow. In the midst of the flowing incense, resonant chanting, and jangling bells, the worshippers exchange a kiss of peace. For Dmitri and Katusha, that kiss becomes the portal to the ecstasy of erotic and romantic love.

Much of what follows is uneven and off key. When Katusha is jailed, the scene resembles a Hollywood prison picture from the 1930s. Mamoulian seemed strangely unwilling to step in and repair the problems of an often-uncomprehending screenplay. Perhaps flushed with so much attention and success, the director lapsed into a period of self-absorbed arrogance. Sturges laughed when Mamoulian said "he could make the audience interested in whatever *he* showed them. I told him he was mistaken. It is true that he can bend my head down and force me to look at a door knob . . . but it is also true that it arrests my comprehension of the scene, destroys my interest and gives me a *pain* in the neck."[25]

The marketing campaign for *We Live Again* was as oversize as Goldwyn's ambition, but testifies to Mamoulian's name recognition among moviegoers. "The greatest motion picture in film history, by the world's most outstanding writer," the ad began. "The directorial genius of Mamoulian, the beauty of Anna Sten and the producing genius of Goldwyn have combined to make the greatest entertainment in the world." The public did not agree. *We Live Again* faired poorly at box offices and marked the beginning of the end for Sten in Hollywood, a career lavishly promoted by Goldwyn but rejected by the American public. "Sam Goldwyn wanted to make her a star in the worst way," Mamoulian said. "That's just what he did."[26]

Mamoulian broke new ground with his next project, *Becky Sharp*, the first three-strip Technicolor feature. Shortly after completing *Applause*, Mamoulian told the *New York Times* that color filmmaking did not interest him. With the magnificent spectrum in grays and black available to cinematographers, he saw no reason to venture into color until the technology was greatly improved.[27] He had good reason to bide his time. From cinema's inception, many movies included hand-tinted color scenes, which were often more intrusive than aesthetically pleasing. In 1914 Massachusetts Institute of Technology instructor Herbert Kalmus and his partners founded the Technicolor Motion Picture Corporation to develop and market a process for filming in color. They made their first film with a two-color system involving green and red filters in 1917. Cumbersome and visually unimpressive, the two-color process was improved by the 1920s. Technicolor sequences were added to *The Ten Commandments* (1923) and *The Phantom of the Opera* (1925), but the system was plagued with technical problems. By 1928 Kalmus had discovered how to dye film prints in color, which reduced many of the glitches.[28] Many films were produced in the aftermath but the colorization remained unsatisfactory until the development of the "three-strip" full-color process.

After Walt Disney's success in using three-strip Technicolor for animated shorts in 1932, an independent studio called Pioneer Pictures, funded by Technicolor investors and distributed by RKO, was established to apply the process to live-action film. Pioneer launched its program with a short subject in the summer of 1934, *La Cucaracha*, and provided color segments for *The House of Rothschild* and *Kid Millions.* Determined to produce a full-length feature, Pioneer began shooting *Becky Sharp,* an adaptation of William Makepeace Thackeray's novel *Vanity Fair,* on December 3, 1934. The project halted when the director, Lowell Sherman, who had made pictures with Mae West and Joan Blondell, died from pneumonia on December 28.

Mamoulian snapped up the offer to fill the director's chair and went to work immediately, closely collaborating with cinematographer Robert Edmond Jones. On January 14, 1935, the production resumed. "I read the script and I didn't like it," he said. "I saw the two weeks rushes and I didn't like them. It started out with a red set. To me that was crazy. Red is a climax. Where do you go after red?" He demanded a new screenplay and began filming from scratch.[29] The subtle palette used in most scenes reflected the pale shades of Wedgwood pottery, creating an appropriate setting for a period comedy in early nineteenth-century England. The color was used throughout for dramatic rather than decorative ends.

Mamoulian explained his ideas on color at a meeting of the Technicians Branch of the Academy of Motion Picture Arts and Sciences. "Colors convey to us subtly different moods, feelings, and impulses," he reminded the gathering. "It is not an accident that we use the expressions 'to see red,' 'to feel blue,' . . . the artist should take advantage of the mental and emotional implications of color and use them upon the screen to increase the power and effectiveness of a scene, situation, or character."[30]

In making *Becky Sharp,* Mamoulian was confronted by the specter of Natalie Kalmus, the divorced wife of Technicolor's inventor, who by contract with all Hollywood studios served as "color supervisor" on every Technicolor production until 1949. Outraged at the prospect of being told how to paint with his colors, Mamoulian claimed he stormed off to the producers and said, "Look, tomorrow, either she is not there, or I am not there."[31] If so, Mamoulian had better luck fending off her interference than other directors. Vincente Minnelli, forced to work with Kalmus on *Meet Me in St. Louis,* complained, "My juxtaposition of color had been highly praised on the stage, but I couldn't do anything right in Mrs. Kalmus's eyes."[32]

Becky Sharp opens theatrically with the parting of a blue curtain as the students of a girls' boarding school emerge to watch the graduation of a pair of morally contrasting characters, the dutiful Amelia (Frances Dee) and the sexually voracious Becky (Miriam Hopkins). For many stretches, *Becky Sharp* seems to violate Mamoulian's axiom that movies should never be merely theater on film, but he was forced to wrestle with the bulky heft of early Technicolor cameras, slowing the kineticism he loved. He employed close-ups of letters, diaries, and handbills the way intertitles had been used in silent movies, yet *Becky Sharp* is largely driven by dialogue between a superb cast numbering such respected character actors as Nigel Bruce, Sir Cedric Hardwick, and Billie Burke. At last, in a spectacular scene midway through the picture, Mamoulian achieves the cinematic sweep that had always been his goal. A grand ball on the eve of Waterloo is disturbed by distant sounds that could be thunder or artillery; along with a rushing gale comes news of French cannons to the crowded dance floor. The civilians are seized by panic and the officers, answering the call of duty, gather their wits and hurry from the hall to their garrison. The windblown curtains, rushing feet, and terror and dismay on the faces of the five hundred actors in the scene divert the conscious mind from an unconscious impression caused by the players exiting the ballroom according to the color of their costumes. "Start the first one in black and white, next dark blue, dark green, then come the yellows and greens, then come the orange, and at the end the officers in red," Mamoulian told his puzzled assistant director, Argyle Nelson. "He said, 'That doesn't make sense. How can you have all the same color people running out at the same time?' I said, 'I'm not arguing with you. I feel the same way in my brain, but I feel differently in my bones.'" [33] By moving from the coolest colors through mounting shades of anxiety, Mamoulian used Technicolor to build tension in the ballroom scene.

An expensive film for its time, *Becky Sharp* was completed on March 20, 1935, at a cost of nearly $1 million. The theatrical trailer presented the film as a cinematic milestone. "RKO Radio has the honor to announce a signal achievement in the art of motion pictures. At last the screen becomes the palette for life's great canvas," it trumpeted. *Becky Sharp* introduced the public to the saturated, richer-than-life hues of Technicolor, yet would be lost in the forward rush toward such full-color classics as *The Adventures of Robin Hood* (1938), *The Wizard of Oz* (1939), and *Gone with the Wind* (1939). The critics did not care for *Becky Sharp.* Most agreed with the *New York Times*' assessment. "Although it is dramatically tedious, it is a gallant and distinguished outpost in an almost uncharted domain."[34] In other words, boring movie, great color.

At the 1935 meeting of the Academy's Technicians Branch, Mamoulian said, "One thing that is going to push color very far ahead is television." He accurately predicted the course of events that would occur two decades after his speech. "People can turn a little button and sit at home and be entertained, but they are going to get that entertainment in black-and-white for a good many years. Color television will come undoubtedly, but it will come late, and in the meantime the screen will be able to use color against the competition of television. There will be an added sense of vividness in the theater that will not be apparent upon the home screen."[35]

In the aftermath of *Becky Sharp,* producer Irving Thalberg assigned Mamoulian to direct what might have been the only Armenian-themed film of his career. With William Powell and Clark Gable in mind for starring roles, MGM had purchased the rights to the international bestseller *The Forty Days of Musa Dagh,* a novel by Austrian Jewish author Franz Werfel dramatizing the true story of heroic resistance by Armenian villagers faced with mass murder at the hands of the Ottoman Turks during World War I. Thalberg pressed forward with the project despite threats by the Turkish regime, which adamantly denied that the Armenian genocide had occurred, and assigned prolific screenwriter Frances Marion to write a script with Mamoulian. After the Breen Office fretted about offending "the history, institutions, prominent people, and citizenry of other nations," and the U.S. State Department expressed concern when the government of France worried that the film might cause unrest in its Near Eastern mandates, the project was shelved. *The Forty Days of Musa Dagh* was never produced.[36]

As it happened, Mamoulian had already received an attractive offer while working on *Becky Sharp.* He was asked by the Theatre Guild to return to Broadway to direct the premiere of *Porgy and Bess.*

Chapter 7

I Loves You, Porgy

Rouben Mamoulian was not everyone's first choice to direct the Theatre Guild's premiere of George Gershwin's opera *Porgy and Bess.* Despite the success of *Porgy* and his relatively smooth working relationship with Mamoulian, DuBose Heyward decided that the original play was "not my idea of good art."[1] He preferred a relatively new face in theater fresh from directing the Virgil Thompson–Gertrude Stein opera *Four Saints in Three Acts,* John Houseman, years away from his career as a Hollywood producer. Gershwin "had heard that I worked well with Negroes in the theatre," Houseman recalled and invited the director to his art deco Manhattan penthouse to hear the songs. "I asked questions and made a few guarded suggestions," Houseman continued. He realized Gershwin was not favorably impressed only weeks later, he recounted, upon reading "the Theatre Guild announcement that Rouben Mamoulian . . . had arrived from California to prepare for the production of *Porgy and Bess.*"[2]

The Guild was eager to draw Mamoulian back to Broadway and Mamoulian was interested in returning if the script was right and time permitted between film productions. They considered offering Mamoulian Eugene O'Neill's *Mourning Becomes Electra* in 1931 and Mamoulian later suggested directing a play starring Greta Garbo, but a suitable script was never found.[3]

The Theatre Guild was not unaware of the publicity value of bringing back *Porgy*'s original helmsman, who had since become a big name in Hollywood, for the unveiling of *Porgy and Bess.* The Guild's production manager Warren Munsell held firm with Heyward. "The matter of the director has been discussed at some length and while we were considering John Houseman, the feeling here is that this is a very big show for Houseman to undertake. We would all be very much better satisfied if Mamoulian were to do it." Munsell added that while he recalled "some minor misunderstandings" between Mamoulian and Heyward, he believed "that the values of the present version will be brought out far better by him than by Houseman, and it would be greatly to your advantage, as well as ours, to have him produce the play." Munsell concluded: "We want to close the arrangements now, so that he will hold the time open for us." Gershwin, who had first met Mamoulian in Rochester in 1923, was convinced from early on that the man who brought *Porgy* to the stage was the best choice.[4]

Mamoulian claimed he was doubtful at first over the project. "I felt the play was so pure and complete in its form, had such a direct simplicity and strength, that any attempt to translate it into operatic form might spoil it," he claimed. "However, my second thought was that if there was a composer in the whole world equipped by the quality of his talent to achieve this end, George was that composer." Mamoulian's claim that he signed a contract with the Theatre Guild "without having heard a single note" of *Porgy and Bess* is contradicted by the spirit of his communications with the Guild, haggling with them for many months over compensation and time. Mamoulian wanted an unusually high fee for an already expensive production while wanting to spend as little time on the project as possible.[5]

Even before *Porgy* was produced as a play, Gershwin had been in touch with Heyward. After reading the novel, he recognized the story's potential as an American opera and became fascinated with setting it to music. Gershwin began his career during the 1910s in New York's Tin Pan Alley, where popular songs were penned for sheet music publishers and phonograph recordings. Al Jolson scored a hit with Gershwin's "Swanee" and the writer developed a talent for popular musical comedies such as *Lady, Be Good* and *Funny Face*. Gershwin was a student of classical music who prowled the Harlem nightclubs, absorbing elements of the European tradition while falling in love with jazz, especially the great stride piano players Eubie Blake and Lucky Roberts. Gershwin was the child of Russian Jewish immigrants who aspired to culture; his ambition was to do for American vernacular music what the great Russian composers had done with the folk music of their homeland by distilling it into compositions for the symphony and opera house.

As early as 1922 Gershwin wrote *Blue Monday (Opera à la Afro-American)*, a half-hour piece about a Harlem gangster shot dead by his jealous lover. It made only a slight impression. Two years later, however, Gershwin's *Rhapsody in Blue* successfully fused the vocabulary of jazz with the grammar of classical music. With the worldwide acclaim of *Rhapsody* as the anthem of the Jazz Age, Gershwin "was to America's music what F. Scott Fitzgerald was to its literature."[6]

The opera that became *Porgy and Bess* would be Gershwin's rebuke to the Mayflower Americans who continued to bristle at immigrants from eastern and southern Europe as well as blacks and Jews. In September 1927, as Mamoulian was putting *Porgy* into rehearsal, the Heywards and Gershwin met for the first time. The composer spoke of his dream to turn the novel into an opera, but his many moneymaking commitments to Broadway, Hollywood, and network radio prevented him from making good on his promise. Heyward's frustration with Gershwin's hesitation to move forward was expressed in the climactic scene of his 1929 novel *Mamba's Daughters,* which fantasized about an all-black opera at the all-white Metropolitan Opera. An audience member commented enthusiastically about the imagined production, "Can't you feel it's something of our own—American—something . . . that Gershwin actually got his hands on in spots of *Rhapsody in Blue.*"[7]

The collaboration finally began to inch from hope to reality in March 1932, when Gershwin wrote Heyward about starting work on *Porgy.* "It is still the most outstanding play I know about colored people," he said. While Gershwin continued to move slowly toward commitment, Al Jolson approached the Theatre Guild with a scheme to stage *Porgy,* starring himself in blackface, with music and book by Jerome Kern and Oscar Hammerstein II. Foreseeing a profitable run, the Guild pressed Heyward to accept the offer, which gave the author reason to renew contact with Gershwin, who still claimed to be unable to clear his schedule. "If you can see your way to making some ready money from Jolson's version, I don't know that it would hurt a later version done by an all-colored cast," Gershwin advised. Heyward felt constrained to negotiate with Jolson, but the blackface *Porgy* never materialized. Kern recalled that by the time Jolson "had assembled [his] thoughts on the idea for the Theatre Guild, Gershwin had beaten him to it."[8]

Finally, in the fall of 1933, Heyward and Gershwin began writing. The Metropolitan Opera was interested in producing the show, but

Gershwin wanted an all-black cast and the doors of the Met were barred to black performers. Since the Theatre Guild was more liberal and capable of hosting a longer run as long as the crowds kept coming, Gershwin approached the Guild. Afraid that calling it an "opera" would scare away ticket buyers, the Guild insisted on terming the production a "folk opera." The description stirred some comment, but was defended as evidence of the tradition Gershwin worked in. "When Mussorgsky conceived *Boris Gudunov* as a folk opera he certainly did not use the designation as an excuse for relaxing his artistic discipline," wrote critic Isaac Goldberg. "It meant to him a sense of inspiration. Gershwin, at his proper distance, regarded the piece the same way."[9]

Ira Gershwin, George's brother, was brought in to help shape Heyward's book into song lyrics, although many of the songs would be credited only to DuBose Heyward and George Gershwin. Following in Mamoulian's footsteps, George visited Charleston in the summer of 1934 to learn firsthand about the Gullahs. "But the most interesting discovery," Heyward wrote, "as we sat listening to their spirituals, or watched a group shuffling before a cabin or country store, was that to George it was more like a homecoming than an exploration. The quality in him which had produced the *Rhapsody in Blue* in the most sophisticated city in America, found its counterpart in the impulse behind the music and bodily rhythms of the simple Negro peasant of the South." The Guild granted Heyward and Gershwin a relatively free hand in choosing cast and crew but insisted on one point: the folk opera would not be called *Porgy*. Heyward explained, "There was a feeling in the publicity department that this would lead to a confusion in that amorphous region known as the public mind, and that *Porgy* in lights might be construed as a revival of the original play." With the example before them of *Tristan and Isolde* and *Samson and Delilah,* they decided on *Porgy and Bess*.[10]

By the time Mamoulian arrived in New York to begin rehearsals in mid-August of 1935, casting and staffing had been completed. Although Gershwin rejected Houseman as director and dismissed the all-black opera *Four Saints in Three Acts,* mocking Stein's libretto for having "the effect of a 5-year old child prattling on" and the music as "early 19th century," he eagerly recruited from the production's cast and crew.[11] Gershwin hired a pair of Russians, Alexander Smallens as conductor and

Sergei Soudeikine as set designer. From the black actors and singers he cast Edward Matthews as Jake the Fisherman and the Eva Jessye Choir. Gershwin and Heyward scoured theater and film for additional African American talent, finding J. Rosamond Johnson (the co-composer of "Lift Every Voice and Sing") as Lawyer Frazer, Ruby Elzy (from the film version of *The Emperor Jones*) as Serena, and a pair of singers with opera experience, Abbie Mitchell as Clara and Warren Coleman as Crown. The vaudeville entertainer John W. Bubbles, who had taught Fred Astaire to tap dance a decade earlier, became Sportin' Life. Gershwin wanted Paul Robeson as Porgy but settled on Todd Duncan, a Howard University music professor who had sung in an all-black production of Mascagni's *Cavalleria Rusticana*. Like many from the African American middle class of the day, Duncan disdained blues, jazz, and popular music, but would gradually warm to *Porgy and Bess*.

The cast was accomplished. Georgette Harvey (Maria) had been in Mamoulian's original *Porgy* and had recently starred in the theater version of Hayward's *Mamba's Daughters*. Anne Wiggins (Bess) was a Julliard graduate and Elzy a Julliard student. Even so, Gershwin's impresario Merle Armitage was correct in saying, "The cast had to use virtually 'unknown singers' in the leading roles, as there were few Negroes at that time with professional operatic experience."[12]

Mamoulian professed to feel about *Porgy* "the way I imagine a mother feels about her first born. If it were to be 'clothed' in music, I was jealously anxious for that music to be good," he said. He was invited to Gershwin's penthouse to hear that music the evening after his arrival in New York. "George sat down at the piano while Ira stood over him like a guardian angel," he recalled. "I found it so exciting, so full of color, and so provocative in its rhythm that after this first piano section was over, I jumped out of my armchair and interrupted George to tell him how much I liked it." Mamoulian remarked that George attained an expression of "Nirvana" while singing "Summertime" with Ira.[13]

Gershwin had taken a page from Wagner by creating leitmotifs for most major characters, yet the opera never sounded Wagnerian. Closer to Bizet in its lightness and local color, it incorporated echoes of Berg, Stravinsky, Schoenberg, and other modernists admired by Gershwin. In the gentle melancholy of "Summertime" the blues was married to the cry of Jewish cantors. "*Porgy and Bess* is a folk tale. Its people naturally would sing folk music," Gershwin explained, adding, in words that could have come from Mamoulian, "I decided against the use of original folk material because I wanted the music to be all of one piece."[14]

Given Mamoulian's lack of input into the opera's preproduction and the insistence of Heyward and Gershwin in choosing key personnel, *Porgy and Bess* could have been the project over which the director exerted the least control since his arrival in the New World. However, Mamoulian characteristically and substantially reshaped the existing text to his aesthetic. The opera's length was already at issue before Mamoulian's involvement. Gershwin continually urged Heyward to shorten it. "I had a play which needed to be cut forty percent for the libretto, yet nothing of dramatic value could be sacrificed," Heyward wrote. "The dialogue had to follow that of the drama, but it had to be arranged to form a new pattern, to escape monotony and adapt itself to the music."[15]

Mamoulian pushed to trim *Porgy and Bess* to a manageable scale and infuse it with greater dynamism. The director stepped into a production that was, to his mind, at loose ends. After the first day of rehearsal, which he compared to "breaking mountains of ice," Mamoulian felt "completely exhausted and . . . a little depressed. Everything seemed awkward, disorganized, almost hopeless," he recalled, his grim mood at odds with his usual irrepressible nature. Lying in bed in his hotel room that evening, "indulging in rather melancholy and misanthropic thoughts," he was cheered by an unexpected phone call from Gershwin. "I just had to call you and tell you how I feel," the composer began. "I am so thrilled and delighted over the rehearsal today!"[16] Mamoulian's depression lifted and he and Gershwin began to work harmoniously.

"George didn't want to interfere during rehearsals, he let us do what we knew how to do," recalled choral director Eva Jessye. Usually, Gershwin sat in the rear of the hall, cracking and eating peanuts. Problems were caused by John W. Bubbles's "negligence over rehearsals and promptness," reported Gershwin's friend, pianist Oscar Levant. In his account, conductor Alexander Smallens's "exasperation with the absent Bubbles caused him to fling down his baton and shout to Mamoulian, 'I'm sick of this waiting. We'll have to throw him out and get someone else.'" Before Mamoulian could respond, however, "Gershwin bounded from his seat a few rows back in the darkened theater and rushed down the aisle. 'Throw him out?' he said. 'You can't do that, Why, he's—he's the black Toscanini!'"[17]

Mamoulian conducted rehearsals with a copy of the score before him, adding touches that could not be notated. He told the cast to "regulate your movement by the rhythm and character of the music at the moment," directing the chorus to move forward on a certain chord during the fight scene. When Bess's movements were too vigorous during the wake, "Mamoulian aided her by saying, 'You're the accompaniment, not the melody. What we want here is an obbligato.'" According to musicologist Charles Hamm, "*Porgy and Bess* was not so much staged as choreographed; and as Mamoulian developed a clearer sense of what he wanted, he had no hesitation in changing what Heyward and Gershwin had given him to work with."[18] Aside from working with the rhythm of the dialogue and music, Mamoulian eliminated dramatic dead spots and clarified dramatic situations.

With the backdrop of Soudeikine's elaborate stage settings, described by the Theatre Guild's Lawrence Langner as "just far enough away from realism to provide the requisite picturesqueness," Mamoulian restaged *Porgy*'s symphony of noises on a larger scale.[19] He choreographed "I Got Plenty o' Nuttin'" as a dense web of sight and sound; a chorus of women rocked and sewed in time to the music while their neighbors on Catfish Row kept time by wielding carving knives, rug beaters, dishrags, shoes, and hammers while others, from the windows above, shook bedding to the beat. That Mamoulian imagined *Porgy and Bess* as a performance rather than a concert confined to the composer's score is lost on some conductors who, a century after Wagner, fail to comprehend opera as a Gesamtkunstwerk, a totality encompassing many media.

More cuts had to be made before the premiere. A piano jazz overture called "Jazzbo Brown" was deleted at the Theatre Guild's behest to save the cost of building a set for a single song. Gershwin ordered "The Buzzard Song" dropped from act 2 because it was sandwiched between two other arias sung by Porgy, "Bess You Is My Woman" and "I Got Plenty o' Nuttin'." He explained, "You won't have a Porgy by the time we reach New York. No one can sing that much, eight performances a week."[20]

Porgy and Bess was given an invitation-only run-through at Carnegie Hall before its September 30, 1935, opening at Boston's Colonial

Theatre, a society event benefiting the New England Hospital for Women and Children. The opera received a thunderous ovation from the audience. At the end of the curtain call, Gershwin, Heyward, and Mamoulian emerged to take their bows and remained onstage for fifteen minutes until the applause finally ended. A sold-out one-week run followed. From Todd Duncan comes the story that Mamoulian, Gershwin, and Smallens "spent the night walking in the Boston Common discussing cuts that must be made before we reached the Alvin Theatre in New York. Their toughest customer was George; but who could blame him."[21]

Hamm studied the various surviving scores from 1935 and found that "nuanced cuts and major changes were made in the course of rehearsals and after the tryout performance in Boston," many at Mamoulian's behest. It was a work in progress until opening night, contrary to the beliefs of a later generation of "purists" who thought they could uncover Gershwin's original intentions by restoring the excised parts. In the jacket notes to his 1976 recording of the "complete" *Porgy and Bess,* conductor Lorin Maazel wrote, "How glorious it is to hear the entire opera, without dozens of cuts, which have mutilated form, flow, dramatic function." Hamm calls this a "myth" of restoration.[22]

At Mamoulian's birthday party two days before the October 10, 1935, Broadway opening, Gershwin presented the director with a sheaf of pages deleted from the score, rolled up and tied with red ribbon. "This is my thank you for making me take out all that stuff in Boston," he said. Recent Gershwin biographers have heard a note of sarcasm in that birthday present, but Gershwin acknowledged that Mamoulian's decisions were correct. "It was Mr. Mamoulian who staged the original production of *Porgy* as a play," the composer said. "He knew all of its values. What was even more valuable, he knew opera as well as he knew the theatre and he was able to bring his knowledge of both to this new form. In my opinion, he has left nothing to be desired."[23]

Mamoulian cited Gershwin's support in defending his decisions. "George, who loved his own stuff as much as he did, never hesitated to make any cuts that were necessary. . . . He did this because he had no false vanity about his work and also because George was one of the best showmen I have ever known. He knew the theatre. He knew the audience."[24]

The first night on Broadway was crowded with Hollywood celebrities, including Katharine Hepburn, Leslie Howard, and Joan Crawford, along with playwrights Robert E. Sherwood and Ben Hecht, novelists Edna Ferber and J. B. Priestley, violinists Fritz Kreisler and Jascha Heifetz, bandleader Paul Whiteman, and publishers Condé Nast and Harold Ross. "One of the most excited audiences in the history of the New York theatre attended the opening and their expectations were fully realized," Langner said. *New York Times* music critic Olin Downes agreed, but added, "It must be admitted that in spite of its cuts there are still too many set songs and 'numbers' which hold back the dramatic development." However, he praised many of Mamoulian's contributions, contrasting *Porgy and Bess* with conventional operatic staging that was "usually as out of date as the dodo." Downes added that if "the Metropolitan chorus could ever put one-half the action into the riot scene in the second half of 'Meistersinger' that the Negro cast put into the fight that followed the crap game it would not merely be refreshing but miraculous. And when did Isolde wave a scarf more rhythmically from the tower than those who shook feather dusters and sheets from the windows to accompany Porgy's song."[25]

Other critics were less kind. Composer Virgil Thomson decried it as "straight from the melting pot. At best it is a piquant but highly unsavory stirring-up together of Israel, Africa and the Gaelic Isles."[26] *Porgy and Bess*'s New York run was exceptional for an opera but not a great success by Broadway standards. Overhead was high, especially because of its larger-than-usual pit orchestra. Finally, admission was lowered from $4.40 to $3.30 for top tickets in an effort to fill seats.[27] The investors, including the Gershwin brothers, lost money, but the Gershwins recouped their investment through musical recording royalties and road shows. Several of the songs gained popularity apart from the opera and were soon on their way to becoming standards.

On January 27, 1936, *Porgy and Bess* opened in Philadelphia and traveled from there to Pittsburgh, Chicago, and Washington, D.C. Washington's National Theatre was a segregated house, prompting a strike from Duncan and other cast members despite threats from the Theatre Guild. With the help of Ralph Bunche and other African American leaders with ties to the Roosevelt administration, the National Theatre was temporarily desegregated for *Porgy and Bess,* although it reverted to the old rules once the opera left town.

In February of 1938 Armitage brought *Porgy and Bess* to the West Coast with performances in the Pasadena Auditorium, Los Angeles's

Philharmonic Auditorium, and San Francisco's Curran Theatre. Directed by Mamoulian with Alexander Steinert conducting, it featured most of the original cast, with Avon Long replacing Bubbles as Sportin' Life. According to Armitage, the "importance of these performances . . . was the interest aroused in the motion picture industry."[28] It would take Hollywood twenty years to film *Porgy and Bess,* however, and by that time Mamoulian's intransigent commitment to his aesthetic ideals cost him the job. During negotiations for a 1951 tour mounted by Robert Breen of the American National Theatre and Academy, Mamoulian's name was also put up as director. Breen told producer Blevins Davis, "[Ira] Gershwin would like to have Mamoulian, but every time he starts talking about him he begins to talk himself out of it. He says what a nice, charming fellow Mamoulian is, but whenever he gets into a theatre he thinks he invented the stage and that he superseded the Greeks." He continued nevertheless to negotiate with Mamoulian, but the director finally bowed out.[29]

The New York premiere of *Porgy and Bess* was an epochal event, remembered for introducing the first significant American opera and the first important operatic performance by an all-black cast. So many professional black singers had never performed together on a Broadway stage; despite the qualms of some African American critics about its contents, *Porgy and Bess* opened new doors for black performers. As an opera on Broadway it crossed barriers at a time when the hedges between high and low art were carefully maintained by the groundskeepers of American culture. Essayist Terry Teachout wrote in 2000, "To date American opera has produced one masterpiece, George Gershwin's *Porgy and Bess* (1935)."[30] Mamoulian was instrumental in shaping as well as presenting that opera to the world.

Chapter 8

Golden Boy

On the night of December 23, 1935, director King Vidor summoned a handful of prominent colleagues to his Beverly Hills home to discuss their concerns. Probably the rumor of a pay cut for all studio employees was as worrisome as the recent edict at Paramount ordering its directors to accept any picture offered them or lose their contracts.

By January 16, Mamoulian had joined some forty other directors at the Hollywood Athletic Club to form the Screen Directors Guild. Vidor was elected president and Mamoulian was named to the board of directors. The founders followed the steps of the Screen Actors Guild and the Screen Writers Guild at a time when rising trade unionism in all fields was met by intense opposition from industrialists and conservatives. Hollywood would be no different. "It was tough to get important directors in because they had a lot to lose, big salaries to lose," Mamoulian said, adding that the Directors Guild's mission was "to lift the position of the average director," who earned relatively little.[1]

Mamoulian recalled years later that the organizers "kept discussing the sad fact that while everybody had a union or a guild, the directors didn't have any. We thought that was a very sad situation," he said. Characteristically, he also saw the Directors Guild as a way of leveraging artistic autonomy from the studio heads. "The idea that moved us was not just to get more salary for the director and to get directors more authority. The ultimate purpose was better films. We were thinking about the quality of films." The studio moguls reacted by threatening to fire directors who joined the Directors Guild, but membership grew rapidly as the founders met prospects over dinner and convinced them to join.[2]

At the guild's second meeting, at the Hollywood Athletic Club on January 22, only the politically conservative Cecil B. DeMille attacked the project "when he cautioned those present not to rush in and sign application blanks for membership until they had carefully studied the purposes and benefits."[3] He objected to any collaboration with the Screen Actors Guild, an affiliate of the American Federation of Labor. According to Laurence Beilenson, attorney for the actors and directors guilds, DeMille "thought this was practically Bolshevism to have a union among directors. And he made an impassioned speech at the meeting denouncing unionism in general."[4] It would not be the last time DeMille and Mamoulian were on opposite sides in the politically divisive field of Hollywood union politics.

The studio heads agreed with DeMille's assessment and fought to ignore the claims by the guilds to negotiate on behalf of writers, actors, and directors. Mamoulian, along with Howard Hawks and Edward Sutherland, were members of the guild's negotiating committee.[5] Finally, on March 13, 1939, the National Labor Relations Board recognized the guild as a legitimate union for directors and assistant directors, two years after the guild thwarted an attempt by studio bosses and mobsters to impose a puppet union on the directors. The recognition of the Directors Guild was a step, if almost imperceptible at the time, toward the dissolution of the studio system that had governed Hollywood like a factory town.

The unending struggle between commerce and art was a theme in Mamoulian's first picture after returning to Hollywood from Broadway. *The Gay Desperado* (1936) began with an idea whose potential for satire appealed to Mamoulian. Producer Jesse Lasky, working in a business partnership with silent star Mary Pickford, had Italian opera singer Nino Martini under contract and planned to star the tenor in a comedy for United Artists, a prestigious and financially successful distribution company for independent-minded producers. At one time or another David O. Selznick, Alexander Korda, Howard Hughes, and Mamoulian's mentor Walter Wanger produced pictures for UA. Searching for a suitable project for Martini, who was having more success at the Met than in Hollywood, Lasky showed Mamoulian a screenplay based on Gounod's *Faust*. "It intrigued me but the script was all wrong," the director recalled. "Jesse was desperate: Martini's first film had flopped, and he couldn't think of another vehicle. Then while we were talking, a man

Rouben Mamoulian during the filming of *Gay Desperado* with the movie's stars, Ida Lupino and Nino Martini, 1936. (Getty Images)

called [Leo] Berinski arrived with the idea for a Mexican film." The concept involved Chicano banditos, inspired by Hollywood gangster movies to modernize their methods, who take as hostage a singer played by Martini. "The idea caught my imagination: a great premise, and charming as a subject for a satire; but the rest of the story was the dreariest you have ever heard," Mamoulian said. He convinced Lasky to retain the idea of banditos emulating tough-talking hoodlums from north of the border while procuring a new script by the prolific screenwriter Wallace Smith.[6]

The film opens with a brilliant spoof of Hollywood gangster conventions at a screening in a Mexican bijou. The local banditos, headed by Braganza (Leo Carrillo), engage in animated discussion of an American crime movie whose hardboiled mannerisms seem just slightly exaggerated. "Bravo! Bravo!" they shout as Tommy guns blaze and cars careen through an American city. Unlike Mamoulian's entry into the crime genre, *City Streets,* death is seen on camera. In the overheated atmosphere triggered by the movie, a knockdown fight erupts with fists and folding chairs, juxtaposed against the violence on-screen. When Chivo (Martini) soothes the passions by singing a familiar Mexican tune, Braganza is overwhelmed by the performance, takes the aspiring opera singer at gunpoint to a local radio station, and interrupts the programming by thrusting Chivo at the microphone to sing "Celeste Aida." Parodying his own experience in Hollywood, Mamoulian teases with the idea of an artist's career advanced through brute force by uncultured men who admire culture.

The comical romp soon entangles a young American couple running away to Mexico to get married. Jane (Ida Lupino) is a down-to-earth girl engaged to the wastrel son of an American millionaire. When she is kidnapped by Braganza's gang and held for ransom, the situation ensures the rapid flowering of romance between Martini, the picture's star, and Lupino, an ingenue who had not yet made her mark on Hollywood.

The Gay Desperado carefully restricts its arrangement of Mexican clichés to the banditos, with their sly smiles beneath enfolding sombreros and their comic mangling of English. The local authorities and ordinary citizens are treated respectfully. When real as opposed to cinematic American gangsters arrive on the scene, another contrast becomes apparent. The Yankee gang members, with many allusions to popular genre stars such as Edward G. Robinson and James Cagney, are heartless products of a materialistic society. Braganza's crew is soulful by contrast, bound to certain codes of conduct and respectful of the muse that whispers in Chivo's ear. The Hays Office worried about *The Gay Desperado*'s lawless tone, expressing the eternal concern that audiences could be influenced in criminality by Hollywood pictures, but passed the film nevertheless.[7]

Although the *New York Times* called *The Gay Desperado* "a first-rate musical comedy," the reviewer added perceptively, "Mr. Martini is a much better tenor than he is a comedian." British novelist Graham Greene, moonlighting as a film critic, was normally no fan of Mamoulian but called *The Gay Desperado* "one of the best light comedies of the year" and praised its visuals. "Eisenstein's Mexico was no more sensuous than this."[8] The film earned Mamoulian the best director's award from the New York Film Critics Circle.

Mamoulian would return to musical comedy for his next film, *High, Wide and Handsome* (1937), working this time with the authors of the groundbreaking Broadway musical *Show Boat,* Jerome Kern and Oscar Hammerstein. The story was a light treatment of a historical turning point, the development of America's first commercially viable oil well in Pennsylvania in 1859. Listening to the music in its raw form at Kern's Beverly Hills home, Mamoulian was perturbed by the resemblance of one tune to a Gershwin melody. Hammerstein resolved the problem by phoning Gershwin for permission to steal eight bars from *Porgy and Bess* for *High, Wide and Handsome.*[9] Kern and Hammerstein composed a light operetta with Americana influences for the film, which was among the few musicals before the 1940s in which song and dance were integral to the plot, rather than standing apart as showcases for the stars. Mamoulian cut the rhythm of his editing to the cadence of the songs.

Paramount mogul Adolph Zukor told producer Arthur Hornblow Jr. to spare no expense on a picture uniting two of Broadway's most popular songwriters with a successful director whose ear for music and visual flair were widely respected. The A-list cast was led by an actress borrowed from RKO, Irene Dunne, the star a year earlier of the film adaptation of *Show Boat.* Having aspired to opera before going to Hollywood, Dunne enjoyed one of her rare singing roles as Sally, the spirited daughter of a mountebank who peddles patent medicine made from Pennsylvania crude, a natural resource whose value has not yet been discerned. She marries an enterprising local farmer, Peter Cortlandt, who has a "crazy notion about oil," as his skeptical neighbors put it. Randolph Scott, the square-jawed hero of many films with frontier settings, was cast as Cortlandt, the man who foresaw the day when oil would drive the world. Dorothy Lamour, still working as a character actress in dark, exotic roles, played a dancehall girl drawn to the boomtown that erupts around Cortlandt's oil derricks.

Hammerstein devoted most of the fall of 1937 to the screenplay, working closely with Kern to integrate the score with the plot, and with Mamoulian on a shooting script that married romance with fact and fantasy.[10] Emerging from their collaboration was an archetypal Hollywood story of an individual whose determination moves mountains and overcomes all obstacles. Cortlandt's boomtown project is menaced from two sides. On one hand are torch-wielding Protestant fundamentalists outraged by the gambling dens and saloons clustered around the derricks. More dangerous is a cabal of banking and railroad plutocrats whose amiable ringleader (played by Alan Hale) is determined to seize Cortlandt's wells by financial pressure, legal chicanery, or violence if necessary. The plot assumes Capraesque dimensions as little people from many backgrounds, including oil workers, farmhands, circus performers, and women of loose morals, band together to block the juggernaut of big business. *High, Wide and Handsome* includes several well-choreographed fight scenes, especially the climactic Armageddon pitting a circus troop, complete with charging elephants, against bullwhip-cracking thugs in black hats dispatched by the tycoons to destroy Cortlandt's oil pipeline.

Mamoulian recalled *High, Wide and Handsome* as "a very difficult story to film." While praised by the *New York Times* for telling a colorful chapter of American history "in vividly cinematic terms," audiences mostly agreed with Graham Greene's assessment of "this long, dumb and dreary picture." On the night of its sneak preview, Adolph Zukor crossed the floor of Hollywood's Riviera Country Club to shake Hammerstein's hand and say, "That's the greatest picture we ever made." A few months later, after failing to recoup his investment, Zukor walked past Hammerstein in a restaurant and looked through him as if he were a stranger. Paramount did not renew Hammerstein's contract, but the lyricist went on to greater success on Broadway, including work with Mamoulian on the debuts of *Oklahoma!* and *Carousel.* For *High, Wide and Handsome,* Mamoulian received the highest salary of his career, $178,000 at the rate of $7,500 per week, a considerable sum for a movie that lost money. By comparison, David O. Selznick signed director William Wellman for a one-year contract in 1937 at only $2,750 a week, and in that same year Louis B. Mayer hired producer Mervyn LeRoy at a weekly salary of $6,000; to avoid the envy of other producers, MGM claimed LeRoy made only half as much.[11] *High, Wide and Handsome* would be Mamoulian's final picture for Paramount.

Mamoulian continued his work on behalf of the Directors Guild while casting for a movie to direct for Columbia Pictures. His relations with Harry Cohn's studio would not be happy, however. "After I did *Porgy and Bess* on Broadway I was fired with the idea of doing a film version, and [studio head Harry] Cohn lured me to Columbia on a ruse, pretending to want to do it," Mamoulian complained. The gestation of *Porgy and Bess* in Hollywood was long and troubled, culminating two decades later. Meanwhile, Columbia's story department showed Mamoulian a treatment called *The Gentleman from Montana,* a proposed screenplay already drawing fire from the Breen Office for its unflattering depiction of American politics. Mamoulian loved it, saying, "In America we make fun of ourselves and criticize ourselves," and threatened to purchase the rights if Cohn refused to assign the film to him. In the end, the movie was made by another director under a different title and became a classic, *Mr. Smith Goes to Washington.* "I traded him *Golden Boy* for it," claimed Frank Capra, explaining how *Mr. Smith* became his film. Capra had been eager to direct what became Mamoulian's next picture, *Golden Boy;* by one account, Mamoulian, who owned the rights to *Golden Boy,* turned down an offer from Capra: the astonishing sum of $75,000.[12]

Golden Boy mirrored the spirit of the director's organizing work with the Directors Guild and the questioning attitude of the American public during the Great Depression. The protagonist, Joe Napoleon, is torn between playing violin, which touches the most human dimension of his personality, and his attraction to the dehumanizing sport of boxing with its lure of riches. Fresh from a seven-month run for the Group Theatre on Broadway during 1937–38, *Golden Boy* was popular enough for Hollywood even if its socialist perspective would inevitably be softened to suit both the censors and the moguls. The playwright, Clifford Odets, considered himself a voice of the proletariat, albeit his own relations with the working class were never close. Although he left the Communist Party after less than a year, finding its line too restricting, the author of *Waiting for Lefty* and *Awake and Sing!* continued to critique the economic underpinnings of a corrupt, money-mad society.

Mamoulian's first brush with the playwright came during the production of *R.U.R.,* in which Odets played a small part onstage. "He is no good!" the director exclaimed.[13] Although *Golden Boy* was a stage play fashioned in cinematic terms and Odets was living in Hollywood, he allegedly refused to work on the adaptation, fearing his vision would be compromised. Mamoulian offered the script to a fellow Armenian, novelist William Saroyan, but recalled that the writer "hated the studio and gave up." Finally, Mamoulian hired a pair of New Yorkers who had won a screenwriting contest sponsored by the Hollywood studios, Daniel Taradash and Lewis Meltzer. According to Taradash, Mamoulian tried out both men by asking them to script the first twenty minutes of *Golden Boy* and, enthusiastic about the results, hired them as a team over the objections of studio mogul Harry Cohn, who wanted a seasoned writer.

Early drafts included Mamoulian's name, indicating his hands-on role in developing the screenplay, but in Taradash's memory, "Mamoulian never wrote anything, but he talked about it all the time as we went along. He was so intelligent, and he had a very private, very charming sense of humor. Harry Cohn was driving him crazy!" Annoyed when Cohn told Taradash and Meltzer to "make it sound like Capra," Mamoulian isolated them from the mogul's influence by bringing them to the Mojave Desert to write.[14]

Taradash and Meltzer transformed the female lead, Lorna Moon, into a wisecracking gal suitable for the actress who played her on-screen, Barbara Stanwyck; they transformed a social drama into the personal struggle of a sensitive artist in an uncaring world; and they diluted the tragedy of the play with a requisite Hollywood happy ending. Even so, the Breen Office vetoed the adulterous relationship between Lorna and boxing manager Tom Moody, played with suave melancholy by Adolphe Menjou. Rewritten several times to suit the censors, the screenplay was eventually credited to Lewis Meltzer and Daniel Taradash along with Sarah Y. Mason and her husband, Victor Heerman, who had won an Oscar for their screenplay of *Little Women*.

To cast Joe Napoleon, the Columbia publicity department mounted a public campaign to find an unknown everyman suitable for the part, and some sixty young men auditioned as a result, but Mamoulian was unhappy with the ballyhoo surrounding the casting and insisted on anointing his own star. "What you want is the best actor for the part that you have, and frequently the unknown supplies that," Mamoulian recalled. "In *Golden Boy* I was stuck. I didn't have the lead. And I finally found this young fellow, who was at Paramount getting $50 a week on a scholarship. . . . And I thought he had something, so I made a test and I decided that I would try him." The young fellow was William Holden and *Golden Boy* was the break the actor was looking for.[15]

Before the filming was completed, however, Holden seemed headed for a breakdown. He worked a seventeen-hour day, learning to box at the Hollywood Athletic Club and learning violin well enough to perform the fingering in close-ups. Cohn and Mamoulian viewed the early rushes "in an uneasy silence"; soon enough, the mogul pressed Mamoulian to replace Holden, whose grasp on the role appeared uncertain. Given his headstrong personality, Mamoulian naturally fought the move, but by all reports it was Stanwyck who eventually rescued Holden by coaching his body language and dialogue. Confronting Cohn in a scene that might have been scripted for one of her movies, she demanded, "Leave him alone and he'll find himself. He's a very sensitive, intelligent young man. I don't know what other qualities you want. None of us can walk on water."[16]

The year of *Golden Boy*'s release, 1939, has been called Hollywood's annus mirabilis on the strength of *Gone with the Wind, The Wizard of Oz, Wuthering Heights,* and the movie that slipped through Mamoulian's hands, *Mr. Smith Goes to Washington*. Against such an array of riches, little wonder *Golden Boy* has been overlooked. Some critics nonetheless found the movie better than the play. Praising Mamoulian for dispensing with Odets's political "hooey," Graham Greene extolled his "vigorous hard-hitting close-up effect" and ranked the climactic fight scene "among the finest sequences of the talking film." However, the film's reputation was set when the *New York Times* called *Golden Boy* "an interesting, entertaining, dramatic, but scarcely first-rate motion picture."[17]

Putting his brief, stormy interlude with Columbia behind him, Mamoulian began the first of three pictures for 20th Century Fox. *The Mark of Zorro* (1940) was dynamic and sumptuous and became the Mamoulian film that left the deepest impression on popular culture the world over, even becoming part of the DC Comics' origin story for Batman. Although it was a remake of the 1920 Douglas Fairbanks Sr. silent movie, Mamoulian's *Mark of Zorro* established the baseline for all Zorros to come, including a popular television series, B pictures, and a high-budget remake starring Antonio Banderas, *The Mask of Zorro* (1998).

Enchanted by the silent version, Mamoulian jumped at the chance to direct a remake. The setting appealed to his visual aesthetic and probably tapped childhood memories of Tiflis, much as *Porgy* had. "I had fallen in love with California as a boy through the stories of Bret Harte, and *The Mark of Zorro* was set there, at a time when it was Spanish, when it had a great picturesque quality and languor, and wonderful *haciendas* and oak-trees and manor-houses," he recalled. Mamoulian was also attracted to the story's theme of fighting oppression. When the dastardly Captain Pasquale (Basil Rathbone) and his sergeant are shown extorting taxes from the poor, Mamoulian reversed the normal order for establishing a scene by pulling the cameras back frame by frame instead of moving them forward. "I'd like to show it the way these villains look to the poor peons," he said. "So I showed a large close-up of a peon trembling and then cut to a large close-up of the monsters. After a few of these, I went to long shots." As Pasquale, Rathbone took up where he left off as the villainous sheriff of Nottingham in *The Adventures of Robin Hood* (1938), which set the bar for Hollywood swashbucklers. Mamoulian was determined to outshine that movie's unforgettable fencing scenes. "Those Errol Flynn films had duels through castles, up and down stairways. Where do you go from that?" he demanded. The solution was to stage the climactic battle between Zorro and Pasquale in confined spaces.[18]

Mamoulian claimed he rejected the screenplay Fox mogul Darryl F. Zanuck handed him and won an unusual degree of control over the final cut. Worried over setting a precedent with other directors, Zanuck agreed to absent himself from the lot during the editing process, giving himself a chance to pretend he was unaware of what Mamoulian was up to.[19]

The Mark of Zorro was Tyrone Power's first taste of swashbuckling, and the presence of Fox's brightest star in the title role was a mark of its prestige within the studio. He was Zanuck's favorite leading man, accorded the privilege of the mogul's company off the lot as well as access to his private steam room. Despite his Irish heritage, the dashing, handsome actor possessed a "Latin look." Even in his stage debut at age seven, Power played a Mexican boy.[20]

Zorro ("fox" in Spanish) draws from a deep well of trickster archetypes. The story of an aristocrat who takes up arms on behalf of the impoverished is Robin Hood transplanted to the New World. Pulp fiction writer Johnston McCulley created his masked rider in 1919 in the aftermath of D. W. Griffith's innovative if historically distorted film *The Birth of a Nation* (1915), which depicted the Ku Klux Klan as masked crusaders punishing the oppressors who descended on the fallen South after the Civil War. The probable inspiration behind Zorro's mask was lost on 20th Century Fox and Mamoulian, whose remake struck a chord against the rise of fascism. The Breen Office joined in, praising the film for rallying spectators to stand and fight at a time when "freedom and right" were "precious and endangered things."[21]

Mamoulian found Zanuck "a dream to work with" and the good feelings were mutual; *The Mark of Zorro* was one of the highest-grossing films of 1940. Mamoulian's next production for 20th Century Fox was essentially a follow-up, with Tyrone Power in another "Latin lover" role as the matador Juan Gallardo; several supporting cast members and much of the crew returned. Like *Zorro, Blood and Sand* was a remake of a popular movie from the silent era, but while successful upon its release in 1941, it has not endured in the mythology of pop culture. The original Rudolph Valentino matador melodrama already drew snickers from the audience at its 1922 premiere and a redux under the strictures of the Hollywood Production Code, dampening the story's sexuality, was almost bound to be little more than two fleeting hours of escapism.[22]

Mamoulian expressed little interest in the story by Spanish novelist Vicente Blasco Ibáñez, reshaped for the screen according to Zanuck's calculations, but relished the opportunity to return to Technicolor. As with *Becky Sharp,* Mamoulian was concerned with the emotional significance of color and painted from his knowledge of art history. Gone were the cool Wedgwood tones of *Becky Sharp*'s English interiors. *Blood and Sand* was set in Spain, a land of intense sunlight and shadows. "The greatest truths are conceived intuitively, not through the brain. The greatest truths can never be proven, but they can be felt," Mamoulian explained, discussing his "color script" for *Blood and Sand,* which was "as much worked out in detail as the dialogue."[23] The drama of a bullfighter's ascent from poverty to the stardom of the ring and the self-destruction of celebrity was better expressed by color than words. Mamoulian's efforts were honored when his cameramen, Ernest Palmer and Ray Rennahan, shared an Oscar for Best Color Photography.

"I tried to emulate the mood of great Spanish painters for various scenes," the director said. Zanuck embraced Mamoulian's concept, agreeing to Murillo bronzes, browns, and black for the bullfighter's impoverished childhood; Goya for the bullring; Velázquez for the richness of temptress Doña Sol's mansion; El Greco for the matador's chapel; Sorella for street and market scenes; the luxurious color and bustling motion of Titian and Veronese for the matador's ceremonial vesting. "I had the whole chapel painted in greens and greys and blues, no whites, a real El Greco color scheme," said Mamoulian of one of *Blood and Sand*'s memorable scenes. He did much of the painting himself with a set of spray guns (the "Mamoulian palette") and treated the film as "a series of moving paintings."[24]

When Tyrone Power entered the matador's chapel, his natural skin tone upset Mamoulian's concept of "El Greco faces, green and blue."

To maintain the color scheme, the director "used gelatins on the lenses and they turned [the actors' faces] half blue, half green. . . . We shot it and it looked perfect on the screen." For the banquet in Doña Sol's mansion, Mamoulian painted the green leaves in a flower bowl black to fully achieve the colors of Velázquez. "I think when they saw me painting them black they went and told Mr. Zanuck I'd gone out of my mind," he said of the startled reaction from his crew.[25] No visual detail was left to chance. Hermes Pan, with whom the director would work on his final completed film, *Silk Stockings,* choreographed the fiesta scenes. Mamoulian's use of gongs for an eerie sonic dimension in the film's second half was reminiscent of his experiments in *Dr. Jekyll and Mr. Hyde,* and his concern for the emotional resonance of sound dates from his work with the Theatre Guild.

Zanuck wanted to borrow Jane Russell from Howard Hughes to play "the other woman" in Juan Gallardo's life, but the mogul refused. Many actresses tested for the part, including Maria Montez. Mamoulian claimed the Dominican-born beauty sat on his desk, "hiked up her skirt to show me her legs, winked at me suggestively and went into a first-rate vamp act." Her screen test was not as impressive. "But the moment I saw Rita Hayworth walk I knew I had my Doña Sol," the director said, admiring her "feline sort of movement that was subtle and insinuating." Mamoulian borrowed Hayworth from Columbia, where she had appeared in B pictures, and thrust her into stardom. Relentlessly enforcing his color scheme, Mamoulian had Hayworth dye her brunette hair to the coppery red she retained through her career.[26]

For his part, Tyrone Power learned the capework but was never allowed near a bull. Although Ibáñez's novel was critical of the blood sport, neither Hollywood version of his book focused on the bulls aside from their value as kinetic spectacle. The American Humane Society worried about the treatment of the animals in Mamoulian's picture, whose fight scenes were shot during a real bullfight in Mexico City's Plaza de Toros. According to technical consultant Budd Boetticher, a onetime bullfighter who went on to direct in Hollywood, close-ups showing the banderillas pricking the bulls were achieved while draping the animals with thick hides. Mamoulian's crew harmed no bulls. Boetticher did not enjoy working with Mamoulian, accusing him of being more concerned with El Greco colors than accurately depicting the sport of bullfighting and complaining of the bell the director rang on the set to summon him for consultation during the filming.[27]

Mamoulian's final film for 20th Century Fox, *Rings on Her Fingers* (1942), was a project for which the director felt little engagement. The movie was Zanuck's effort to replicate the success of Preston Sturges's screwball comedy *The Lady Eve* (1941); he even brought Henry Fonda back from the earlier movie to play, once again, the victim of genial confidence artists. According to his costar, Gene Tierney, Fonda "detested the script" and *Rings* was "the beginning of his unrest with Hollywood." It was not the first time Fonda had toiled under Mamoulian. He was a $15-a-week extra in the Theatre Guild's production of *The Game of Love and Death* (1929), a production that coincided with the stock market crash and closed after six weeks.[28]

Rings on Her Fingers was similarly doomed. As Tierney put it, the movie "was my first comedy part. But it was not a good time for comedy—the time being the final weeks of 1941." The December 7 filming on Catalina Island was interrupted, Tierney recalled, "when an assistant came running down the beach. 'The Japanese have bombed Pearl Harbor,' he yelled." The cast and crew evacuated the island for the mainland.[29]

For Mamoulian, however, *Rings on Her Fingers* produced an unexpectedly positive outcome. Tierney introduced him at a party in her home to the portrait artist and bicoastal, transatlantic socialite Azadia Newman, cousin of Wallis Simpson and daughter of Edwin A. Newman, Washington, D.C., real estate baron and chairman of the Democratic National Committee during the time of Woodrow Wilson. Her family came of old settler stock in the New World and claimed ancestry from Alfred the Great and Charlemagne. Newman had studied at several schools, including the Art Students League and the Pennsylvania Academy of Fine Art, and was "much in demand on both sides of the Atlantic" as a portrait artist for wealthy clients, including members of Congress and Hollywood celebrities. In 1938 she exhibited a collection of portraits at Los Angeles's Stendahl Galleries, the city's leading art venue, and afterward sojourned often in Hollywood, where she painted Carole Lombard and other stars for the short-lived magazine *Cinema Arts.* A mutual love for cats may have drawn the couple together. When Newman sailed for London aboard the *Normandie* to accept a series of commissions, she was accompanied by her tabby cat because she refused to be parted from him. Her previous marriage to actor Scott Colton assumed the character of a Howard Hawks screwball comedy when he captured a California lynx and presented it to her as a gift. With the fellow tenants of her exclusive Manhattan apartment building in revolt, she was forced to donate the creature to the Staten Island Zoo.[30]

At the time Newman met Mamoulian, she was still married; her divorce from Colton was decreed on January 15, 1943. Meanwhile, in the early months of 1942, gossip columnists repeatedly spotted Mamoulian with Carole Landis, who had been cast to star in *Blood and Sand* but was removed from the picture by Darryl Zanuck after she refused to sleep with him. After Landis left Mamoulian for producer Gene Markey, his interest in Newman grew more serious.[31]

Nearly fifteen years his junior, Newman would be employed by Mamoulian to create a visually prominent painting for the film *Laura* (1944) and studies for the costumes worn in his Broadway play *Sadie Thompson* (1944). In March 1945, Mamoulian, described in *Time* magazine's announcement as the "lean, owl-eyed stage & screen director," married the "comely, lynx-eyed socialite portraitist" in Peekskill, New York. The marriage was reported along with other society events in *Town & Country*. According to the Armenian American press, "Very few people expected him to walk to the altar, but he surprised every one when . . . he married Azadia Newman, descendent of an old Quaker family, a prominent and highly paid society portraitist."[32] The daughter of old money became Mamoulian's wife and companion whenever he ventured from Hollywood to work in New York. She would be with him in London for his final film, *Cleopatra*. The relationship ended only with his death.

Chapter 9

Lost in the Stars

Mamoulian refused all requests to work for the Theatre Guild during his busy Hollywood years of the late 1930s and early 1940s.[1] Lacking an interesting movie project after *Rings on Her Fingers,* however, he returned to New York in the early months of 1943 to direct the Guild's premiere of one of the most important, enduring shows to emerge from Broadway, Richard Rodgers and Oscar Hammerstein's *Oklahoma!*

With *Oklahoma!* Rodgers and Hammerstein transmuted the raw material of American musical comedy into a musical theater whose song-driven stories played with larger themes and were inhabited by characters that cast a psychological shadow in the limelight. With the best of their musicals, and *Oklahoma!* was among the best, Rodgers and Hammerstein acted as artists and advocates as well as entertainers, amusing the audience while offering them something to think about and to feel. *Oklahoma!* might not have been the first production of its kind—Hammerstein's collaboration with Jerome Kern, *Show Boat* (1927), is a good contender—but *Oklahoma!* set many precedents on Broadway when it opened on March 31, 1943.[2]

Oklahoma! was also the next step in the project begun by Gershwin with *Porgy* to produce an American answer to European opera in an entirely vernacular idiom. Verdi penned his operas to entertain a mass audience in his homeland, not only a thin elite at the top of society, and American composers dreamed of similarly bridging the chasm between high and low culture with eager marriages of words and music. In contemporary press accounts, *Oklahoma!* was called a "folk operetta" in distinction to Gershwin's "folk opera," *Porgy and Bess,* and was important for bringing a veneer of the folkloric music of white America to the popular stage, an analogue to the more authentic revival already begun in the circles of Woody Guthrie, Pete Seeger, and the Almanac Singers as well as compositions for symphony and ballet by Aaron Copland. *Oklahoma!* was the spirit come to life of the WPA murals painted in courthouses and post offices across the United States during the New Deal, with their heroic allegories of the common man and woman at work in a landscape of hope.

Oklahoma! reinvented an earlier Theatre Guild play, Lynn Riggs's *Green Grow the Lilacs* (1931), which Mamoulian had turned down an invitation to direct. According to the Guild's Lawrence Langner, the downbeat play about settlers in the Oklahoma Territory "called for a colorful chorus which sang cowboy songs to cover the changes from scene to scene." Langner's partner, Theresa Helburn, persuaded Rodgers to adapt the modestly successful *Green Grow the Lilacs* into a new musical and since his usual collaborator, Lorenz Hart, was recovering from illness, she suggested Oscar Hammerstein II.[3]

Facing financial ruin after several unprofitable seasons, Langner and Helburn desperately needed to present the Guild with a hit; they suggested casting prominent stars, such as Groucho Marx, as box office bait, but Rodgers and Hammerstein insisted on employing only Broadway talent. It was a testimony to the Guild's dedication to the art of theater that it persevered with a production largely shorn of musical comedy's burlesque roots and inimical to the infamous Broadway maxim: "No gags. No girls. No chance." "As our treasury was so depleted, it was obvious that we could not produce *Oklahoma!* without outside capital," Langner admitted. After complicated negotiations with MGM, which had long before purchased the film option for *Green Grow the Lilacs,* Helburn finally convinced Harry Cohn of Columbia Pictures to invest $15,000 in the project. Rodgers and Hammerstein, along with cast members Joan Roberts (Laurey) and Alfred Drake (Curly), performed their songs in the apartments of wealthy patrons to raise cash, which trickled in slowly. Choreographer Agnes de Mille complained that Helburn even interrupted rehearsals to show unfinished scenes to prospective backers.[4]

"Finally came the question as to who should direct the play," Langner recalled. "Rouben Mamoulian, the hero of *Porgy and Bess,* came to town from Hollywood, and he was engaged as the director on our suggestion." However, this account obscures the fact that Mamoulian was not the first but the fourth choice to stage the musical. Rodgers preferred Joshua Logan, who had directed several of his shows with Lorenz Hart. The composer wanted an American-born director for such an all-American show, but Logan was about to enter the service. Elia Kazan and Bretagne Windust turned down the job, telling Helburn they were not interested.[5]

Rodgers had worked successfully with Mamoulian on *Love Me Tonight*, one of the brightest musicals from Hollywood, and Hammerstein had partnered with the director on *High, Wide and Handsome*, another folkloric staging of American history. Rodgers and Hammerstein's concept for a total work of theater encompassing costume and set design along with story, song, and dance was thoroughly in line with Mamoulian's aesthetic. The director stepped into a project well under way, if still incomplete, by the time he began rehearsals on February 8, 1943. The score was mostly written. Along with Roberts and Drake in the starring roles, Celeste Holm had already been cast as Ado Annie, Betty Garde as Aunt Ellen, Joseph Buloff as Ali Hakim, and Howard Da Silva as Jud. The crew members had been delegated their tasks. Guild veterans Lemuel Ayers and Miles White were handling the scenery and costumes, and choreographer Agnes de Mille, who had danced the lead in the premiere of Aaron Copland's ballet *Rodeo* (1942), was in charge of the *Oklahoma!* dancers. A clash of temperaments was inevitable, especially given the anxious backdrop of the Guild's financial concerns. The show's star, Joan Roberts, praised Mamoulian for bringing out the best in her, but complained of too many directors. "I would have been happy just to have Mamoulian, Rodgers, and Hammerstein. But then I had Jay Blackton, who was music director, Langner, and Helburn—six people saying do it this way or that," she recalled. "I remember Mr. Mamoulian standing up and saying, 'There can only be one captain of this ship and I am the director,' and it [the arguments] stopped."[6]

De Mille, who viewed *Oklahoma!* as an opportunity to draw from an untapped well of modern dancers rather than the usual Broadway hoofers, remembered many heated discussions during the casting of the chorus. "Helburn and Rouben Mamoulian wanted slim legs above all," she said. "I wanted talent and personality. Rodgers wanted faces, but was inclined to stand by me." Mamoulian tried to block her candidates for the chorus. "They're certainly not pretty," he said. "They can't act. Possibly they can dance." After de Mille threatened to quit, Mamoulian backed down, shrugging, "Then just keep them out of my way."[7]

Clashes between Mamoulian and de Mille continued through rehearsals at the Guild Theatre on Fifty-second Street. "He was used to complete, unquestioned authority and total obedience," she said, conceding, "I was used to the same." She credits the good judgment of Rodgers, his "authority for running interference," for keeping the process moving forward. Rehearsals were chaotic and creative, a workshop whose final product was shaped and pounded red hot on the anvils as the deadline hung overhead. In de Mille's memory, "Lawrence Langner expounded. Terry Helburn snapped and badgered and barked at our heels, with a housekeeper's insistence on detail. Mamoulian created in spite of the hour and other people's nerves. But Oscar [Hammerstein] just quietly pointed the way." Langner recalled Rodgers and Hammerstein "writing new songs without any apparent effort during rehearsals, whenever they were needed," including the "rousing song of the earth" that became "Oklahoma!" When designer Miles White was out of the room, Langner and Mamoulian had the cutter reveal a little more neck and bosom in the women's costumes.[8]

Many ideas were tried and discarded. Dancer George Church told the story that Mamoulian, wanting a crowd-pleasing spectacle for the finale, hired an "honest-to-goodness cowboy from Oklahoma" to lasso Roberts and Drake in a rope of love. He was dismissed after lassoing Mamoulian by accident. Even the title underwent much tailoring. It was still called *Away We Go* on March 11, 1943, at its out-of-town tryout in New Haven's Shubert Theatre, where it was warmly received. Hammerstein suggested *Oklahoma,* which struck most everyone as sounding downbeat. "Lawrence declared himself satisfied if an exclamation point was added," de Mille said with a note of dry sarcasm. At the debut of *Away We Go,* the bucolic first scene opened cinematically with a flock of white pigeons flying across the stage. "The Guild got hold of a pigeon expert who told me he could manage my effect with the greatest of ease," Mamoulian explained. But instead of flying across the stage as expected, "the perverse birds shot straight up like Roman candles and landed on pipes at the top of the stage. There they stayed through the three days of our New Haven engagement, causing repeated and unexpected embarrassment to actors and much white and fluffy damage to scenery and costumes."[9]

On March 15, *Oklahoma!* arrived at Boston's Colonial Theatre, minus the pigeons but still advertised as *Away We Go.* By contractual obligation, Mamoulian's name appeared in the same-size font as Rodgers and Hammerstein's, while everyone else was relegated to tiny type. Langner declared the show "in excellent shape, and in practically the exact condition in which it opened in New York," albeit act 2 was rewritten on the fly during a two-week run in Boston. Mamoulian recalled much animosity from his last-hour reshaping of the material, complaining, "No one even spoke to me. Rodgers thought I was destroying his music. He couldn't accept the singers having their backs to the audience. Everyone wanted me to restage it as an ordinary musical comedy. I refused, and they did not even invite me to the opening night party." Langner later credited Mamoulian with "integrating all the talents involved in the production, and merging them into the final form of *Oklahoma!* This was illustrated not only in the way the songs were directed by him . . . but also in the way the play was lighted" to produce dramatic effects.[10] *Oklahoma!* might have made a less striking impression, and may even have been a different play, if not for Mamoulian's contributions.

Oklahoma! magnified the optimistic mood of Americans at war and distilled the national ethos into songs. It would fill the St. James Theatre for years to come and endure as a staple of American theater, adding new numbers to the American popular songbook. Much of the early press it received focused on the "unusual features" of the production, including the larger-than-normal twenty-eight-piece pit orchestra and the "generous sprinkling of graduates of the Julliard School of Music and various ballet schools." The idea of such an American story being directed by the foreign-born Mamoulian, "with an almost cherubic smile that sits oddly on his dark Armenian face," struck some pundits as worthy of notice.[11]

No one acted more surprised by the success of *Oklahoma!* than Richard Rodgers. "Everyone connected with the show, except me, had had a string of failures," he seemed to grouse. "The Theatre Guild had made no secret of the fact that this was really their last gasp. Our choreographer, Agnes de Mille, had withdrawn from two Broadway musicals before they had come to New York. . . . All we really knew about her was that we liked her ballet, *Rodeo,* and we thought she would be right for the dances. Rouben Mamoulian had had nothing on Broadway since *Porgy and Bess*, and that was in 1935. The cast was completely unknown."[12]

Happy to divide his time between Broadway and Hollywood, Mamoulian was engaged by 20th Century Fox to direct *Laura* (1944), but acrimony between him and producer Otto Preminger led to his firing. Preminger would take charge of the picture. Afterward, Mamoulian returned to New York to direct a string of new productions, some of them footnotes and others storied chapters in Broadway history. His first project was to direct and help write the book for *Sadie Thompson*, a lighthearted musical based on W. Somerset Maugham's short story "Rain." The story had literary cachet and was familiar, twice staged in different versions on Broadway and adapted into Hollywood movies for Gloria Swanson and Joan Crawford. However, after only five rehearsals *Sadie Thompson*'s star Ethel Merman pulled out. Her problem was with the lyrics of Howard Dietz, the Broadway tunesmith and longtime MGM publicist credited with choosing the studio's roaring lion mascot. The diva felt his words were beneath her dignity as a performer.

Despite the loss of Merman, whose name was expected to draw crowds, Mamoulian staged a lavish and challenging production with musical numbers and story ballets in the form of montages that exposed the folkloric primitivism of its setting, Pago Pago. The sets included a "water curtain" along with what Mamoulian called a "human sculptural frieze" acting in rhythmic counterpoint to each other as scenery changed in full view of the audience.[13] Opening at the Alvin Theatre on November 16, 1944, *Sadie Thomson* closed after only sixty performances.

Mamoulian would enjoy much greater success with his next production, *Carousel*. The musical was based on *Liliom*, a highly regarded work by Hungarian playwright Ferenc Molnár successfully performed twice by the Guild in past years. As early as 1937 Kurt Weill spoke to Mamoulian about adapting it as a musical. "He was enthusiastic when I told him about the *Liliom* idea and said we absolutely would have to get Molnar's permission," Weill told his wife, singer Lotte Lenya. No one easily obtained Molnar's permission. "It was common knowledge that he'd already turned down offers from both Puccini and Gershwin to adapt his work for the musical stage," said Rodgers, who in any event felt that "a musical *Liliom* seemed totally impossible." A pessimistic fantasy would never light the Great White Way. Langner disagreed, insisting, "*Liliom* would make an excellent libretto for a musical." Helburn and Langner hoped to gain Molnar's permission by bringing him to see *Oklahoma!* "At an interview with Theresa Helburn and myself after he had seen the musical, he confessed that if Rodgers and Hammerstein could treat the subject of *Liliom* as tastefully and charmingly as they had treated *Oklahoma!,* he would give his consent," Langner said. Rodgers conceded that the "persistence" of Langner and Helburn as well as their idea to change *Liliom*'s locale from Hungary to nineteenth-century New England finally swayed him.[14]

This time there were no second thoughts over who would helm the production. According to Rodgers, "We reasoned—rightly, as it turned out—that with *Oklahoma!* behind them, both director Rouben Mamoulian and choreographer Agnes de Mille would feel secure enough to work smoothly together this time."[15]

Darker in theme than *Oklahoma!* and more sophisticated musically, *Carousel* operatically evoked each character through Rodgers's music. Mamoulian, who insisted on no break in character when a performer switched from song to dialogue, avidly embraced the stylization. "The nearer it comes to a song the more rhythmic the speech becomes," he said. "And the movement must all be rhythmic too. Realistic movement would be terrible in this musical."[16]

Once again, the cast had been chosen before the director was picked and was largely unknown. John Raitt, the father of singer Bonnie Raitt, played the protagonist, the abusive Billy Bigelow, who kills himself after a botched robbery and redeems himself from beyond the grave through an act of love. As with *Oklahoma!, Carousel*'s New Haven tryout prompted a great number of changes, including the elimination of scenes and characters. "With some excellent suggestions from Molnar and Mamoulian on the book, we arrived in Boston with a second act which was on its way toward the perfection which it later achieved," Langner declared.[17] *Carousel* opened on April 19, 1945, at the Majestic Theatre, a considerably larger venue than the St. James. It played for two years.

Rodgers had only happy memories of the collaborative process and Molnar, who attended several rehearsals and the New Haven tryout, was impressed by "the directorial ability of Rouben Mamoulian, who stood motionless on the stage, instructing actors, chorus, and ballet with perfect calm, speaking softly and displaying ingenuity in everything he said."[18] The collaboration with Mamoulian, however, did not continue.

Plans for Rodgers and Hart to subsequently adapt Anita Loos's play *Happy Birthday* with Mamoulian as the director never materialized; Broadway favorite Josh Logan directed the play instead.[19]

Mamoulian was not asked to direct the next Rodgers and Hammerstein premiere, *Allegro* (1947); the task fell to de Mille. "The same teamwork which had resulted in the success of *Oklahoma!* and *Carousel* was missing, and the results were unwieldy and unconvincing," Langner concluded.[20]

Bertolt Brecht's American publisher, Samuel French, forwarded financial backer Jules Leventhal's suggestion that Mamoulian direct the planned 1945 production of *Caucasian Chalk Circle.* Brecht had been in New York for the debut run of *Porgy and Bess* and expressed admiration for Mamoulian's direction, but the production never got beyond the talking stage and *Caucasian Chalk Circle* would not receive its premiere until 1948. Although Mamoulian returned to Hollywood for the final months of 1945, where he signed with MGM to work under the acclaimed producer of musicals Arthur Freed, he returned to New York early the following year to help the Theatre Guild rejuvenate the tired casts of *Oklahoma!* and *Carousel.* Despite their eagerness to work together, the Guild and Mamoulian sparred periodically during the next several years over what the director considered "the minimum obligatory requirements of my contract" to be given full acknowledgment for all *Oklahoma!* and *Carousel* productions, even road shows where he played no continuing role. The Guild groused that Mamoulian had failed to fulfill his end of the bargain by offering advice and troubleshooting, and was insufficiently helpful in maintaining high performance levels for the newer productions.[21]

Freed struck a bargain with Mamoulian before he departed for New York to assist the Guild and to meet with Eugene O'Neill to obtain the playwright's blessing for his current Hollywood project, a musical adaptation of *Ah, Wilderness!* The producer, who had just conceded to one of Mamoulian's concepts for *Ah, Wilderness!* wanted something in return. "You're going East, you want to see O'Neill, right? Since I've done you a favor, would you do one for me?" he asked. "Come up to Boston and tell me what can be done with the show."[22]

The show was a floundering stage musical with an all-black cast, *St. Louis Woman.* Freed and his MGM colleague Sam Katz had invested in the production as a vehicle for Lena Horne, a rising star at the studio after the success of *Stormy Weather* (1943). The problems began when Horne, a woman determined to break the color barrier and overcome stereotypes, pulled out of the project, protesting that although she "had fallen in love with the music" by Harold Arlen and Johnny Mercer, she hated the script, especially her intended role as "a flashy whore." She disdained the script as "melodramatic and old fashioned" and "resented its pidgin English" and one-dimensional characters. "In fact the play seemed just another of those tired rehashes with *Porgy and Bess* overtones."[23]

What had seemed liberating to many African Americans only a decade earlier now drew the ire of activists. "I believe Arthur Freed's motives were good," Horne said, assuming he was positioning her for greater success at MGM, including a film version of *St. Louis Woman*. "They kept telling me that it had been a long time since Negroes had had a chance to work on Broadway—which was certainly true. . . . On the other hand, people representing the Negro organizations were telling me that I must not do the part. They were concentrating very hard just then on trying to end cliché presentations of Negro life." Horne's decision had repercussions on her career. Afterward, MGM "ceased giving me permission to work in cabarets. They also forbade me to work on Broadway in a revival of *Show Boat*," she said.[24]

St. Louis Woman originated in an important novel of the Harlem Renaissance, Arna Bontemps's *God Sends Sunday* (1931). The acclaimed Harlem Renaissance poet and essayist Countee Cullen had already adapted the text into a play under that name in the 1930s, which was produced to little notice by the Federal Theater Project. Cullen was working to modify the expansive plot into a musical for Freed and Katz at the time of his death shortly after rehearsals began. Although he spent several nights at the Boston tryout of *St. Louis Woman* in February 1946 and wrote a critique for Freed, Mamoulian was reluctant to seize the director's reins from his old Guild colleague Lemuel Ayers and concerned about a prolonged absence from MGM. When Freed assured him there would be no problem with the studio and Ayers, who felt he was in over his head, stepped aside to become the show's designer, Mamoulian assumed the task of directing the production and rewriting the book. His wife, Azadia, accompanied him to rehearsals at New York's Martin Beck Theatre.[25]

St. Louis Woman was familiar territory for the director of *Porgy* and

Rouben Mamoulian with his wife, Azadia Newman, at a Theatre Guild New Year's Eve party, 1944. (Getty Images)

Porgy and Bess. Set in the black community of St. Louis in 1900, its protagonist, the jockey Little Augie, is a short man menaced by Bigelow Brown, a hulking saloonkeeper. Little Augie is in love with Bigelow Brown's mistress, Della Green. Mamoulian reconfigured Cullen's two-act play into three acts, each ending at a dynamic peak. He clarified the story, quickened the pace, integrated music and dance into the plot, and eliminated Bontemps's theme of racial snobbery by light-complexioned African Americans toward their darker brothers and sisters. "I told them we had to change all that," Mamoulian insisted. "I reminded them that we were all engaged in the struggle for equality. It is ridiculous to act with snobbery to someone who is darker than you." The cast resisted Mamoulian's efforts to impose racial solidarity on the play until newcomer Pearl Bailey, in her Broadway debut as Butterfly, a waitress for Bigelow Brown, shouted, "Wake up! Can't you see this man is for us, you fools?" Bailey also remembered the cast being concerned with the melodrama of certain scenes. "So I told him [Mamoulian] what the trouble was," she said. "He stopped the rehearsal, came onstage, took a chair, and asked us all to sit in ours. Then he proceeded to tell us of his coming to this country, how he got nothing much at first, then came *Porgy,* which became a classic. He reminded everyone of the great contribution the Negro had made to America, giving the country its only original art: music. Then he dismissed us, and out of that came some new feelings and better relationships."[26]

The out-of-town tryout was a familiar ordeal for Mamoulian and may even have been more exhausting than *Oklahoma!* or *Carousel.* The cast had little time for sleep, including Ruby Hill, who replaced Horne; Cotton Club tap dancer Harold Nicholas; June Hawkins, who had played in *Carmen Jones* on Broadway; and the prolific stage and screen actor Rex Ingram. Mamoulian met with Arlen and Mercer after each performance to evaluate the cast and the rapidly changing production. Several songs were cut, but new ones were added.

On the morning of the show's New York premiere, March 30, 1946, Bailey led a mutiny over the replacement of the leading actress, Ruby Hill, by the more experienced Muriel Rahn, who had played the title role in *Carmen Jones.* The producers backed down and hastily reinstated Hill. *St. Louis Woman* opened despite an NAACP picket line in protest of the show's alleged stereotypes outside the opulent Martin Beck Theatre and played for 113 performances, a modest run but not a smashing success. The *New York Daily News* called it "the Best Negro musical in many seasons" and credited Mamoulian for his "handling the movement of groups" into an "exciting and intricate spectacle," but the *New York Times* dismissed the plot as "a curse" and Arlen's music as second rate. Writing for the leftist newspaper *PM,* the respected drama critic

Louis Kronenberg reprimanded the authors, albeit "two very reputable Negro authors," for relying on "glib characterizations" and "stock humor and melodrama." Although *St. Louis Woman* would leave behind a pair of classic songs, "Come Rain or Come Shine" and "Any Place I Hang My Hat Is Home," at the time it felt like failure to a director of Mamoulian's stature. "No one with any intelligence or any real authority was left in New York to run the thing properly, or to handle the business part of it," he said angrily.[27]

In between completing work on his film *Summer Holiday* for MGM in October 1946 and his January 1949 staging of *Leaf and Bough* by young playwright Joseph Hayes, who achieved success the following decade with *The Desperate Hours,* Mamoulian worked neither on stage nor screen. At least on Broadway his inactivity was his own decision. Mamoulian was seldom eager to undertake a production unless convinced of its merit or of its potential to challenge him. A number of projects with the Theatre Guild were discussed during the late 1940s. Mamoulian rejected as frivolous a script for an updated version of *The Barber of Seville* and the Guild rejected his proposal for a musical based on Puccini's opera *Manon Lescaut.*[28] His return to the stage was inauspicious. *Leaf and Bough,* produced by Charles Heidt, a financial backer of the Guild, closed after only three performances at the Cort Theatre in Jamaica, New York. Mamoulian blamed the demise on the young playwright's failure to accept his advice, while Hayes resented Mamoulian's interference.[29]

Mamoulian would find a more congenial partner in a fellow cosmopolitan émigré, Kurt Weill. Arriving in the United States in 1935 after fleeing Nazism, Weill was renowned in his homeland as Germany's leading composer for theater but largely unknown in America, where only a small number of American aficionados knew *Mahagonny* and *Three Penny Opera.* Weill was determined to become a naturalized citizen of Broadway, translating his aesthetic, which already owed much to the Weimar glamorization of Jazz Age America, into the idiom of his new home. "Providentially, one of the first musicals Weill saw was *Porgy and Bess.* . . . For the rest of his life *Porgy and Bess* remained for Weill at once a model of the kind of American opera he wanted to create and a reminder of the Broadway musical's flexible boundaries." Weill was pleased to meet Mamoulian as early as 1937, when the director introduced him to Paramount executives at a Hollywood party, and commented to his wife that he found the director "very nice" company.[30] Mamoulian's kind words may have paid off. Weill's first Hollywood assignment was for a Paramount picture, Fritz Lang's *You and Me* (1938).

The aesthetic and worldviews of Mamoulian and Weill were compatible. "I want to use whatever gifts I have for practical purposes, not waste them on things which have no life, or which have to be kept alive by artificial means," as Weill explained.[31] Both men sought to focus the strategies of modernism in music and performance to reach a popular audience. Weill would open eight musicals on the Great White Way, "Broadway opera" he called them, beginning with *Johnny Johnson* (1936) and ending with his final production before death, *Lost in the Stars* (1949).

Mamoulian and Weill continued to talk about collaborating, whether in Hollywood or on Broadway. "Jess Lasky . . . showed me a letter from Mamoulian saying he wants to direct *Venus* if Lasky will produce it. . . . I am very excited about this possibility," Weill wrote Lenya.[32] Nothing came of those plans, however, and Weill's musical *One Touch of Venus* was ultimately adapted as a film for Universal in 1948 by director William Seiter. Mamoulian was also Weill's first choice to direct his social problem drama *Street Scene*. "Excellent idea," Mamoulian wired him from Hollywood on January 19, 1946. He was at work on *Ah, Wilderness!* but had agreed to travel to New York to troubleshoot ongoing productions of *Oklahoma!* and *Carousel* for the Guild, which grew into a larger than expected undertaking, and he was unable to pursue the offer.[33]

Weill was especially keen to adapt Alan Paton's *Cry, the Beloved Country* into a musical. The antiapartheid novel explored a black pastor's loss of faith after the execution of his son for murdering a white advocate for civil rights. Weill worked with playwright Maxwell Anderson to simulate the story's South African setting. The black cast would not attempt to replicate South African dialect and Weill's music, while not without an African flavor, was written for Broadway with an ear for African American spirituals. "Mamoulian, in effect, became the show's third author—a circumstance for which Weill, but not Maxwell Anderson, was grateful."[34]

Returning from the West Indies in the early months of 1949, where they had immersed themselves in the black culture of Haiti and the Bahamas, Rouben and Azadia found an apartment in New York and he prepared for his next project, the Theatre Guild's *Arms and the Girl.* The Revolutionary War musical comedy was an ill-starred idea from a Guild anxious to mount another hit. It began life as the 1934 play *The Pursuit of Happiness* by Lawrence Langner and his wife, Armina Marshall, which was turned into a 1935 movie starring Joan Bennett. Langner approached Herbert and Dorothy Fields to write the libretto and lyrics for the musical version. Dorothy Fields, known for such standards as "I Can't Give You Anything but Love" and "Exactly Like You," was a professional who tried her best with what proved a difficult assignment. The original composer, Broadway veteran Burton Lane (*Finian's Rainbow*), was replaced by a relative lightweight, Morton Gould (*Billion Dollar Baby*). Meanwhile, the Fields were having trouble molding the play into a musical and constantly rewrote the thin story of romance between a high-spirited Yankee girl and a Hessian mercenary fighting for the British during the Revolution.[35]

Mamoulian had turned down the Theatre Guild's offer to direct *Arms and the Girl* in 1948 but was finally persuaded to try to salvage the project in the spirit of maintaining good relations with the Guild.

Shortly before Mamoulian began rehearsing *Arms and the Girl,* Weill and Anderson invited him to lunch at the Plaza Oak Room. He was asked for advice on developing *Lost in the Stars.* After reading the script, Mamoulian excitedly dashed off many pages of analysis and accepted their offer to direct the first musical ever staged on the topic of apartheid. Langner was understandably annoyed at Mamoulian for relegating his production to secondary consideration. The director insisted he was "honor-bound" to work on a project with the moral and aesthetic potential of *Lost in the Stars* but also felt it was his "duty" to complete work on *Arms and the Girl* after devoting eight weeks to Weill's musical.[36]

Despite the joint effort of Weill, Anderson, and Mamoulian, a trio of familiar names on Broadway, finding financial backing for a musical on racism in South Africa proved difficult. According to Mamoulian, Rodgers and Hammerstein attended one audition and walked out without a word of explanation. Finally, Weill and Anderson persuaded a group to which they belonged, the Playwrights Producing Company, to produce *Lost in the Stars.* With members such as Robert Sherwood and S. N. Behrman, the company was a collective of distinguished artists dedicated to bypassing the usual Broadway producers by presenting their own works. Even so, Anderson and Weill were forced to invest a substantial amount of their own money in a show whose commercial prospects were doubtful at best. Given all the difficulties, the Playwrights Company appreciated Mamoulian's participation as a stroke of good fortune. "We were told by those who knew his work best that the time to get him was after a bad flop; he was a phoenix-like director who rose from the ashes sturdier than before," recalled the company's founder, John F. Wharton. "We were lucky to get him when we did; he had just had a failure with *The Leaf and the Bough;* he gave us a first-rate job."[37]

Weill, Anderson, and Mamoulian were determined to use the operatic musical to dramatize the injustice of apartheid and encourage the audience to feel the plight of its characters. *Lost in the Stars* was part of a wave of postwar American plays, screenplays, and novels written to move the consciences of people who often accepted, without much reflection, injustice in the United States, even after fighting overseas in freedom's name. Mamoulian told a reporter that in the shadow of the atom bomb and the gathering gloom of the cold war, he hoped *Lost in the Stars* would "provide some psychological compensation for the state of the world," arousing "a hidden hunger for beauty, love, romance and faith. . . . People are ashamed of feelings that go so deep."[38] If audiences could identify emotionally with people suffering under a repressive society, they would be moved more deeply to repent of their own attitudes and begin working for positive change.

While Anderson and Mamoulian shared the same goal, they strongly disagreed on how to dramatize the story. Anderson wanted the protagonist, the pastor Stephen Kumalo, depicted as a fist-clenching political rebel. Mamoulian's vision was subtler, imagining Kumalo as a Gandhi-like figure and emphasizing the spiritual dimension of his character. Todd Duncan, cast as Kumalo, had starred as Porgy in Mamoulian's production of *Porgy and Bess* and shared the director's understanding of his character. "Mamoulian wanted my part played sweet, Anderson wanted a brick in the hand," Duncan recalled. "I think Mamoulian was right, because honey will do the job better than vinegar." The director offered Sidney Poitier his first lead role on Broadway as Kumalo's son Absalom, but before the production began, Poitier accepted an offer from Hollywood, leaving the part to Julian Mayfield.[39]

Mamoulian's insistence on a more emotional, less explicitly political presentation of racist oppression was in line with his perspective that social issues are inevitably manifested in personal relations and are more effectively expressed in those terms. Under the darkening clouds of McCarthyism, at a time when the censorship board of Memphis banned *Annie Get Your Gun* because its cast included a black railroad conductor, Mamoulian's approach was probably the wiser. The perception of radicalism would have sunk the production within weeks of its opening.

Although Anderson was Weill's neighbor as well as his friend, the composer accepted Mamoulian's concept without complaint. His heart-tugging music for *Lost in the Stars* was a snug fit for Mamoulian's aesthetic of empathy. The director pushed for rewrites that brightened the early scenes in preparation for the stark drama to come. "Every laugh, chuckle or smile that can be honestly brought into the play will be like a drink of water in the desert," Mamoulian told his collaborators. Once Kumalo is confronted with the tragedy of his son, "no light strokes can be applied to him."[40]

Sparked by arguments over the tone of the play, the rancor at rehearsals was barely restrained. Anderson's entourage despised Mamoulian. The playwright's son Alan, the production coordinator, described the director as a "flamboyant, overpowering Hollywood character . . . an autocrat who wanted a larger-than-life quality." Duncan remembered the personalities differently, finding Weill quiet and amenable to suggestions but Anderson as "angry" and "arrogant." He added, "Mr. Mamoulian really ran the show; he was the director in every sense" and he understood Mamoulian's interpretation of Kumalo as "more difficult, but by far more artistically rewarding than the expediency of giving in to hatred."[41]

Mamoulian's choreography for *Lost in the Stars* included scenes with masses of people in motion; others featured two or three characters silhouetted against open space. Two choruses, one black and the other white, stood on each side of the proscenium arch and commented in song on the story; platforms extending from the stage allowed the action to overspill from the proscenium toward the audience; with that in mind, Mamoulian removed the front-row seats. As always in his stage productions, stylization was key. Designer George Jenkins's two dozen sets, painted like WPA murals from the New Deal era to allegorize everyday life, were wheeled onstage in view of the audience. Cast members were arranged in sculptural tableaux.

When *Lost in the Stars* opened at New York's Music Box on October 30, 1949, the critics gave a mixed assessment. The *Saturday Review* damned Mamoulian with faint praise, calling his staging "stunning" and admitting that he "had to reach inescapably for a theatrical substitute" for Alan Paton's prose, but complained the effect was "far too studied. . . . His strivings for the simple are strangely elaborate." The *New York Times* lauded *Lost in the Stars* as the equal of Weill's previous work, "a memorable musical drama," but condemned the book, much of it rewritten under Mamoulian's pressure, as "routine story-telling in the form of a thriller" with "little dramatic vitality." While praising Mamoulian's "vivid color and flaring motion," the *Times* concluded that "half as much might have been twice as good." The *Nation* chastised the musical as a distortion of *Cry, the Beloved Country* located "somewhere between Harlem and South Africa."[42]

Lost in the Stars ran for a respectable 281 performances, but was costly to mount and ultimately unprofitable at the box office. Its climactic reconciliation between blacks and whites might have been prophetic, but *Lost in the Stars* imagined whites moved by the error of their ways, rather than through decades of black struggle and international opprobrium. The musical has been called an artifact of "yesterday's liberalism," but was revived several times as apartheid came to an end in the 1980s and 1990s.[43]

For their next collaboration, Weill and Anderson planned to adapt *Huckleberry Finn* as a musical, tentatively called *Twain on the River.* Despite the often-tense collaboration with Anderson, Mamoulian was asked to direct.[44] Weill's sudden death on April 3, 1950, ended all thoughts of bringing the project to fruition. It would not be the last time Anderson and Mamoulian would work together, but the two men were never able to bring another production to the stage.

After *Lost in the Stars,* Mamoulian returned as promised to *Arms and the Girl,* but the production was unhappy for all parties concerned. Morton Gould claimed cast member Nanette Fabray complained about Mamoulian's tyrannical style. *Arms and the Girl* opened February 2, 1950, at the Forty-sixth Street Theatre and closed after 134 performances as a money loser. One critic described the contrived plot and the

Fields song "A Cow and a Plough and a Frau" as "just plain thud," even if choreographer Michael Kidd's dances were "pretty wonderful."[45] After *Arms and the Girl,* Mamoulian would never again direct a world-premiere play.

Chapter 10

Summer Holiday

In between *Oklahoma!* and *Carousel,* in the midst of his greatest commercial successes on Broadway, Mamoulian returned to 20th Century Fox in the spring of 1944 to direct a movie based on a popular contemporary novel. The film, *Laura,* would become a classic of Hollywood's golden age, an exemplary work among the nascent and still-unnamed genre French critics would later call *film noir.* Mamoulian was fired during the early weeks of production, and while his standing in Hollywood seemed unaffected at first, with hindsight he had reached a watershed. After *Laura,* Mamoulian completed only two movies during what would become a long coda to his career in filmmaking.

With *Laura,* Mamoulian's aesthetic vision collided with another aesthete's will to power. Otto Preminger, *Laura*'s producer, was a cosmopolitan émigré from a privileged Viennese family whose career paralleled Mamoulian's in some respects. Before *Laura,* he had directed and acted for Broadway and Hollywood, and his strong views on theater and film gained him a difficult reputation. Like Mamoulian, he believed the director's vision should be definitive, but in contrast, Preminger imposed his ideas by bullying his casts and crew.

Preminger wanted *Laura* for himself. Years later, he claimed to have "practically forced" 20th Century Fox's executive Darryl F. Zanuck to purchase rights to the novel.[1] Zanuck had a testy relationship at best with Preminger and was unwilling to employ him as director of an A-list film. John Brahm, Walter Lang, and Lewis Milestone had all turned down *Laura* before Mamoulian accepted Zanuck's offer; meanwhile, the script underwent many revisions by Jerry Dratler and Ring Lardner Jr., who had just won an Oscar for *Woman of the Year.*[2]

According to Preminger, Mamoulian "didn't like" the movie, "but he wanted the money." Arguments between the two men flared almost immediately. "When he found out that I was not particularly in Zanuck's good graces, he started to ignore me," Preminger complained. When Mamoulian began, as always, to rewrite the screenplay, Preminger claimed to have said, "'You accepted the script, you've got to do it.' I had no hopes of directing it, however."[3] Despite his denials, Preminger showed every sign of wanting to direct *Laura,* seeing it as his ticket to the higher ranks of the Hollywood hierarchy.

The production was a brutal wrestling contest between the director and the producer during the development of the screenplay. Zanuck weighed in and deserves credit for crystallizing the personality of the title character. "Laura should be everything they [the scheming characters in her circle] are not . . . she is neither bright, nor witty, nor particularly smart." Her charm "should be in her frankness and honesty. Where the others are Park Avenue cutthroats, she should be fresh as a child," he said.[4] Jennifer Jones was sought for the title role, but the part ultimately fell to a Fox contract player well known to Mamoulian, Gene Tierney. Another actor under contract, Dana Andrews, was assigned the role of the police detective, Mark McPherson. Preminger schemed to subvert Zanuck, who wanted to cast Laird Cregar or Monty Woolley as the acid-tongued critic Waldo Lydecker, and shot a screen test of Clifton Webb, who happened to be playing in Noel Coward's *Blithe Spirit* at Los Angeles's Biltmore Theatre. "You must have a man who is either unknown or has never played heavies before," Preminger insisted. "Otherwise, the audience will know right away, and there will be no chance to suspect Gene Tierney."[5]

Preminger's judgment was better, and the casting helped maintain suspense over who was guilty among the story's many dubious characters. Webb had played in a few silent pictures but was virtually unknown to moviegoers in 1944. *Laura* established his Hollywood career.

Tension increased when the cameras began to roll on April 27, 1944. "Mamoulian started to direct the picture, and he ignored me completely. He didn't even let me on the stage, said I made him nervous because I was also a director," Preminger said. The situation deteriorated rapidly. Claiming the rushes were "so bad you couldn't believe it," Preminger said that Zanuck told Mamoulian, "Try again tomorrow. I'll give you another chance." On May 15, the well-connected Hollywood gossip columnist Louella Parsons announced that Mamoulian "has asked to be released from directing *Laura*, and Otto Preminger, the producer of this much discussed movie, will direct the picture himself." She explained the trouble as "a difference of opinion on the psychological treatment of the story and character. The two men could not see eye to eye, and so Mamoulian stepped out."[6]

The final explosion between Preminger and Mamoulian shook the set. According to Dana Andrews, the argument was over his character and both Mamoulian and Preminger had instructed him to play McPherson as a college-educated criminologist, not the streetwise cop of the finished film. In his recollection "a great commotion was heard" when Zanuck saw the rushes, "and suddenly in the middle of the afternoon the picture was stopped, and the director and the producer were over with Mr. Zanuck. And the word came to us that they were going to take Mamoulian off the picture." Andrews was called to Zanuck's office during the fracas and witnessed this exchange. When Zanuck said he wanted McPherson played as a hardboiled detective, Preminger replied, "Why, that's what I was telling Rouben." Mamoulian was outraged by the duplicity. "That's a lie. You did not. You explained to me that you wanted this man played the other way," Andrews recalled him saying.[7]

Reaction on the set to Mamoulian's firing was largely negative. According to Preminger, cinematographer Lucien Ballard "ignored me completely" and ostentatiously read the newspaper and smoked cigars on the set before he was replaced with Joseph LaShelle. Dana Andrews recalled that Mamoulian's firing "upset everybody in the picture, because we were very fond of Rouben. . . . Judith Anderson practically refused to act." Anderson, who played Laura's sexually voracious aunt, said, "Preminger's direction was Germanic in approach. He saw the picture his way. There was a change of everything. I much preferred Mamoulian's direction. It would have been a happier experience had he been directing."[8]

However, Vincent Price, playing one of Laura's gigolo suitors, believed that Preminger's ascendancy was for the best. *Laura* might not have been a film noir classic under Mamoulian. It might not have been film noir at all. "What Otto added to the film—and none of us could figure it out at first—was the ability to give each one of the characters an underlying sense of evil," Price said. "Nobody in that picture is normal. Mamoulian hadn't done that; he was a very good director and a nice man, but he had no concept about these kind of upper class scum people."[9]

Preminger fired Mamoulian's costume designer, scrapped most of the sets, and even replaced the film's central visual image, the portrait of Laura by Mamoulian's future wife Azadia. He "felt that it lacked the mystic quality he insisted on having," Tierney recalled. "He sent me instead to pose for Frank Poleny, the studio photographer whose pictures of me as a starlet had appeared in so many magazines. Otto had this one enlarged and lightly brushed with paint to achieve the effect he wanted."[10]

With *Carousel* to occupy him, Mamoulian had little time to rue the loss of *Laura,* and with the phenomenal success of *Oklahoma!* and *Carousel,* the director was considered a hot property by MGM, the studio most closely associated with lavish cinematic musicals at a time when millions of Americans wanted their movie stars to sing and dance. By November 1945 Mamoulian was under contract to MGM and on the lot, waiting for an assignment from musical production head Arthur Freed. The producer was planning to offer him *Jumbo,* a 1936 Rodgers and Hart circus musical, but their lunch meeting at the studio commissary on Mamoulian's first day at work was interrupted when a phone was brought to their table. The message was that Freed's colleague Jerome Kern had been stricken by a heart attack. The composer's death on November 11, 1945, derailed *Jumbo,* which would not be made into a film until 1962.[11]

A month later, meeting once again in the hubbub of the MGM commissary, Freed asked Mamoulian's opinion on adapting Eugene O'Neill's *Ah, Wilderness!* into a musical. After a lengthy silence, Mamoulian replied he would think about it. "At first I thought—it's an excellent play, so why monkey with it? If you take something written for the stage and put it on the screen, you're going to lose certain values," he said. "But then I went through the play again and got very excited about it."[12]

In a memo to Freed, Mamoulian declared he wanted to transform *Ah, Wilderness!* into "a story which will be told through the medium of integrated dialogue, songs, dance and music, with each of these elements taking an organic and vital part in the telling of the story." He wrote of translating the dialogue "into [its] musical equivalent" in song and dance, not cutting the story but changing the manner of telling and adding emotional values through the music. "The only valid reason for transforming *Ah, Wilderness!* into a musical would be to tell that story in richer, more colorful and more imaginative terms, without sacrificing any of its true values, but on the contrary, bringing it more beauty and excitement than was there before."[13]

The memo summarized the aesthetic principles Mamoulian had brought with him to America and reiterated throughout his career on stage and in Hollywood. Freed halted development on a tentative plan for Mamoulian to direct Fred Astaire and Judy Garland in *The Belle of New York* and reassigned the movie's top talent to *Ah, Wilderness!* including screenwriter Irving Brecher, who had written for the Marx Brothers; prolific composer Harry Warren, who had won an Oscar for "Lullaby of Broadway"; and lyricist Ralph Blane, who had just completed work on *Meet Me in St. Louis.* Mamoulian's vision soon clashed with many of MGM's tenets. Because the play was a wistful reminiscence of O'Neill's coming-of-age in small-town New England at the turn of the century, Mamoulian rejected the usual bright color scheme of MGM musicals for shades of yellow, beige, and green. "This I considered to be the colors of 'Americana'—like Thomas Benton, John Curry and Grant Wood." Mamoulian explained, "Since this was a color film I would work on the color scheme of the whole picture as thoroughly as I do on a script, which means meetings with all the departments." Many arguments with those departments ensued, but Freed supported Mamoulian and the director responded gratefully. "If you come up with something that is tough to do he does what a producer should do," Mamoulian said. "He'll fight for you—most of the time."[14]

MGM had filmed *Ah, Wilderness!* a decade earlier, but the restrictions of censorship on its story of adolescent growing pains only seemed to have tightened over the years. Mamoulian complained of his encounter with an emissary from the Breen Office. "'We suggest you cut the prostitute out—cut this out—cut that out—cut this word out,' etc.," he recalled, growing angrier by the moment. By then Mamoulian was a practiced hand at working within the suggestive spaces left by the censors. "'Look,' I said, 'you want all these words out. Fine.' I took my red pencil and started cutting every phrase—I'd keep the first half, but cut the second, so that not only the censorable words would be cut, but even the innocent ones." As a result, Mamoulian scripted a climactic scene "in which the father finds himself embarrassed with the subject of sex to such an extent that he is never able to finish a sentence."[15]

Mamoulian's vision of *Ah, Wilderness!* as a total work of art, with the rhythm of song and dance integral to the structure, and every detail enhancing the whole, was largely implemented. Inspired by Grant Wood's *Daughters of the Revolution,* he told the casting department to find actresses resembling the women in the painting. Mamoulian clashed with Freed and his technicians over a fantasy scene in which a tawdry barroom is gradually transformed into the dream world of the boy protagonist Richard Miller (Mickey Rooney), only for the illusion to fade and the world to turn shabby again. Freed struck a deal with Mamoulian. The scene would be shot as he wished if the director helped salvage Freed's investment in the stage musical *St. Louis Woman.*[16]

Mamoulian coupled his work on Freed's new musical with a visit to Eugene O'Neill and a consultation with the Theatre Guild in early 1946. On February 1, 1946, Mamoulian sent a cheery memo to Ralph Blane, Irving Brecher, and Harry Warren. "As you know, I am leaving for New York because my little children Oklahoma! and Carousel seem to be in need of a little brushing and tuning up."[17]

After directing the premiere of *St. Louis Woman,* Mamoulian returned to Hollywood, where work on *Ah, Wilderness!* resumed in June. Filming was soon halted by violence between rival Hollywood unions, the racketeer-run International Alliance of Theatrical Stage Employees (IATSE) and the leftist Conference of Studio Unions (CSU). The battle for control over the studios' craft employees and stagehands had already begun in the spring of 1945, with the moguls paying protection money to IATSE in exchange for suppressing the CSU. Screenwriters and actors were deeply divided over the ongoing conflict around the negotiating table as well as at the picket line. When the CSU struck in the summer of 1946, bricks and stones flew outside the major studios, including MGM, as IATSE fought to break the strike. Mamoulian was prepared to keep working on *Ah, Wilderness!* but the refusal of Walter Huston (playing paterfamilias Nat Miller) and Selena Royle (Mrs. Miller) to cross the picket line brought filming to a halt. Shooting resumed later in July, although the atmosphere in Hollywood was tense as a film noir drama. The head of CSU was reportedly picked up by henchmen and beaten as they drove him around town; Ronald Reagan, the recently elected president of the Screen Actors Guild, took to wearing a .38 in a shoulder holster.[18]

By the time it was completed in October 1946, *Ah, Wilderness!* had gone $405,000 over budget owing to strike delays and Mamoulian's fussiness, which included a lavishly detailed twelve-day shoot depicting an Independence Day celebration and eight days on the barroom scene where Rooney's alcohol-altered imagination transformed the "floozy" into a dream woman who, by Mamoulian's design, grew "bigger and bigger and redder and redder; he's drunk, and she's overpowering him." In a marker of his declining status in Hollywood, Mamoulian was paid $163,000 for directing the picture, less than he had received ten years earlier for *High, Wide and Handsome*.[19] Despite Freed's support, MGM's front office was unhappy with Mamoulian's vision and cut three songs from the final print, including "Omar and the Princess," exquisitely fashioned in the manner of a Persian print by costume designer Walter Plunkett. MGM retitled the picture *Summer Holiday* and kept it on the shelf for eighteen months before finally releasing it on April 16, 1948.

Mamoulian called *Summer Holiday* "the most difficult and fascinating task of my directorial career." He approached the musical adaptation of O'Neill with great care, stressing that "there was no question of cutting out big hunks of the play to make room for song and dance routines of the usual film musical." He castigated that approach as "vandalism" and added that O'Neill's play "had to be transposed into a new form that glowed with a beauty of its own." Mamoulian's goal was to "create a new type of musical film wherein no singing, dancing, or music was used unless it adequately replaced the play's dialogue and consistently advanced the story." Harkening back to *Love Me Tonight*, *Summer Holiday*'s introductory song, "Our Home Town," begins with Walter Huston singing before a map of the United States in his office, and continues through dissolves showing him strolling down shady streets and arriving home while singing. Mickey Rooney and Gloria DeHaven (as his girlfriend Muriel) finish the song at a soda fountain. The sequence was exemplary in its graceful movement, which introduced all the principal characters and whisked the viewer through the town. Addressing its failure at the box office, Mamoulian wrote, "Whether or not the results are successful, I am convinced that within this approach lies the future of the musical theatre. It is high time for the standard film musicals to be put away in moth balls."[20]

The film received mixed reviews upon its release with much of the criticism directed at the casting of Mickey Rooney, who had starred a decade earlier in the previous movie adaptation of *Ah, Wilderness!* and, despite his boyish face, was already too old at twenty-seven to play the teenage protagonist. He lacked the gravitas of an O'Neill character. "And where the youngster in the play was a human, he is simply Mr. Rooney, in this film," the *New York Times* complained, adding, he "is given to clowning in his familiarly broad and impish way . . . exactly as Andy Hardy does,"[21] referring to Rooney's role in the Andy Hardy movies as a boisterously good kid in an idyllic small town. MGM banked on his popularity and hoped Rooney's stardust would rub off on *Summer Holiday,* but a chill had entered the postwar climate and the Hardy movies already began to feel old-fashioned. The long-running series ended in 1946, around the time *Summer Holiday* was completed. The film would become Rooney's first flop. As a result, Mamoulian was no longer considered bankable in Hollywood despite his recent successes on Broadway.

Mamoulian may have grown cautious by the end of the 1940s in the face of the anxiety that saturated the entertainment industry after the House Un-American Activities Committee (HUAC) began holding hearings in late 1947 on "subversive" influences in Hollywood and elsewhere. The anti-Communist crusade unfurled its banners against the backdrop of Soviet nuclear spies and cold war conflict in Europe and Asia, but for many of its proponents, anti-Communism was an excuse to settle scores with the New Deal, turn back Roosevelt-era reforms, and abort the civil rights movement before it came to term. HUAC suggested the blacklisting of suspected Communists working in Hollywood, a move the studio moguls, cowed by the anti-Semitism of some committee members, initially resisted but soon endorsed. Such prominent actors with whom Mamoulian had worked as Adolphe Menjou and Gary Cooper testified to the Communist presence in Hollywood.

Mamoulian might have been nervous to learn that when MGM's chief, Louis B. Mayer, declared Russia as his birthplace under HUAC questioning, spectators in the Old House Caucus Room stirred ominously in their seats. A "friendly witness" at the hearings, film critic John Charles Moffit, condemned the New York stage as a breeding ground for Communist propaganda.[22] One of Mamoulian's erstwhile colleagues from the Theatre Guild, Herbert Biberman, was named as a Communist, along with an actress from *Dr. Jekyll and Mr. Hyde,* Rose Hobart, and two writers with whom he was associated, *Laura*'s cowriter Ring Lardner Jr. and *Golden Boy*'s playwright Clifford Odets. According to one of his colleagues at the Screen Directors Guild, Joseph C. Youngerman, Mamoulian was considered one of "the unholy eleven" by the studios for his role in founding the guild. He added that one of the guild's blacklisted members, Irving Pichel, was indeed a Communist "and, except for Mamoulian, the other directors didn't go near him."[23]

Like many in Hollywood, Mamoulian was under surveillance. The FBI had begun to investigate the director as early as 1943, its suspicions aroused by his role in the Screen Directors Guild, his contacts with a representative of the Soviet film industry in Hollywood, his presence at National Council of American-Soviet Friendship dinners, and his work as an instructor at the Hollywood Writers School of the League of American Writers, identified by the FBI as a Communist front organization. At various times the agency tracked Mamoulian's phone calls, gained access to his mail, and kept tabs on his parents and his home. The FBI was mollified after recording a conversation between two Communist Party members who agreed that Mamoulian was not a Communist but "held the Roosevelt view of things." The agency closed its investigation in 1950 but kept Mamoulian's file open.[24]

In 1950 Mamoulian found himself standing against the rightist forces in Hollywood during the contentious battle for control of the Directors Guild. Cecil B. DeMille, a dominant figure in the guild, had become a noisy watchdog in the hunt for Hollywood Communists; his DeMille Foundation compiled dossiers on the suspicious affiliations of screen directors, which he happily shared with the Un-American Activities Committee of the California legislature. DeMille was opposed by the guild's moderate president, Joseph L. Mankiewicz, who won a pair of Oscars in 1950 for writing and directing *A Letter to Three Wives* and had just completed his masterpiece, *All about Eve.* DeMille impugned Mankiewicz's father for supporting a Socialist for mayor of New York in 1914, declaring, "these tendencies are very often inherited."[25] DeMille and his allies on the guild's board of directors were correct in suspecting that Mankiewicz would oppose their move to impose a loyalty oath on all members. Guild officers had already taken the oath to comply with a recently enacted federal law requiring all union officers to affirm that they had never been affiliated with any organization seeking the overthrow of the U.S. government. DeMille sought to extend the controversial provision to rank-and-file members.

With Mankiewicz out of the country, DeMille called on guild members to approve the oath, which they did in an open ballot on a vote of 547 to 14. It was less a victory for DeMille's idea than the triumph of fear at a time when writers and directors were being jailed, forced into exile, or forced to keep quiet on penalty of losing their jobs. Mankiewicz questioned the legality of DeMille's move. "According to the Taft-Hartley Act, we have not the right to deny a man the right to work because he won't sign an affidavit," he insisted. The argument between DeMille and Mankiewicz played out in the press and in a mendacious power struggle led by DeMille, who was determined to remove his opponent from the guild's presidency through another open ballot.[26]

The struggle for control of the guild came to a conclusion during a dramatic, eight-hour membership meeting on October 22 at the Beverly Hills Hotel. Over the course of the evening, Mankiewicz gradually rallied the majority to his side and defeated DeMille. One of the long evening's most memorable and impassioned speeches was given by Mamoulian, who stood up to say how nervous he felt for speaking in an accent after enduring DeMille's pronouncements on 100 percent Americanism.

> I don't remember any time when a fellow director had to get up and before expressing what he had to say he had to declare himself to be an honest, reputable man. He had to mention how far back he goes of any generations to be born in this country. That leaves me hanging in the air, because I was not born in this country. I came here and I am a naturalized citizen. . . . I wanted to be an American, and I would not want anyone challenging my being a good American so I will forget the embarrassing feeling on being shy about my accent.
>
> I have known Mr. DeMille for a long time, not very well. He has always been most cordial to me. . . . Tomorrow it is I who may be the subject of your remarks. I think it is wrong for a member of the Guild within the family to accuse anyone even anonymously without actual data or actual direct knowledge, because it is that that suddenly sows seeds of a terrific mistrust, fear and anxiety and suspicion.[27]

Although his assignments were increasingly scarce, Mamoulian continued to make the rounds of Hollywood society. Playwright and screenwriter Anita Loos recalled a "rather spooky incident" concerning Mamoulian and Aldous Huxley's "favorite psychic," who accurately predicted an accident involving the director's brand-new automobile. A photograph from the period shows Mamoulian in his study with Azadia, dressed like Grace Kelly in *Rear Window,* sketching his portrait. The room is elegantly appointed and lined with books. An icon of Mary and the infant Jesus before the twin peaks of Ararat, the sacred mountain of the Armenians, hangs on the wall. Mamoulian continued to draw media attention during this time despite his relative inactivity. *Life* magazine devoted a color photo spread to the portrait collages he made of his wife, whimsical outlines of her face assembled from shells, dried leaves, flowers, postage stamps, and pieces of maps.[28]

Happily married to a woman of great wealth, Mamoulian felt little compulsion to work unless tempted by the pleasure of artistic satisfaction. He told a reporter that unless he was offered a film "I'm nuts about, I would rather do another play." He decried most Hollywood movies as divorced from "people in the world" and praised the new wave of Italian neorealist films such as Roberto Rossellini's *Open City* and Vittorio De Sica's *The Bicycle Thief* and the stark power of Carol Reed's *The Third Man.*[29]

If Mamoulian had been driven by a more powerful ambition, he could have found work as a director in Western Europe, where joint production deals with Hollywood studios were becoming common and his acute sense for stylization coupled with a willingness to use actual locations might have resulted in his own neorealist project. As it was, the changing climate of Hollywood in the 1950s offered fewer opportunities for a man of his sophistication. It is difficult to imagine Mamoulian embracing the dark world of film noir or being sufficiently interested in the sort of melodramas directed by Douglas Sirk. He might not have worked easily with method actors such as Montgomery Clift and Marlon Brando, whose Lee Strasberg iteration of Stanislavski's search for theatrical truth involved too much immersion in individual character for Mamoulian, who focused on the truth of the ensemble. A Technicolor Mamoulian western would be interesting to contemplate. Although he predicted the rise of television, Mamoulian expressed no interest in working in a medium whose visual quality seemed so inferior, and besides, he was concerned about its social influence. "What will happen to us if television finally kills off the theatre's live audience and with it, our ability to gather together in civilized groups to share civilized experiences?" he asked.[30]

Mamoulian, however, kept his hand in the game. In 1950 David O. Selznick employed him to help "salvage" a British film he had coproduced with his business partner from *The Third Man,* Alexander Korda. *Gone to Earth* was a prestige project by writer-director Michael Powell and Emeric Pressburger, whose *Red Shoes* (1948) remains a classic film on the world of dance. The mystic story of a Gypsy woman married to a rigid minister was drawn from the novel by Mary Webb satirized decades later by Stella Gibbons's *Cold Comfort Farm.* Powell described the film version as "fantasy based on the atmosphere." Selznick, who was hoping to use it as a star vehicle for his wife, Jennifer Jones, felt it had no commercial appeal. He tried to block its U.K. release on the grounds that it "varied in substance from the novel" but when a British court dismissed his action, he exercised his right to reedit the film for the North American market. Selznick cut thirty-five minutes and eliminated entire characters from the story. Mamoulian was then asked to film several new scenes to restore *Gone to Earth* to feature length. In an interview years later, Powell, who steadfastly refused to watch the American version, defended Mamoulian, calling him "a very good director," and blamed Selznick, "one of these producers who feels obliged to change something in all of the films that he produced." The Hollywood reshoot did not go well. As cameraman Christopher Challis recalled, "Tremendous disagreements about the script caused a lot of reshooting—pretty well the whole of the end sequence and additional scenes too."[31]

Selznick gave the new *Gone to Earth* a catchier title, *The Wild Heart,* but his rendition sank at the box office with little trace upon release in 1952 while Powell's original cut has since been regarded as a masterpiece. *The Wild Heart* was marked against Mamoulian as another commercial failure.

Despite the acrimony between them during the production of *Lost in the Stars,* the backers of that musical, Playwrights Producing Company, announced a new musical by Mamoulian and Maxwell Anderson. The play, *The Devil's Hornpipe,* was essentially *Faust* in modern dress. "With Rouben's help I started from the beginning, saving nothing but the background and the names of the characters—and we're getting near the end of a new version in which the story is changed, the motivations are different and the good people have enough brains to outsmart the devils in the end," Anderson wrote playwright Robert E. Sherwood in 1953. Allie Wrubel, whose Hollywood career included Disney's *Song of the South* (1947), wrote the music for *The Devil's Hornpipe*. Although Playwrights rejected their first draft in 1953, Mamoulian and Anderson continued working. Playwrights rejected it a second time in January 1959, but by then the play had been transmogrified into a screenplay for director Charles Lederer's musical comedy about labor racketeering, *Never Steal Anything Small* (1958), starring James Cagney. As Cagney biographer John McCabe put it, "The Anderson-Mamoulian material got swallowed up in a mélange of pseudo-Damon Runyon fiction and pseudo-Kurt Weill."[32]

During those years the Metropolitan Opera offered *Carmen* to Mamoulian with Rise Stevens in the title role, but Mamoulian, anticipating the direction of opera by the end of the twentieth century, wanted an actress who could sing, not a singer who emoted from a rigid position. Mamoulian was never engaged for the production despite his great fascination with restaging or filming *Carmen* with an eye toward recovering its roots as a popular musical, not a grand opera. A script completed with Maxwell Anderson interpolated dialogue into the sung libretto, incorporated pantomime, and emphasized the emotions conveyed by sound and color.[33]

Most of his creativity in the early through mid-1950s was expressed on the stage. Working with Agnes de Mille, he directed the Theatre Guild's revival of *Oklahoma!* opening at the Broadway Theatre on May 9, 1951, and running for one hundred performances. A tenth-anniversary revival opened August 31, 1953, at the New York City Center, also with Mamoulian and de Mille. It ran for a limited engagement of forty shows. In 1953 he organized an evening of entertainment in the Hollywood Palladium for Adolph Zukor's Golden Jubilee. The following year, he directed the Los Angeles and San Francisco revivals of *Carousel*. In 1955, Mamoulian was commissioned by the U.S. State Department to direct a European tour of *Oklahoma!* as part of its program of international goodwill tours, which showcased major American performers such as Louis Armstrong, Benny Goodman, Dizzy Gillespie, and Duke Ellington to promote America's image as a dynamic society in contrast to the dour, inert Soviet bloc. Indirectly, Mamoulian even helped inspire the State Department's project. When President Eisenhower requested a special appropriation from the Senate for "cultural and artistic fields," he cited the "fabulous success of *Porgy and Bess,* playing to capacity houses in the extended tour of the free countries of Europe."[34]

Reeling at the box office from the impact of television, Hollywood in the mid-1950s turned to wide-screen, Technicolor spectacles to draw patrons from their living rooms and into theaters. Colorful adaptations of popular Broadway musicals became part of Hollywood's strategy to shore up sagging ticket sales. In that spirit, Arthur Freed hired Mamoulian to direct an adaptation of Cole Porter's most recent musical, the modestly successful cold war comedy about a no-nonsense female commissar seduced by the West, *Silk Stockings.* Porter based what would be his final work for the stage on the much-loved Ernst Lubitsch–Greta Garbo film *Ninotchka* (1939).

The Hollywood business model Mamoulian had known since *Applause* had come apart in the years since *Summer Holiday.* When the U.S. Supreme Court ruled against the movie industry in a landmark antitrust case, *U.S. v. Paramount Pictures, et al.* (1948), the court's decree effectively began the dismantling of the old studio system by banning block booking and divesting the studios of their theater chains, which deprived the system of its economic basis. As a result, MGM's producers were no longer under contract but became free agents. Arthur Freed Productions had already invested in the Broadway show of *Silk Stockings* and the Cole Porter musical became Freed's first independent production released through MGM. The studio was opposed to allowing Mamoulian to direct the picture, given his recent failures, but at that uncertain moment in the industry, Freed had more clout than the once-mighty lion of Hollywood. MGM's talent roster was being disbanded, but *Silk Stockings*'s stars, Fred Astaire and Cyd Charisse, were still on the payroll.[35] Astaire would play a suave Hollywood producer working in Paris and Charisse a disapproving Soviet commissar, determined to bring home an errant Russian composing the score for Astaire's "decadent" film production.

A long-legged, ballet-trained beauty, Charisse had recently emerged from the obscure ranks of contract players opposite Astaire in the popular musical *The Band Wagon* (1953). When given the choice of working with Gene Kelly on *Les Girls* or Astaire on *Silk Stockings,* Charisse eagerly chose the older man. Astaire, however, worried that the twenty-two-year age gap would result in a painful-looking romantic pas de deux. He was also nervous about Mamoulian's reputation as a perfectionist. Freed arranged for Astaire and Mamoulian to discuss *Silk Stockings* over lunch. The director charmed the aging actor, insisting he accepted the movie only for the chance to work with the dancing stars of *The Band Wagon.* Regarding the age difference, Mamoulian said, "What kind of nonsense is that! I see all the young actors today on the screen and none of them can match you in charm and romantic appeal." The spell Mamoulian cast worked its magic. Astaire wrote to Freed, "I was delighted to meet with Rouben M. yesterday. He is of course a wonderful man and I'm so pleased with his viewpoints on the picture."[36]

The screenplay's first draft by Leonard Spigelgass proved unsatisfactory. "We should be concerned at this time only with the essence of our theme and story and, most importantly, with the characters involved in it," Mamoulian wrote in a memo, echoing Stanislavski. "In other words, we should work from the inside out. Create the soul and body first, then adorn it with clothes and jewels (if any)!"[37] Harry Kurnitz and Leonard Gershe took turns on the screenplay after Spigelgass. In the end, Mamoulian was less concerned with dialogue than with pantomime and wanted to relate the story through song and dance, not extended conversation.

Freed made most of the decisions over hiring, signing Gene Loring to re-create his choreography from the Broadway *Silk Stockings* and Hermes Pan to collaborate on the dances with Astaire. André Previn became music director. Cole Porter contributed two new songs to the film, "Fated to Be Mated" and, at Astaire's request, an ill-conceived concession to the younger generation, "The Ritz Roll and Rock," which became the great dancer's final bow in top hat and tails.

On the strength of Janis Paige's Broadway role in *The Pajama Game,* Freed signed her as the empty-headed Hollywood star who comes to Paris to make a film. She remembered Mamoulian as "a very elegant, lovely man," adding, "the age of the gentleman, it's gone. I don't think we'll ever have it again."[38]

Jules Munshin, Joseph Buloff, and Peter Lorre played the three comical commissars. Mamoulian was responsible for casting Lorre, whose career was in steep decline. Fascinated by the gap between the real Lorre and his screen persona, the director wanted to play both with and against typecasting. "'Now Peter Lorre,' everybody said, 'Oh, well, he's for these mystery stories and these strange people.' Actually Peter was a very cultivated man," Mamoulian said, "a very sensitive person, a very loveable man, and with a great sense of humor." *Silk Stockings* was not Lorre's final performance, but it was his last of any significance. Although he was beset by ailments, "he seemed full of joy and vigor," Mamoulian recalled. "I never knew about his health because he was always sliding through like a kid, mischievous, but always serious."[39]

The Hollywood censors were concerned with the sly humor of Porter's lyrics and made several changes, clipping the reference to a "five-foot-wide bosom" in "Stereophonic Sound," intended by Mamoulian as an ironic spoof of Hollywood's love affair with technical gimmickry (this in a film shot in CinemaScope and Metrocolor), and insisting that the thoroughly erotic "All of You" be sung in a "nonsuggestive manner." With his usual self-confidence, Mamoulian prodded Astaire and Hermes Pan to rechoreograph "Paris Loves Lovers," telling them, "It's a good dance but it's not dramatic enough." He was thrilled by the revised version. "You'd think that his entire life and future depended on the outcome of each dance. He keeps at the top because he does the impossible. He improves on perfection," Mamoulian said of Astaire.[40]

Principal photography began on November 7, 1956, and the film was completed by January 31, 1957. Mamoulian worked with great efficiency, editing as he shot, delivering the movie at a cost of under $2 million. After its release on July 18, *Silk Stockings* would gross over $4 million during its initial run and, during its six weeks at Radio City Music Hall, became the biggest-grossing musical ever to play the venerable theater. The *New York Times*' Bosley Crowther named *Silk Stockings* one of the year's best films. "Under the direction of Rouben Mamoulian the whole thing moves with a suave and graceful flow."[41]

Mamoulian managed to bring a touch of warmth to the cold war and a close reading of the film reveals its political sophistication. "The picture has a tendency to laugh *at* communism and *with* capitalism," critic David Parkinson recently wrote. "But although Mamoulian ridicules the Marxist emphasis on utility over beauty, he also exposes the dehumanizing impact of faddish materialism and vulgar populism on the complacent West."[42]

Silk Stockings was a colorful, stylish finale for Astaire, who never appeared in another full-blown song-and-dance role, and would be the Hollywood high point for Janis Paige, who was never allowed to develop her cinematic potential. As for Charisse, her Hollywood career soon dissolved; she was a better dancer than an actress and found only few roles in the United States and Europe after 1960. *Silk Stockings* might not have been the final curtain for the Hollywood musical, but it marked the beginning of the genre's long endgame. The times were changing rapidly as the 1950s turned into the 1960s and the panache of the old musicals would soon be out of step.

Yet at the time, *Silk Stocking*'s success seemed to position Mamoulian for a comeback. Hollywood producer Samuel Goldwyn had seen Mamoulian direct the Broadway premiere of *Porgy and Bess* and had long dreamed of giving the world a cinematic masterpiece in tribute to George Gershwin.[43] For Mamoulian, translating *Porgy and Bess* for the screen was a dream come true.

Goldwyn's project had a long prehistory that began with Robert Breen, general director of the American National Theatre and Academy, producer of the 1952 revival of *Porgy and Bess,* and organizer of the successful State Department–sponsored European tour that followed. Breen, ambitious, energetic, and imaginative, had dismissed the idea of working with Mamoulian, whom he saw, with justification, as a difficult collaborator. He had his own ideas of how to interpret the opera.

Breen had earned the confidence of Ira Gershwin and Dorothy Heyward and made himself a key player negotiating the lucrative film rights. By the time Goldwyn announced his purchase of those rights in May of 1957, Breen was named as his associate producer. The deal was negotiated by Irving "Swifty" Lazar, the agent for both Gershwin and Mamoulian, who according to legend obtained the prize of *Porgy and Bess* for Goldwyn in exchange for the gift of a Rolls Royce.[44] The oral agreement made Breen a partner in the film's production and its probable writer and director, but after his arrival in Hollywood in July, Breen began hearing disconcerting rumors of other directors being considered and realized that a verbal agreement was not the same thing as a written contract. He had signed away his controlling option over the film without a legally enforceable commitment in return to a producer infamous for having allegedly said, "A verbal agreement isn't worth the paper it's printed on."

Sam Goldwyn Jr. remembered that Breen "wanted a picture close to the way he had directed the production. My father had never seen that version. What he had seen was the original opera as it had been done in nineteen thirty-five, and he retained a fond memory of it and wanted it done in that way."[45] Although Breen reported rumors that Goldwyn had offered the project to Elia Kazan, King Vidor, and Frank Capra, it follows from the mogul's way of thinking that Mamoulian would be the obvious choice.

The collaboration between Goldwyn, Mamoulian, and the project's screenwriter, N. Richard Nash, who had enjoyed success on Broadway and Hollywood as writer of *The Rainmaker*, began on a good footing. In November 1957, Goldwyn wrote Nash, "Mr. Mamoulian and I had a couple of lengthy and stimulating discussions. . . . I found his ideas extremely exciting—and I had the clear impression that he found my ideas exciting too. As a matter of fact, it was a totally enjoyable experience." Nash worked on the screenplay for *Porgy and Bess* in New York, but visited Hollywood periodically to meet with the mogul and the director. "Goldwyn, Mamoulian and I are still hitting it off wonderfully well," Nash wrote a friend in January 1958. "In my revision of the play I shall endeavor to scale the scenes so that the proportions of the screenplay more nearly approximate the scale that the personal and human story of 'Porgy and Bess' demands," Nash obediently told Goldwyn. In keeping with his aesthetic, Mamoulian insisted on further cuts; as Nash understood his directions, "the purposes of the screen do not require such a full elaboration of dialogue" as in the stage production.[46]

The first problems with *Porgy and Bess* came from outside the studio. If Freed and Mamoulian found African Americans wary of how they might be depicted in *St. Louis Woman,* Goldwyn and Mamoulian were met with even greater resistance over *Porgy and Bess.* The NAACP and the Council for the Improvement of Negro Theater Arts were up in arms over a film of *Porgy,* claiming it perpetuated negative stereotypes by depicting blacks as murderers, drug dealers, gamblers, and faithless women, essentially the same reproach African American elites expressed in those years to blues and other forms of vernacular music created by African Americans. The Negro Theater Council even placed ads in the *Hollywood Reporter* condemning any black actor for considering a role in the picture. After Harry Belafonte announced he would refuse the role of Porgy, Pearl Bailey and Dorothy Dandridge, two of Hollywood's brightest female black stars, wrestled quietly with the question of their involvement. Dandridge spoke of her concerns with other probable cast members and concluded "if Goldwyn was dead set on doing the picture, he might as well do it with me." Although Goldwyn wanted Cab Calloway as Sportin' Life, Sammy Davis Jr. eagerly campaigned for the part and won it after the producer caught his nightclub act, which included a medley from *Porgy and Bess* cooked up for the occasion. Sidney Poitier, the face of a new black generation in Hollywood for his roles in *No Way Out, Blackboard Jungle,* and *Cry, the Beloved Country,* sent word that he wanted to hear Goldwyn's concept from the producer's own lips. After meeting with Mamoulian and Goldwyn, Poitier declared he was "happy to say that my reservations were washed away." Mamoulian told the African American press that he spoke to the actor of "the poetry and emotional richness of the character, and of the wonderful opportunity for the Negro artist to express himself." With Poitier on board, Bailey and Dandridge embraced the roles of Maria and Bess, and the NAACP quietly withdrew its protest. Only the Negro Theater Council remained adamant.[47]

Goldwyn spared no expense in bringing his dream movie to the screen, hiring jazz pianist André Previn, who had just won an Oscar for his work on *Gigi* (1958), as music director. The almost inevitable clashes began when the producer spent $2 million re-creating Catfish Row on Stage 8, the second-largest sound stage in Hollywood. Mamoulian would have preferred to film on location in Charleston. Dandridge agreed with Mamoulian, complaining about Goldwyn's "attempt to clean up Catfish Row . . . to make life on Catfish Row look not so bad." Early in the morning of July 2, the date of the first scheduled dress rehearsals, a fire broke out on Stage 8, consuming the sets as well as Irene Schaff's costumes. Goldwyn would not be put off by the catastrophe. Later on the day of the fire, he called together Mamoulian, the principal cast, and production staff and vowed to rebuild everything. Mamoulian upset Goldwyn by choosing that moment to press the case for location shooting. Goldwyn held firm.[48]

The delay in filming while Catfish Row was reconstructed gave the producer time to fret. "What worried him most of all was Rouben Mamoulian," Goldwyn biographer Arthur Max wrote. Despite the director's track record, Goldwyn wondered whether Mamoulian really "understood life on Catfish Row" and "had the right rapport with the all-black cast." As the set was rebuilt, the time the producer would otherwise have devoted to the day-by-day business of the movie became time spent brooding on his anxieties over the project, especially his conflicting vision with Mamoulian for the film. Goldwyn finally fired the director on July 27, paying him the full salary of $75,000 as specified in his contract. He immediately hired Mamoulian's nemesis, Otto Preminger, by then one of Hollywood's most successful filmmakers, for $150,000. As director of *Carmen Jones* (1954), an all-black adaptation of Bizet's opera *Carmen* with Harry Belafonte and Dorothy Dandridge, Preminger seemed a good choice for *Porgy and Bess.* In a press release, Goldwyn claimed "the greatest respect" for Mamoulian as a director, but "basic differences of opinion" had forced his hand.[49]

"What surprised me was that those two men could *ever* have gotten along!" Nash said years later. "Rouben is a man of *enormous* talent, *meticulous* in his ideas. He speaks with such specificity, you know *exactly* where his mind is. Their conflict was basic: Rouben, the articulate, and Sam, the inarticulate." Mamoulian brought the firing on himself, according to Nash. "Rouben got into the habit of scoffing at everything Sam had to say," Nash recalled. "They finally got to the point where neither of them heard what the other was saying. Their battles slowed everything up. We weren't getting anywhere. Rouben, the intellectual, demanded the precise phrase for what you meant; Sam hoped you would understand what he meant, instead of what he was saying."[50] Goldwyn was also upset when Mamoulian disobeyed his dictate on giving no interviews of his own about the film; both men vied to be recognized as the sole creative mind behind the project. Seeing *Porgy and Bess* as his child, the director even hired a press agent, Russell Birdwell, to trumpet his role in the production. Quotes from Mamoulian circulated widely, not only in the entertainment media but also in African American magazines and even the daily newspaper of Charleston, South Carolina.

Claiming he learned of his firing through reports in the press, Mamoulian fought back tenaciously and brought his case before the Screen Directors Guild. The hurt of being deprived of directing the play he had brought to the stage twice, as *Porgy* and as *Porgy and Bess,* was made more painful by the humiliation of being replaced once again by Preminger. One can only wonder if Mamoulian suffered a breakdown in reason as he stood before the guild's board of directors and cast his employment dispute with Goldwyn as an issue "important to our national life—whether we still have a democracy or whether we have a dictatorship." Mamoulian told the guild that he had been responsible for auditioning actors in New York for the smaller parts, worked with the set and costume designers, the music director and the vocal coach, and directed the prerecording of the film's musical score. "I am not going to buckle down to this toy dictator," he said of Goldwyn. "Even if he pays me in full, I am going to sue him. I have already directed ¾ of this picture already. I cannot conceive of somebody else's walking in and shooting this and saying 'directed by.'" He demanded that the credit for *Porgy and Bess* read, "Directed by Rouben Mamoulian and Otto Preminger."[51]

Witnesses supported some of his claims. Praising Mamoulian as "one of the finest directors," Dandridge viewed Bess as a "whore's role," but said the director "gave me sound ideas on how to approach the role." Ivan Dixon, one of the smaller players discovered by Mamoulian, called Goldwyn "a shrewd man" who tricked Mamoulian into serving as casting director. The Screen Directors Guild agreed at first with Mamoulian, condemning Goldwyn for dismissing him for "frivolous, spiteful, or dictatorial reasons" and ordering its membership not to work for the producer. The Screen Producers Guild rushed to Goldwyn's defense, however, protesting "with shock and dismay the hysterical assaults upon the dean of American producers, Mr. Samuel Goldwyn, for exercising his prerogatives as an employer by changing directors on 'Porgy and Bess.'"[52] Wisely, Goldwyn maintained silence, fully expecting, as owner of the film property, to win the battle.

Mamoulian overplayed his hand when his press agent produced the race card at a press conference. A veteran of the 1927 premiere of *Porgy,* Leigh Whipper, president of a benevolent society called the Negro Actors Guild of America, praised Mamoulian's 1935 stage production of *Porgy and Bess* for achieving "the heights of human dignity and spiritual content." He announced his resignation from the role of the Crab Man, claiming the film was now in the hands of a man "unsympathetic to my people," adding, "I have first-hand information concerning the new director which brands him, to me, as a man who has no respect for my people." Goldwyn immediately marshaled cast members such as Sammy Davis Jr., Pearl Bailey, and Brock Peters to rebut the accusation. "I think that is an awful statement," said Bailey, a longtime friend of Mamoulian. "I think Mr. Preminger is going to do a wonderful job." Goldwyn's agents were also able to cast doubt on Whipple's character by showing how he had exaggerated the importance of his Negro Actors Guild and his role as an African American spokesman. Dorothy Dandridge kept quiet and, years later, made only an ambiguous remark on Preminger. "If Otto was prejudiced, he didn't know it."[53]

Mamoulian lost another battle in the war for sympathy when "Swifty" Lazar, vacationing in Paris, cabled the Screen Directors Guild to contradict Mamoulian's version of the events. Lazar, whose potential conflict of interest as agent for both Goldwyn and Mamoulian should have disqualified him from taking sides, claimed the director had been notified in advance of his firing and had drafted, along with Birdwell, the statement Goldwyn released to the press. The agent also insisted that he had tried to reconcile the director with the producer, an entirely plausible claim given Mamoulian's stubbornness on all questions relating to *Porgy and Bess*.[54] Mamoulian failed to understand that he did not possess special rights over the presentation of that property.

Preminger completed work on *Porgy and Bess* despite the controversy and finally appeared before the board of the Screen Directors Guild on February 2, 1959. Under questioning from Frank Capra, Preminger reprised the claims he had made about *Laura*. "None, absolutely none," he said of what was retained from Mamoulian's work. He also produced affidavits from the cinematographer and other crew members supporting his claim as sole director of *Porgy and Bess*.[55]

The guild was persuaded by Preminger's testimony and ruled against Mamoulian, concluding a drawn-out episode that reflected well on none of its participants, but received many pages of attention in the national press. "I couldn't get along with him," Goldwyn said of Mamoulian. "It's an intimate organization. I'm spending the money." The troubled project did not do well at the box office after its release in the summer of 1959, and Hollywood insiders whispered that Goldwyn had made a mistake by firing Mamoulian and hiring Preminger.[56]

Despite all the bad publicity, Mamoulian soon began work on another major motion picture. It would be his last. Producer Walter

Wanger, who had introduced Mamoulian to filmmaking with *Applause* in1929, hired him to direct *Cleopatra,* a movie designed to capitalize on the recent success of historical epics such as *The Ten Commandments* (1956) and to compete with television through its brilliantly colored wide-screen spectacle. Mamoulian's radical idea was to include African American actors in the picture. Mamoulian cast veteran player Elisabeth Welch as one of Cleopatra's handmaidens, but she was cut from the film after Mamoulian was replaced as director. He even wanted Dorothy Dandridge as Cleopatra, proposing the role to her over lunch at Romanoff's in Hollywood. "You won't have the guts to go through with this," she told him. "They are going to talk you out of it."[57] She was correct, and Mamoulian cast Elizabeth Taylor in the role over the objections of Wanger and Fox's president Spyros Skouras, who worried that the public had turned on the star for breaking up the marriage of singer Eddie Fisher to actress Debbie Reynolds. Taylor was not interested in the part and made Fox an offer she was certain they would refuse, demanding $1 million. She was startled when the studio accepted, setting a new record for an actor's salary and setting off the mounting costs of a picture that would never sell enough tickets to become profitable.

The project stumbled from the onset. "Originally, when I signed for Cleopatra, the conditions were that I could shoot the interiors in Hollywood and the exteriors in Italy and Egypt," Mamoulian insisted. To his dismay, he found that art director John De Cuir had begun building Alexandria on the 20th Century Fox back lot, a cost-saving scheme cut short before filming could begin when the property was sold to real estate developers. Returning to the original plans, De Cuir began again from scratch in Rome, where he constructed Egyptian temples and enlarged a lake to accommodate galleys, until Fox ordered a halt and transferred him to London without Mamoulian's knowledge. Several reasons have been given for the decision, including the impending 1960 Summer Olympics in Rome, which could have made accommodating the cast and crew difficult, and, probably more to the point, the generous subsidies offered by the British government to foreign film productions in the United Kingdom. According to one story, when Mamoulian flew to London to fix the hopeless screenplay by English novelist Nigel Balchin, he turned gray and vomited at first sight of the palm tree–

Rouben Mamoulian discussing the troubled script of *Cleopatra* with novelist Lawrence Durrell, 1960. (Getty Images)

fringed set of Pinewood Studios, realizing this was where *Cleopatra* would be filmed. "I'll decide where we'll spend $6 million. Go ahead and shoot," Skouras commanded.[58]

The troubles only continued. Mamoulian hated the new script by the acclaimed author of the Alexandria Quartet, Lawrence Durrell, calling it "absolute crap . . . nothing but sensationalism."[59] Regardless, filming began on September 28, 1960, and before long Mamoulian's single enduring contribution to the finished movie, Elizabeth Taylor, fell too ill to continue working. While filming outdoors in the impossible effort to re-create Egypt in London, Taylor contracted a severe bronchial infection from the rain and wind and chill of an English fall.

Skouras may have considered closing down the production to collect the insurance, cutting his losses before the costs continued to climb. "The insurance company panicked," Mamoulian recalled. "They said shoot some scenes while waiting around" for Taylor to recover. "We tried—in rain, sleet, cold, and mud, and with seven hundred extras. Whenever a word was spoken, you could see the vapor from their mouths. It was the North Pole, not Egypt."[60]

Work with the principal stars finally resumed on January 3, 1961; Mamoulian shot six takes of Cleopatra introducing herself to Caesar by rolling nude out of a carpet, as well as a dinner scene between the two rulers. With the script continuing to unravel and the weather persistently unsuitable, Mamoulian resigned on January 18, hoping to force the studio to bring the troubled production in line under his guidance and confident that Skouras and Wanger would decline to accept his resignation. The threat of resignation had won Mamoulian success four decades earlier when he used the ploy to gain the director's seat on his first London play, *The Beating on the Door*, but this time, he overplayed his hand. The director did not realize that Taylor wanted him replaced with Joseph L. Mankiewicz, with whom she had enjoyed working on *Suddenly Last Summer* (1959).[61]

By September 25, 1961, the first day of principal photography, Rex Harrison had replaced Peter Finch as Caesar and Richard Burton stepped in for Stephen Boyd as Mark Antony. The script was still unfinished but the production was switched to the Cinecitta studio in Rome, where Mamoulian had hoped to shoot the film all along. Given the many casting changes and the difficulties with the London setting, none of Mamoulian's footage could be salvaged. When it was finally released in 1963, *Cleopatra* was the highest-grossing film of the year but the biggest money loser of all time, a monument to the extravagance and indecisiveness of Hollywood executives uncertain of where the times were headed. Mamoulian became a casualty and symbol of the wretched excess; his reputation for meticulousness lent itself to the charge that he was partly to blame for the cost.

The remaining twenty-six years of Mamoulian's life after leaving *Cleopatra* turned into a long summer vacation before the inevitable winter of his last days. In 1964 the New York Graphic Society published his children's book, *Abigayil: The Story of the Cat at the Manger*, with color drawings by the respected illustrator Marshall Goodman. The endearing tale was told from the perspective of a cat, a species present in all of his films, at the Nativity, and embraced themes of oppression and random cruelty as well as the potential for kindness among creatures. He dedicated *Abigayil* "to Azadia, as related to me by Sugar, on behalf of all the cats in the world." Sugar was one of the couple's five cats.[62]

Mamoulian worked on other literary projects as well. He had first discovered *Hamlet* in translation as a young man in Tiflis, but upon reading it in English, was dismayed by the language's lack of immediacy for contemporary audiences. His revision of the play into modern English filled his days in the absence of offers from Hollywood or Broadway and was part of a trend, exemplified by Franco Zeffirelli's film of *Romeo and Juliet* (1968), toward softening the language barrier that kept popular audiences from Shakespeare's world. Mamoulian edited 510 lines from the play, rewrote 100 more and replaced nearly 2,000 words with contemporary English terms. He had worked on the project for several years; a 1961 tape recording of Mamoulian reading the text with David Cammack along with a 1963 reading by Mamoulian alone has been deposited in the Library of Congress. His version was published in paperback by Bobbs-Merrill in 1965 and was staged a year later at Transylvania University, a private liberal arts college in Lexington, Kentucky. Mamoulian did not direct the production but was present on opening night. Although his version of *Hamlet* was never revived, British historian and Shakespeare scholar A. L. Rowse praised it, and as late as 1974, there was talk in Hollywood of a film adaptation.[63]

Mamoulian's parents continued to live nearby his home in Beverly Hills. Their longevity was a forecast of his own old age. Zacharie died on December 6, 1966, at age one hundred, and Virginie survived until August 9, 1972, when she was ninety-six.[64] Mamoulian reached a turning point in his long epilogue in 1967 when New York's Gallery of Modern Art honored him with a fortieth anniversary tribute.[65] The event raised Mamoulian's profile at a time when universities were expanding the cultural curriculum to embrace popular culture, including the study of Hollywood movies, and when film societies flourished on American campuses and the cineaste culture of France found its reflection in the United States, complete with an embrace of the auteur theory and its emphasis on the role of the director.

Mamoulian suddenly found himself in demand again, not as a filmmaker but at least as someone who could speak of filmmaking from the time it learned to talk. Mamoulian eagerly embraced his new role as elder statesman and toured the widening circuit of film seminars and festivals during the 1970s, appearing at events as widespread as the Ontario Film Festival, the San Sebastien Festival in Spain, the Teheran Film Festival, and a program in his honor at Paris's Cinémathèque française. In 1974 Mamoulian presented the first annual Rouben Mamoulian Award for Australian film at the Sydney Film Fest. Along with attending festivals under the auspices of Franco and the shah of Iran, he was a guest of the Soviet Union, visiting Tbilisi, as his hometown of Tiflis had been renamed. Like all but the most ideologically driven filmmakers since Mussolini established the Venice Film Festival, Mamoulian was always willing to accept the cordiality of any regime. The director had time on his hands and spent it generously. He invited aspiring film writers to his home, where he presented an unfailingly charming face through the smoke of the cigars he habitually enjoyed. By the 1970s visitors remarked that cats had already overrun the place. By the end of his life over forty of the animals roamed the spacious house, whose handsome furnishings were ruined from their clawing, defecation, and urination.[66]

Rumors of new projects made their way into the press. Mamoulian planned to work with veteran screenwriter Robert Hardy Andrews on translating his novel, *Great Day in the Morning,* into a musical called *Shining Mountains.* The book had already been filmed in 1956 and the title change probably reflected questions of legal rights. *Summer Holiday*'s lyricist Ralph Blane was tapped for the adaptation. There was also talk of Mamoulian directing an Anita Loos screenplay on the life of Puccini for 20th Century Fox.[67] None of these projects materialized.

As late as the early 1980s Mamoulian claimed to be reviewing, and rejecting, scripts. "I don't know why I should waste my time on trash," he declared. In reality, like Billy Wilder and many other directors from Hollywood's golden age, Mamoulian, with his genteel humanism, was out of step with the direction of the movie business and out of touch with the new generation of powerbrokers. "I think today films, not unlike other arts, suffer from psychic depression," Mamoulian told critic Andrew Sarris. "Ours is a peculiar age—while scientists are lifting man into space, most artists keep shoving him into the gutter." He objected to films that focused on the bad in humanity and ignored the good. Unlike some of his peers, Mamoulian was unwilling to play the role of a veteran begging for a chance to prove himself. He was reasonably content to collect honors such as his induction into the Broadway Hall of Fame (1980) and the D. W. Griffith Award for Lifetime Achievement from the Directors Guild of America (1983), the successor to the Screen Directors Guild. The Museum of Modern Art launched its 1986 series honoring great directors with a screening of Mamoulian's *Love Me Tonight*. Too ill to attend a 1986 Directors Guild screening of his films, Mamoulian sent a taped introduction. He was still an elegant, distinguished figure even under the shadow of sickness. In his message he praised "this new art form" as "a kind of international language," adding, "It's rather sad at this time when the world is so fragmented . . . that we don't make enough films that can balance the horror that is going on." For Mamoulian, who had committed his life, like a Russian-trained aesthete, to reaching the masses, "all real art is entertainment" and film should allow viewers to "leave the theater a little better man or a little better woman." Through great filmmaking, "we can save the world from the disgrace of a bad ending." Mamoulian died on December 4, 1987, at the Motion Picture and Television Hospital in Los Angeles, where he had been hospitalized for a short time.[68] Azadia lived another twelve years.

Rouben Mamoulian was among hundreds of émigré directors, actors, and writers who enriched Hollywood in the decades after World War I by bringing a cultivated European sensibility to the cinema. The founders of Hollywood had also been immigrants, but they were men of modest education and great ambition, often admirers of the fine arts but grappling with complicated feelings of cultural insecurity. Some of the new émigrés cast a shrewd eye on American culture and sought ways to package their critique into acceptable entertainment. Between 1927 and 1950, Rouben Mamoulian directed more blacks on Broadway than any other director, white or black, casting more African Americans than John Houseman or Orson Welles.[69] As an Armenian, Mamoulian grew up in a minority culture within the Russian Empire and was dismayed as Armenians in the Ottoman Empire were slaughtered in the massacres his people called the Medz Yeghern, the Great Catastrophe. Mamoulian understood that racism could end in extermination. The status of African Americans was a subject he approached with great empathy.

The cosmopolitan atmosphere of Tiflis gave Mamoulian a model for a society in which different cultures coexist, and the rich education he received at home, and in Paris and Moscow, confirmed the breadth of his sensibility. Mamoulian's work is inscribed with the dignity of the human race, however flawed and distorted the manifestation of that spirit may be in individuals. Influenced by the example of his mother in the Armenian theater, his films from *Applause* through *Silk Stockings* depict women struggling against the constraints of convention. His belief in happy endings was amenable to Hollywood; the sources of his perspective can be traced to the Judeo-Christian tradition, refracted through his upbringing in the symbolic pageantry of Armenian Orthodoxy and strengthened by his reading of the great humanist authors of Russia and Europe. For Mamoulian, art was instrumental in showing the human spirit its potential. Mamoulian stated his credo a few years before his death at the American Film Institute's Center for Advanced Film Studies:

> In this unhappy, fragmented world of ours, overflowing with mutual suspicions, hostilities, violence, and destruction, we need a constructive force. Politics, economics, religions seem to fail. I think our best hope is in the arts. Today, the most universal and powerful medium of art and communication is in the film. In the last few years I've done a great deal of traveling to many countries, and I've been amazed at the impact of films on both the individuals and the societies of different nations. The influence is enormous. So we must all strive to elevate the quality of motion pictures. We must affirm and insist that the ultimate goal of a film, no matter what subject matter it deals with, is to add to the beauty and goodness of life, to the dignity of human beings, and to our faith in a better future.[70]

Mamoulian never entered the top tier in the canon of auteurs as established by film historians in the 1960s and 1970s. In the age before VHS, his most innovative films, *Applause, Love Me Tonight,* and *Becky Sharp,* were generally out of circulation and known mostly by fading memory and rumor. Several of his earlier films had been unseen for years or glimpsed only in versions truncated by the Hollywood Production Code. Academics found it impossible to label Mamoulian's work under the convenient, world-encompassing dogmas of Marxism, Freudianism, or Roman Catholicism. Mamoulian's refusal to remain within one genre or another frustrated some film buffs. Unlike the similarly eclectic career of Howard Hawks, Mamoulian's contained many gaps, both during periods when he returned to theater and from his inability to work consistently after the early 1940s. Writers seeking Hollywood iconoclasts found little material in Mamoulian, who was happy with material comforts and whose rebellions usually concerned new methods of revealing reality. He avoided attachment to any party line and never hurled himself into a life of reckless excess.

The strength as well as the problem faced by Mamoulian in Hollywood and on Broadway began with a well-developed aesthetic grounded in his training at the Moscow Art Theatre. His vision for depicting the world was focused on seeing beyond surface appearances to the underlying essence; his steadfast unwillingness to compromise could succeed only as long as his productions succeeded at the box office. Mamoulian was convinced he could persuade reluctant producers and technicians to embrace his perspective. He sometimes failed, often through lack of diplomacy.

Mamoulian the aesthete was not especially well suited to the rough-and-tumble of Hollywood. Dorothy Dandridge's remarks on Mamoulian's competitor, Otto Preminger, have bearing on his own situation. "Otto was ugly. Truly ugly," she said. "It is the folklore of Hollywood; the ugliness is much commented upon; it is known and understood that out of this ugliness they fashion and armor a toughness with which to prey and rule and succeed, and these alone are the kings of Hollywood."[71]

Despite his difficulty working in Hollywood, Mamoulian created a body of work sensitive to detail and emotional resonance. For him, Technicolor was no mere palette of brilliant hues but integral to the emotions of characters and settings in ways Goethe and other early color theorists would have approved. He was a profound influence on the greatest director of Hollywood musicals, Vincente Minnelli, who found most other work in the genre lacking in sophistication and panache.[72]

In the twenty-first century Mamoulian has attracted attention from a new generation of aesthetes, notably Canadian director Guy Maddin, whose films evoke the conventions of bygone cinema with loving irony. Mamoulian specifically influenced his feature *The Saddest Music in the World* (2004). Maddin wrote that Mamoulian's films "surprise the palate with a tasteful tumult of novelty, a riotous growth-spurt in the newborn filmic syntax, an effervescent revolution of authorial sophistication!" He added, "Mamoulian-viewing [is] as startling and fresh as it ever was, and makes us feel as though we are today speaking with less expressive cameras than we could be" and decried his "being led out to pasture at age 65 by the hipness-desperate studio heads of the 60s. I have a little dream," Maddin continued. "What if Mamoo could have immediately restarted his career right then, somehow as a young man, a flower child, at that time of great political and cultural upheaval. What miraculous tropes would have bloomed in his riotous garden of invention."[73]

Perhaps Mamoulian would have concurred. Commenting on *Dr. Jekyll and Mr. Hyde,* he compared Jekyll's drug-induced quest to the 1960s counterculture, "looking for an expansion of consciousness, for love, for the good things." He called the protagonist's "original purpose . . . very lofty and quite heroic," even if he ultimately fell victim.[74]

While *Dr. Jekyll and Mr. Hyde, The Mark of Zorro, Porgy and Bess,* and *Oklahoma!* are inseparable from the history of twentieth-century Hollywood and Broadway, Mamoulian is probably most remembered for a single scene. In the closing shot of *Queen Christina,* Greta Garbo stares without expression into an uncertain future in one of the great moments of cinema, an unforgettable tabula rasa created from Mamoulian's characteristic coupling of emotional sophistication with technical daring. It remains an enduring image of the potential of film as art.

Acknowledgments

This book grew out of conversation with film historian Patrick McGilligan, to whom I am indebted. I am grateful to film historian Joseph McBride of San Francisco State University for his assistance, and to Bruce Cole of the Marquette University Library, who was tireless in tracking down obscure sources. I would also like to thank John Schneider, who teaches theater history at Marquette University, and Steve Spice, an aficionado of film and theater, for reading portions of the manuscript in progress. I am especially thankful to Mary Manion for her research assistance and encouragement.

Notes

Introduction

1. Dated August 7, 1967, Rouben Mamoulian Papers, Library of Congress, Washington, D.C.; *Brooklyn Daily Eagle,* November 17, 1927.

2. Paul Horgan, *A Certain Climate: Essays in History, Arts, and Letters* (Middleton, Conn.: Wesleyan University Press, 1988), 207, 208.

3. Andrew Sarris, *The American Cinema: Directors and Directions, 1929–1968* (New York: Dutton, 1968), 160.

4. David Thompson, *Have You Seen . . . ? A Personal Introduction to 1,000 Films* (New York: Knopf, 2008), 45.

1. Caucasian Youth

1. The 1886 Russian census reported 55,000 Armenians in Tiflis out of a population of 145,000. H. F. B. Lynch, *Armenia: Travels and Studies,* vol. 1 (London: Longmans Green, 1901), 449.

2. Richard G. Hovannisian, *Armenia on the Road to Independence, 1918* (Berkeley: University of California Press, 1967), 42.

3. Mark Spergel, *Reinventing Reality: The Art and Life of Rouben Mamoulian* (Metuchen, N.J.: Scarecrow, 1993), 18, 26, 28.

4. Nishan Parlakian and S. Peter Cowe, eds., *Modern Armenian Drama* (New York: Columbia University Press, 2001), xi–xiv.

5. Catherine A. Schuler, *Women in Russian Theatre: The Actress in the Silver Age* (London: Routledge, 1996).

6. Hovannisian, *Armenia,* 15.

7. Victor Yezefovich, *Aram Khachaturyan* (New York: Sphinx, 1985), 4.

8. Unpublished notes by Rouben Mamoulian, quoted in Spergel, *Reinventing Reality,* 20–21.

9. Charles Higham and Joel Greenberg, *The Celluloid Muse: Hollywood Directs* (Chicago: Henry Regnery, 1969), 129.

10. Andrew Sarris, *Hollywood Voices: Interviews with Film Directors* (London: Secker & Warburg, 1971), 67.

11. Margaret Case Harriman, "Mr. Mamoulian, of Tiflis and 'Oklahoma!'" *New York Times Magazine,* July 25, 1943; George Stevens Jr., ed., *Conversations with the Great Moviemakers of Hollywood's Golden Age at the American Film Institute* (New York: Knopf, 2006), 183.

12. Rouben Mamoulian, 1958 interview, Columbia University Oral History Collection, New York; Bennett Oberstein, "The Broadway Directing Career of Rouben Mamoulian" (Ph.D. diss., Indiana University, 1977).

13. Spergel, *Reinventing Reality,* 16, 25; Harriman, "Mr. Mamoulian."

14. Hovannisian, *Armenia,* 17–21.

15. "Dialogue on Film: Rouben Mamoulian," *American Film,* January 1983; Paul Horgan, "Rouben Mamoulian: The Start of a Career," *Films in Review,* August–September 1973.

16. "Conversations with Rouben Mamoulian," unpublished manuscript, Department of Theatre and Drama, Indiana University, Bloomington.

17. Stevens, *Conversations,* 168–69.

18. David Robinson, "Painting the Leaves Black: Rouben Mamoulian Interviewed," *Sight and Sound* 30 (Summer 1961): 124; "Rouben Mamoulian on the Exciting Revolution in Musicals," *Times* (London), June 17, 1960; Harry A. Hargrave, "Interview with Rouben Mamoulian," *Literature/Film Quarterly* 10, no. 4 (1982): 265.

19. "Conversations with Rouben Mamoulian."

20. Ronald G. Suny, "The Revolution in Transcaucasia," in *Critical Companion to the Russian Revolution, 1914–1921,* ed. Edward Acton, Vladimir Cherniaev, and William G. Rosenberg (Bloomington: University of Indiana Press, 1997), 719–27; Hovannisian, *Armenia,* 205–6.

2. From West End to Rochester

1. Maurice Zolotow, "Hollywood's Armenian Yankee Doodle Dandy," *Saturday Evening Post,* December 13, 1947.

2. Adrian Cedric Boult, *My Own Trumpet* (London: Hamish Hamilton, 1973), 48; Oliver M. Sayler, *The Russian Theatre* (New York: Brentano's, 1922), 181, 184.

3. Robinson, "Painting the Leaves Black"; Zolotow, "Hollywood's Ar-

menian Yankee Doodle Dandy"; Rouben Mamoulian, "Bernhardt versus Duse," *Theatre Arts,* September 1957.

4. William J. Becvar, "The Stage and Film Career of Rouben Mamoulian" (Ph.D. diss., University of Kansas, 1975), 20; Robinson, "Painting the Leaves Black."

5. Becvar, "The Stage and Film Career of Rouben Mamoulian," 21.

6. Sarris, *Hollywood Voices,* 61.

7. Robinson, "Painting the Leaves Black"; Becvar, "The Stage and Film Career of Rouben Mamoulian," 24; Raymond Rohauer, *A 40th Anniversary Tribute to Rouben Mamoulian, 1927–1967* (New York: Gallery of Modern Art, 1967), Theatre Collection, New York Public Library.

8. Sarris, *Hollywood Voices,* 62; Becvar, "The Stage and Film Career of Rouben Mamoulian," 36.

9. J. P. Wearing, *The London Stage, 1920–1929: A Calendar of Plays and Players,* vol. 1 (Metuchen, N.J.: Scarecrow, 1984), 320–21; Sydney W. Carroll, "The Dramatic World," *Sunday Times,* November 12, 1922; Paul Ibell, *Theatreland: A Journey through the Heart of London's Theatre* (London: Continuum, 2009), 172–73.

10. Nicolas Slonimsky, *Perfect Pitch: A Life Story* (London, Oxford University Press, 1988), 84; For a summary of the Eastman School's early years, see Elizabeth Brayer, *George Eastman: A Biography* (Baltimore: Johns Hopkins University Press, 1996), 442–67.

11. Horgan, "Rouben Mamoulian." In Horgan's roman à clef on his years at the Eastman School, *The Fault of the Angels* (New York, Harper & Bros., 1933), he introduced Colya, a character who sounds inspired in part by Mamoulian. A Russian refugee, Colya was a rebel with "witty malice" who "talked about politics, and art, and music, and science, and mathematics, and personalities, with equal charm and good sense" (27, 109).

12. Sarris, *Hollywood Voices,* 62; Robinson, "Painting the Leaves Black"; Becvar, "The Stage and Film Career of Rouben Mamoulian," 31.

13. "A School for Opera," *Literary Digest,* August 25, 1923; Sidney Skolsky, "Times Square Tintypes," *New York Sun,* June 11, 1928.

14. Horgan, "Rouben Mamoulian."

15. "Concentration Vital in Opera, Producer Says," *Rochester Democrat and Chronicle,* November 26, 1923; Horgan, "Rouben Mamoulian."

16. Horgan, "Rouben Mamoulian"; Robinson, "Painting the Leaves Black"; Brayer, *George Eastman,* 464.

17. "Concentration Vital"; Horgan, "Rouben Mamoulian."

18. Becvar, "The Stage and Film Career of Rouben Mamoulian," 43–44.

19. Horgan, "Rouben Mamoulian"; "Prison Scene from Faust," *Roch-*

ester Democrat and Chronicle, December 18, 1923; the production was also favorably reviewed in the *Buffalo Journal and Post,* December 18, 1923.

20. Interview with James Silke and James Blue, American Film Institute, Los Angeles, April 30, 1970.

21. "The Barber of Seville," *Rochester Democrat and Chronicle,* January 15, 1924; "Eastman Theatre Singers to Put on Excerpts from One of Wagner's Music Dramas," *Rochester Democrat and Chronicle,* February 12, 1924; "Tannhauser," *Rochester Democrat and Chronicle,* March 4, 1924.

22. "Drive Opens for Little Theatre," *Rochester Herald,* November 9, 1924; Becvar, "The Stage and Film Career of Rouben Mamoulian," 57.

23. James H. Thompson, "Faust," *Rochester Herald,* January 30, 1925; A. J. Warner, "American Opera Company Repeats 'Faust,'" *Rochester Times-Union,* January 30, 1925.

24. A. J. Warner, "New Opera Company Gives 'Carmen' at Eastman," *Rochester Times-Union,* March 27, 1925.

25. Nikolai A. Gorchakov, *The Theater in Soviet Russia,* trans. Edgar Lehrman (New York: Columbia University Press, 1957), 42–43, 57.

26. Becvar, "The Stage and Film Career of Rouben Mamoulian," 69, 72; program notes, *Sister Beatrice,* January 17, 1926.

27. Horgan, "Rouben Mamoulian," 411.

28. Don McDonagh, *Martha Graham: A Biography* (New York: Praeger, 1973), 44.

29. "New School Links Dance with Drama," *Rochester Democrat and Chronicle,* July 5, 1925; Robert Tracy, *Goddess: Martha Graham's Dancers Remember* (New York: Limelight, 1997), 3; Becvar, "The Stage and Film Career of Rouben Mamoulian," 66; Martha Graham, *Blood Memory* (New York: Doubleday, 1991), 106.

30. McDonagh, *Martha Graham,* 45, 46–52; Rohauer, *40th Anniversary Tribute.*

3. Young Lion of Broadway

1. For an account of the Guild's early years, see Walter Prichard Eaton, *The Theatre Guild: The First Ten Years* (New York: Brentano's, 1929), 3–42.

2. Lawrence Langner, *The Magic Curtain* (New York: Dutton, 1951), 225–26; Becvar, "The Stage and Film Career of Rouben Mamoulian," 78.

3. "Rouhen Mamoulian" [*sic*] was granted a visa in Paris on September 1, 1926, and sailed from Southampton on the White Star liner *Majestic,* arriving in New York on September 14. His profession was listed as "theatrical director" and his last permanent address was given as Rochester, New York.

Passenger List of Vessels Arriving at New York, National Archives, Washington, D.C., microfilm roll T 715-3925.

4. James R. Silke, *Rouben Mamoulian: Style Is the Man* (Los Angeles: Center for Advanced Film Studies, 1971), 34; Langner, *Magic Curtain,* 226. The Guild ignored an unfavorable review in the trade paper *Billboard,* critical of the play's direction. Gordon M. Leland, "New Plays on Broadway," *Billboard,* May 14, 1927; Eaton, *Theatre Guild,* 86.

5. Nannie Elizabeth Creighton, "DuBose Heyward and His Contribution to Literature" (M.A. thesis, University of South Carolina, 1933), 24; James M. Hutchisson, *DuBose Heyward: A Charleston Gentlemen and the World of Porgy and Bess* (Jackson: University Press of Mississippi, 2000), 39, 49.

6. Eaton, *Theatre Guild,* 98; Langner, *Magic Curtain,* 226; Becvar, "The Stage and Film Career of Rouben Mamoulian," 79.

7. Oberstein, "The Broadway Directing Career of Rouben Mamoulian," 34; Otto Zoff, ed., *Great Composers through the Eyes of Their Contemporaries* (New York: Dutton, 1951), 460; Langner, *Magic Curtain,* 226; Eaton, *Theatre Guild,* 98; Mamoulian on Charleston from an undated clipping from the *Charleston News and Courier,* the Guild Collection, Yale University, New Haven, Conn.; John Bennett Papers, South Carolina Historical Society, Charleston, from a letter dated August 14, 1927; Becvar, "The Stage and Film Career of Rouben Mamoulian," 81–82.

8. For an overview of African American theater in those years, see David Krasner, *A Beautiful Pageant: African American Theatre, Drama, and Performance in the Harlem Renaissance, 1910–1927* (New York: Palgrave Macmillan, 2002).

9. Rouben Mamoulian interview, *Charleston News and Courier,* January 19, 1958; Dorothy Heyward, "Porgy's Native Tongue," *New York Times,* December 4, 1927.

10. Louise Mace, "Harlem in Catfish Alley," unidentified clipping in New York Public Library Theatre Collection; undated clipping, *Charleston News and Courier,* New York Public Library Theatre Collection; Hutchisson, *DuBose Heyward,* 81.

11. Eleanor Ball, "Director and Cast Work for Opening Porgy," *Charleston News and Courier,* October 1, 1927; DuBose and Dorothy Heyward interview, *New York Sun,* October 22, 1927.

12. Brooks Atkinson, *The Lively Years, 1920–1973* (New York: Association Press, 1973), 58; Percy Stone, *New York Herald Tribune,* December 11, 1927; Harriman, "Mr. Mamoulian."

13. Porter S. Woods, "The Negro on Broadway: The Transition Years"

(DFA diss., Yale University, 1965), 74–75; Merle Armitage, ed., *George Gershwin* (London: Longmans, Green, 1938), 51; DuBose Heyward to Jane Screven Heyward, September 21, 1927, South Carolina Historical Society, box 11; letter DuBose Heyward to Jane Screven Heyward, October 6, 1927, South Carolina Historical Society, box 11.

14. Brooks Atkinson, "The Play, Negro Lithography," *New York Times,* October 11, 1927; Brooks Atkinson, "Negro Mystery," *New York Times,* October 16, 1927; Alexander Woollcott, "The Stage," *New York World,* October 11, 1927; Oliver M. Sayler, "The Play of the Week," *Saturday Review of Literature,* October 29, 1927.

15. Hutchisson, *DuBose Heyward,* 77; Eaton, *Theatre Guild,* 151–52.

16. Langner, *Magic Curtain,* 228–31; Alison Smith, *New York World,* October 23, 1927.

17. "Men and Their Shadows: Mamoulian Deals in Both," *New York Herald-Tribune,* December 16, 1928.

18. Oberstein, "The Broadway Directing Career of Rouben Mamoulian," 62–63; Mary Hedwig Arbenz, "The Plays of Eugene O'Neill as Presented by the Theatre Guild" (Ph.D. diss., University of Illinois, 1960), 91.

19. Jack Pulaski Ibee, "Marco Millions," *Variety,* January 11, 1928; program for *Marco Millions,* Theatre Collection, Museum of the City of New York; Percy Hammond, "The Theatres," *New York Herald Tribune,* January 11, 1928; Sayler, "The Play of the Week"; Oberstein, "The Broadway Directing Career of Rouben Mamoulian," 66–67; light cue sheets for *Marco Millions,* Theatre Collection, Museum of the City of New York.

20. Vincent Sherman, *Studio Affairs: My Life as a Film Director* (Lexington: University Press of Kentucky, 1996), 14; Alexander Woollcott, "The Stage," *New York World,* January 10, 1928; Brooks Atkinson, "Eugene O'Neill's Gorgeous Satire," *New York Times,* January 10, 1928.

21. Silke, *Rouben Mamoulian,* 35.

22. According to the census roll, all three family members spoke English. Probably to simplify matters, they gave Armenia as their place of birth and Armenian as the "language spoken in home before coming to the United States." 1930 U.S. Census in New York City, 10th Assembly District, Borough of Manhattan.

23. Oberstein, "The Broadway Directing Career of Rouben Mamoulian," 70.

24. Alison Smith, *New York World,* November 29, 1928.

25. Advertisement in Theatre Guild program for *Wings over Europe,* December 11, 1928, New York Public Library Theatre Collection; Wilella Waldorf, *New York Evening Post,* November 28, 1928.

26. Oberstein, "The Broadway Directing Career of Rouben Mamoulian," 77, 79.

27. Ibid., 78; Roy S. Waldau, *Vintage Years of the Theatre Guild, 1928–1939* (Cleveland: Press of Case Reserve Western University, 1972), 43.

28. Brooks Atkinson, *New York Times,* February 18, 1930; unsigned, undated clipping from *New York Mirror,* New York Public Library Theatre Collection.

29. Howard Barnes, *New York Herald Tribune,* February 18, 1930; Oberstein, "The Broadway Directing Career of Rouben Mamoulian," 91.

30. John Mason Brown, *New York Post,* March 18, 1930; Katharine Hepburn, *Me: Stories of My Life* (New York: Knopf, 1991), 111; Anne Edwards, *Katharine Hepburn: A Remarkable Woman* (New York: Macmillan, 2000), 66–67.

31. Langner, *Magic Curtain,* 248–49.

32. Eaton, *Theatre Guild,* 19; Langner, *Magic Curtain,* 24; Silke, *Rouben Mamoulian,* 3.

33. John Mason Brown, *Upstage: Types of American Direction* (Port Washington, N.Y.: Kennikat, 1969), 181–82.

4. The Sound of Applause

1. For an argument in favor of silent movies over talkies, see the 1928 essay "Sound Film" by German critic Rudolf Arnheim in Arnheim, *Film Essays and Criticism* (Madison: University of Wisconsin Press, 1997), 29–31.

2. Sarris, *Hollywood Voices,* 63.

3. Maurice Bardeche and Robert Brasillach, *The History of Motion Pictures,* trans. Iris Barry (New York: Norton and Museum of Modern Art, 1938), 306.

4. Marguerite Tazelar, "Mamoulian, from the Caucasus, Says 'The Camera's the Thing,'" *New York Herald Tribune,* June 23, 1929.

5. Sarris, *Hollywood Voices,* 63.

6. Silke, *Rouben Mamoulian,* 6.

7. Thomas Schatz, *The Genius of the System: Hollywood Filmmaking in the Studio Era* (New York: Pantheon, 1988), 75; Spergel, *Reinventing Reality,* 96.

8. Silke, *Rouben Mamoulian,* 6. Mamoulian was confused about *A Kiss for Cinderella,* a silent film shot in Astoria in 1925. Richard Koszarski, "The Greatest Film Paramount Ever Made," *Film History,* no. 4 (2003); Eric Sherman, *Directing the Film: Film Directors on Their Art* (Boston: Little Brown, 1976), 12–13; Florey, quoted in Koszarksi, "Greatest Film."

9. Tazelar, "Mamoulian"; Sherman, *Directing the Film,* 33.

10. Silke, *Rouben Mamoulian,* 10–11.

11. "Mamoulian's Camera," *New York Times,* September 22, 1929; Sherman, *Directing the Film,* 292; Tazelar, "Mamoulian."

12. Silke, *Rouben Mamoulian,* 7; Stevens, *Conversations,* 169; Hargrave, "Interview with Rouben Mamoulian."

13. Silke, *Rouben Mamoulian,* 7.

14. Sarris, *Hollywood Voices,* 64; Silke, *Rouben Mamoulian,* 7–8; Hargrave, "Interview with Rouben Mamoulian."

15. Colonel Jason S. Joy to Walter Wanger, September 18, 1929, Production Code Administration Papers, Motion Picture Producers and Distributors of America Collection, Margaret Herrick Library Center for Motion Picture Study, Academy of Motion Picture Arts and Sciences, Beverly Hills, Calif.

16. "Newspaper Life in Film," *New York Times,* October 7 and October 23, 1929.

17. Silke, *Rouben Mamoulian,* 15; John A. Gallagher and Marino Amoruco, "An Interview with Rouben Mamoulian," *Velvet Light Trap,* no. 19 (1982).

18. Mordaunt Hall, "Screen," *New York Times,* October 8, 1929; "Notes on Hollywood Directors (as of 1933)," in *Dwight Macdonald on Movies* (Englewood Cliffs, N.J.: Prentice-Hall, 1969), 81; "Jazz Mad Nights," *New York Times,* November 3, 1929.

19. *Motion Picture Herald,* June 29, 1929; Tazelar, "Mamoulian."

5. Hollywood

1."Sunday News of the Rialto," *New York Times,* November 12, 1929; Cyril Maude, "The New Films & Others," *New York Times,* August 3, 1930.

2. Silke, *Rouben Mamoulian,* 15.

3. Rudy Behmer, ed., *Memo from David O. Selznick* (New York: Viking, 1972), 26–27.

4. Gallagher and Amoruco, "Interview with Rouben Mamoulian"; Richard Layman, *Shadow Man: The Life of Dashiell Hammett* (New York: Harcourt Brace Jovanovich, 1981), 126, 269.

5. I. G. Edmonds and Reiko Mimura, *Paramount Pictures and the People Who Made Them* (San Diego: A.S. Barnes, 1980), 179; Gallagher and Amoruco, "Interview"; Gary Cooper, as told to George Scullin, "Well, It Was This Way," *Saturday Evening Post,* March 24, 1956; Edmonds and Mimura, *Paramount Pictures,* 197; Robinson, "Painting the Leaves Black."

6. Hargrave, "Interview with Rouben Mamoulian."

7. Sarris, *Hollywood Voices,* 65.

8. Gallagher and Amoruco, "Interview."

9. Tom Milne, *Mamoulian* (London: Thames & Hudson/British Film Institute, 1969), 33; Mordaunt Hall, "Screen," *New York Times,* April 19, 1932.

10. By the first quarter of 1932, daily cinema attendance had declined to 6 million from its 1928 height of 10 million, and Paramount Studio was under great financial strain. Peter Baxter, *Just Watch! Sternberg, Paramount and America* (London: British Film Institute, 1993), 41.

11. Joseph I. Breen to Paramount Pictures, December 10, 1936, *City Streets* file, Production Code Administration Papers.

12. Hargrave, "Interview with Rouben Mamoulian"; Silke, *Rouben Mamoulian,* 21–22.

13. "U Has Horror Cycle All to Self," *Variety,* April 18, 1931.

14. Fredric March Papers, Wisconsin Center for Film and Theater Research, State Historical Society of Wisconsin, Madison.

15. John Kobal, *People Will Talk* (New York: Knopf, 1985), 358, 359.

16. Deborah C. Peterson, *Fredric March: Craftsman First, Star Second* (Westport, Conn.: Greenwood, 1996), 61.

17. George Turner, "Two-Faced Treachery," *American Cinematographer,* March 1999; William Stull, "Common Sense and Camera Angles," *American Cinematographer,* February 1932.

18. Robinson, "Painting the Leaves Black." Cinematographer Karl Struss claimed he had devised the technique used to transform Jekyll into Hyde for the scene of lepers being healed in *Ben Hur* (1926), Turner, "Two-Faced Treachery."

19. Clipping from *Hollywood Citizen News,* June 14, 1938, and unidentified, undated clipping, March Papers.

20. *Photoplay,* quoted in Lawrence J. Quirk, *The Films of Fredric March* (New York: Citadel, 1974), 80.

21. *Dr. Jekyll and Mr. Hyde* file, Production Code Administration Papers.

22. Richard J. Anobile, *Rouben Mamoulian's Dr. Jekyll and Mr. Hyde, Starring Fredric March* (New York: Darien House/Universe Books, 1975), 6.

23. Mordaunt Hall, "Screen," *New York Times,* January 2, 1932.

24. Spergel, *Reinventing Reality,* 29; Dickran Kouymjian, "Saroyan Shoots a Film," in *William Saroyan: The Man and the Writer Remembered,* ed. Leo Hamalian (Cranbury, N.J.: Associated University Presses, 1987), 78.

25. John F. Wharton, *Life among the Playwrights: Being Mostly the Story of the Playwrights Producing Company, Inc.* (New York: Quadrangle/New

York Times Book Co., 1974), 191; Richard Griffith, ed., *The Talkies: Articles and Illustrations from Photoplay Magazine, 1928–1940* (New York: Dover, 1971), 282; Kobal, *People Will Talk,* 358; James Kotsilibas-Davis and Myrna Loy, *Being and Becoming* (New York: Knopf, 1987), 72; Lynn Kear and John Rossman, *Kay Francis: A Passionate Life and Career* (Jefferson, N.C.: McFarland, 2006), 114.

26. "Rambling Reporter," *Hollywood Reporter,* December 5, 1933; Karen Swenson, *Greta Garbo: A Life Apart* (New York: Scribner, 1997), 312, 317–18; Barry Paris, *Garbo: A Biography* (New York: Knopf, 1995), 249; "Garbo and Mamoulian Return," *Los Angeles Times,* January 18, 1934; "Rambling Reporter," *Hollywood Reporter,* February 7, 1934.

27. Joseph C. Youngerman, *My Seventy Years at Paramount Studios and the Directors Guild of America* (Los Angeles: Directors Guild of America, 1995), 54; Simon Alexander Morrison, *The People's Artist: Prokofiev's Soviet Years* (New York: Oxford University Press, 2009), 74–75.

28. Richard Rodgers, *Musical Stages: An Autobiography* (New York: Random House, 1975), 149.

29. Kotsilibas-Davis and Loy, *Being and Becoming,* 72.

30. Rodgers, *Musical Stages,* 150; Silke, *Rouben Mamoulian,* 26.

31. Youngerman, *My Seventy Years at Paramount,* 20–21; Gallagher, "Interview."

32. Gene Ringold and DeWitt Bodeen, *Chevalier: The Films and Career of Maurice Chevalier* (Secaucus, N.J.: Citadel, 1973), 111; Edward Baron Turk, *Hollywood Diva: A Biography of Jeanette MacDonald* (Berkeley: University of California Press, 1998), 120.

33. Kotsilibas-Davis and Loy, *Being and Becoming,* 72. Mamoulian told a similar story of rescuing Loy from playing "villainesses and Oriental spies in those B-pictures." Gallagher, "Interview."

34. David Bret, *Maurice Chevalier: The Authorized Biography* (London: Robson Books, 2002), 93; Rouben Mamoulian, foreword to Ringold and Bodeen, *Chevalier,* 1.

35. Joseph I. Breen to Mr. Hammel at Paramount, *Love Me Tonight* file, Production Code Administration Papers.

36. Gallagher, "Interview."

37. Steven Bach, *Marlene Dietrich: Life and Legend* (New York: William Morrow, 1992), 164; Marlene Dietrich, *Marlene,* trans. Salvator Attanasio (New York: Grove, 1989), 97, 173.

38. Charles Higham, *Marlene: The Life of Marlene Dietrich* (New York: Norton, 1977), 102–4.

39. The collaboration "proved to be smooth and friendly," according to Leslie Frewin, *Dietrich* (New York: Stein & Day, 1967), 75, but Mamoulian

was annoyed at Dietrich's star attitude. Donald Spoto, *Blue Angel: The Life of Marlene Dietrich* (New York: Doubleday, 1992), 108; Brian Aherne, *A Proper Job* (Boston: Houghton Mifflin, 1969), 200, 204–5.

40. Rouben Mamoulian to A.M. Botsford, June 5, 1933. *Song of Songs* file, Production Code Administration Papers.

6. Queen Garbo

1. Maria Riva, *Marlene Dietrich by Her Daughter* (New York: Knopf, 1993), 160.

2. Paris, *Garbo,* 285, 290.

3. Salka Viertel, *The Kindness of Strangers* (New York: Holt, Rinehart & Winston, 1969), 175.

4. Ibid., 183; memo, H. M. Harwood to Walter Wanger, *Queen Christina* file, MGM archive, University of Southern California, Los Angeles; Robert Payne, *The Great Garbo* (New York: Cooper Square, 2002), 218.

5. Viertel, *Kindness of Strangers,* 152.

6. Paris, *Garbo,* 294; Swenson, *Greta Garbo,* 304.

7. "Dialogue on Film: Rouben Mamoulian," *American Film,* January 1983; Kevin Brownlow, *The Parade's Gone By . . .* (New York: Knopf, 1968), 12.

8. Brownlow, *Parade's Gone By,* 12; "Rambling Reporter," *Hollywood Reporter,* June 2, 1933. Garbo supposedly liked Olivier's acting and his resemblance to John Gilbert in the 1932 RKO romance *Westward Passage,* Paris, *Garbo,* 295.

9. Laurence Olivier, *Confessions of an Actor* (New York: Simon & Schuster, 1982), 93; Leatrice Gilbert Fountain, *Dark Star* (New York: St. Martin's, 1985), 233–34; Paris, *Garbo,* 297; "Rambling Reporter, *Hollywood Reporter,* September 22, 1933.

10. Robinson, "Painting the Leaves Black"; Lloyd Chesley and Michael Gould, "The Lost Interview Series: Rouben Mamoulian, the 'First Underground Director,' on Technology and Jumping Fences," *MovieMaker,* Winter 2005.

11. Higham and Greenberg, *The Celluloid Muse,* 138; "Dialogue on Film."

12. Milne, *Mamoulian,* 74; Kenneth Tynan, "Garbo," *Sight and Sound,* April 1954.

13. Robinson, "Painting the Leaves Black"; Silke, *Rouben Mamoulian,* 22–23.

14. Robinson, "Painting the Leaves Black"; Silke, *Rouben Mamoulian,* 24.

15. Silke, *Rouben Mamoulian,* 28–29.

16. Viertel, *Kindness of Strangers,* 192.

17. Sven Broman, *Conversations with Greta Garbo* (New York: Viking, 1992), 119; Mordaunt Hall, "Screen," *New York Times,* December 27, 1933; Swenson, *Greta Garbo,* 315.

18. Memo, James Wingate to E. J. Mannix, August 7, 1933, Production Code Administration Papers; memo, Joseph I. Breen to Louis B. Mayer, January 8, 1934, Production Code Administration Papers; memo, John V. Wilson, August 11, 1933, *Queen Christina* file, Production Code Administration Papers; Joseph I. Breen to Rev. FitzGeorge Dinneen, SJ, March 17, 1934, American Catholic University History Research Center and University Archives, Catholic University of America, Washington, D.C.; Martin Quigley, *Decency in Motion Pictures* (New York: Macmillan, 1937), 37.

19. Swenson, *Greta Garbo,* 316, 321.

20. "Rambling Reporter," *Hollywood Reporter,* February 28 and June 6, 1934; A. Scott Berg, *Goldwyn: A Biography* (New York: Knopf, 1989), 240–41.

21. Preston Sturges, *Preston Sturges* (New York: Simon & Schuster, 1990), 278; Donald Spoto, *The Life of Preston Sturges* (Boston: Little Brown, 1990), 120.

22. Rouben Mamoulian, unpublished interview with Jim Curtis, August 3, 1977, quoted in Diana Jacobs, *Christmas in July: The Life and Art of Preston Sturges* (Berkeley: University of California Press, 1992), 135.

23. Vincent Hart to Joseph I. Breen, October 2, 1934, *We Live Again* file, Production Code Administration Papers; memo, Joseph I. Breen to Will H. Hays, October 8, 1934, Production Code Administration Papers.

24. Peterson, *Fredric March,* 82.

25. Sturges, *Preston Sturges,* 275.

26. Arthur Marx, *Goldwyn: A Biography of the Man behind the Myth* (New York: Norton, 1976), 196; Berg, *Goldwyn,* 244.

27. "Mamoulian's Camera," *New York Times,* September 22, 1929.

28. "Moving Pictures in Color," *New York Times,* February 22, 1917; Herbert Kalmus, "Technicolor Adventures in Cinemaland," *Journal of the Society of Motion Picture Engineers,* December 1938.

29. Gallagher, "Interview."

30. Rouben Mamoulian, "Some Problems in Directing Color Pictures," *Journal of the Society of Motion Picture Engineers,* August 1935.

31. Anthony Slide, "The Return of *Becky Sharp,*" *Films in Review,* November 1984.

32. Vincente Minnelli, *I Remember It Well* (New York: Doubleday, 1974), 131–32.

33. Gallagher, "Interview."

34. Andre Sennwald, "The Radio City Music Hall Presents 'Becky Sharp,' the First Full-Length Three-Color Photoplay," *New York Times,* June 14, 1935.

35. Mamoulian, "Some Problems."

36. "Mamoulian Grants Interview to the 'Weekly' Reporter," *Hairenik Weekly,* December 4, 1935; Mark A. Vieira, *Irving Thalberg: Boy Wonder to Producer Prince* (Berkeley: University of California Press, 2010), 39. See also Edward Minasian, *Musa Dagh* (Nashville: Cold Tree, 2007).

7. I Loves You, Porgy

1. Quoted in Hollis Alpert, *The Life and Times of Porgy and Bess: The Story of an American Classic* (New York: Knopf, 1990), 92.

2. John Houseman, *Run-through: A Memoir* (New York: Simon & Schuster, 1972), 165–66.

3. Waldau, *Vintage Years,* 124, 189.

4. Warren Munsell to DuBose Heyward, December 18, 1929, DuBose Heyward Papers, South Carolina Historical Society; Rouben Mamoulian, "I Remember," in Armitage, *George Gershwin,* 47.

5. Mamoulian, "I Remember," 48; Warren Munsell to Rouben Mamoulian, March 7, 1935, Theatre Guild Archives, Beinecke Rare Books Collection, Yale University, New Haven, Conn.

6. Walter Rimler, *George Gershwin: An Intimate Portrait* (Urbana: University of Illinois Press, 2009), 6.

7. DuBose Heyward, *Mamba's Daughters* (Columbia: University of South Carolina Press, 1995), 302.

8. George Gershwin to DuBose Heyward, March 29, 1932, and October 14, 1932, George Gershwin Collection, Library of Congress; Michael Freedland, *Jolie: The Al Jolson Story* (London: W. H. Allen, 1985), 171–72. Jolson still would not give up. In 1950 he negotiated with the Theatre Guild for rights to produce a film with an all-black cast aside from himself as Porgy. Herbert G. Goldman, *Jolson: The Legend Comes to Life* (New York: Oxford University Press, 1988), 289.

9. The Metropolitan Opera would become one of the world's last major opera houses to host a performance of *Porgy and Bess,* which finally played the Met in 1985; Isaac Goldberg, "Score by George Gershwin," *Stage,* December 1935.

10. DuBose Heyward, "Porgy and Bess on Wings of Song," *Stage,* October 1935.

11. Howard Pollack, *George Gershwin: His Life and Work* (Berkeley: University of California Press, 2006), 150.

12. Merle Armitage, *George Gershwin: Man and Legend* (New York: Duell, Sloan & Pearce, 1958), 15.

13. Mamoulian, "I Remember," 47.

14. George Gershwin, "Rhapsody in Catfish Row," *New York Times,* October 20, 1935.

15. Heyward, "Porgy."

16. Mamoulian, "I Remember," 51.

17. Robert Kimball and Alfred Simon, *The Gershwins* (New York: Atheneum, 1973), 184; Oscar Levant, *A Smattering of Ignorance* (New York: Doubleday, Doran, 1940), 179–80.

18. Irving Kolodin, "*Porgy and Bess:* American Opera in the Theatre," *Theatre Arts Monthly,* no. 19 (1935); Charles Hamm, "The Theatre Guild Production of *Porgy and Bess,*" *Journal of the American Musicological Society,* Autumn 1987.

19. Langner, *Magic Curtain,* 265.

20. Isaac Goldberg, *George Gershwin: A Study in American Music,* rev. ed. (New York: Frederick Unger, 1958), 325.

21. Hutchisson, *DuBose Heyward,* 158; Todd Duncan, "Memories of George Gershwin," in Armitage, *George Gershwin,* 62.

22. Hamm, "The Theatre Guild Production"; Lorin Maazel, jacket notes to *Porgy and Bess* (London Records, 1976).

23. Mamoulian, "I Remember," 52; Joan Peyser, *Memory of All That: The Life of George Gershwin* (New York: Simon & Schuster, 1993) 247; Gershwin, "Rhapsody."

24. Mamoulian, "I Remember," 52.

25. Alpert, *Life and Times of Porgy and Bess,* 3; Langner, *Magic Curtain,* 265; Olin Downes, "Exotic Richness of Negro Music and Color of Charleston, S.C., Admirably Conveyed in Score of Catfish Row Tragedy," *New York Times,* October 11, 1935.

26. Peyser, *Memory of All That,* 248.

27. Armitage, *George Gershwin,* 151.

28. Ibid.

29. Alpert, *Life and Times of Porgy and Bess,* 150, 152.

30. Terry Teachout, "American Opera in Progress," *Commentary,* March 2000.

8. Golden Boy

1. Joseph McBride, *Frank Capra: The Catastrophe of Success* (New York: Simon & Schuster, 1992), 288, 325.

2. David Robb, "Directors Guild Born out of Fear 50 Years Ago," *Daily Variety,* October 29, 1985.

3. *Daily Variety,* January 23, 1936.

4. Robb, "Directors Guild."

5. "Film Directors Guild Labor Hearing Opens," *Citizen News,* August 29, 1938.

6. Higham and Greenberg, *The Celluloid Muse,* 139–40.

7. At the first board meeting of the Motion Picture Producers and Directors Association (1922), the trade group resolved to "do everything possible to prevent the production of any new motion picture films which present the Mexican character in a derogatory or objectionable manner," yet Latino stereotypes were so ingrained in American culture that the stereotyping continued. Ruth Vasey, *The World According to Hollywood, 1918–1939* (Madison: University of Wisconsin Press, 1997) 20; *The Gay Desperado* file, Production Code Administration Papers.

8. Frank S. Nugent, "Nino Martini Tries his Hand at Musical Comedy in 'The Gay Desperado' at the Music Hall," *New York Times,* October 9, 1936; Graham Greene, *Spectator,* November 13, 1936.

9. Gerald Bondman, *Jerome Kern: His Life and Music* (New York: Oxford University Press, 1980), 365, 367.

10. Hugh Fordin, *Getting to Know Him: A Biography of Oscar Hammerstein* (New York: Random House, 1977), 147.

11. Higham and Greenberg, *The Celluloid Muse,* 140; J. T. M., "'High, Wide and Handsome,' a Story of the Oil Rush, Opens at the Astor—The Paramount's 'Exclusive,'" *New York Times,* July 22, 1937; Graham Greene, "The Gay Desperado," *Night and Day,* August 26, 1937; Fordin, *Getting to Know Him,* 149; Spergel, *Reinventing Reality,* 167; Schatz, *Genius of the System,* 181, 262.

12. Higham and Greenberg, *The Celluloid Muse,* 140; McBride, *Frank Capra,* 401–2; Axel Madsen, *Stanwyck* (New York: HarperCollins, 1994), 163.

13. R. Baird Shuman, *Clifford Odets* (New York: Twayne, 1962), 22.

14. Madsen, *Stanwyck,* 163–64; Higham and Greenberg, *The Celluloid Muse,* 140; Spergel, *Reinventing Reality,* 173; Patrick McGilligan, *Backstory 2: Interviews with Screenwriters of the 1940s and 1950s* (Berkeley: University of California Press, 1997), 313.

15. Madsen, *Stanwyck,* 165; Hargrave, "Interview with Rouben Mamoulian."

16. Al DiOrio, *Barbara Stanwyck* (New York: Coward-McCann, 1983), 114–15.

17. Graham Greene, "Golden Boy," *Spectator,* December 1, 1939; Frank S. Nugent, "The Screen: Four Films in Review," *New York Times,* September 8, 1939.

18. Higham and Greenberg, *The Celluloid Muse,* 140; Silke, *Rouben Mamoulian,* 27; Chesley and Gould, "Rouben Mamoulian, the 'First Underground Director.'"

19. Higham and Greenberg, *The Celluloid Muse,* 140–41.

20. Dennis Belafonte and Alvin H. Marill, *The Films of Tyrone Power* (Secaucus, N.J.: Citadel, 1979), 9.

21. Joseph L. Breen, memo of January 16, 1941, *The Mask of Zorro* file, Production Code Administration Papers.

22. Higham and Greenberg, *The Celluloid Muse,* 141; Emily W. Leider, *Dark Lover: The Life and Death of Rudolph Valentino* (New York: Farrar, Straus & Giroux, 2003), 204.

23. Gallagher and Amoruco, "Interview."

24. Silke, *Rouben Mamoulian,* 13–14; memo, Darryl Zanuck to Rouben Mamoulian, January 27, 1941, *Blood and Sand* file, University of California at Los Angeles Film Collection.

25. Higham and Greenberg, *The Celluloid Muse,* 142; Robinson, "Painting the Leaves Black."

26. Gene Ringgold, *The Films of Rita Hayworth* (Secaucus, N.J.: Citadel, 1974), 123–24; Hector Arce, *The Secret Life of Tyrone Power* (New York: Morrow, 1979), 157, 159.

27. Ringgold, *Films of Rita Hayworth,* 123; Andrew J. Rausch and Michael Dequina, *Fifty Filmmakers: Conversations with Directors from Rogery Avqry to Steve Zaillian* (Jefferson, N.C.: McFarland, 2008), 37.

28. Gene Tierney with Mickey Herskowitz, *Self Portrait* (New York: Wyden Books, 1979), 100; Henry Fonda with Howard Teichmann, *My Life* (New York: New American Library, 1981), 55.

29. Tierney, *Self Portrait,* 101.

30. *Who Was Who in American Art, 1564–1975* (Madison, Conn.: Sound View, 1999), 2:2142; the Stendahl exhibition was listed in *California Arts & Architecture* (1938); Louis J. Camuti, Marilyn Frankel, and Haskel Frankel, *All My Patients Are under My Bed: Memoirs of a Cat Doctor* (Farmington, Mich.: Cengage Gale, 1980), 203–4; "Zoo Gets Western Lynx," *New York Times,* January 18, 1939.

31. "Divorces," *Billboard,* February 27, 1943; Louella Parsons, *Hollywood Reporter,* March 3 and March 16, 1942; E. J. Fleming, *Carole Landis: A Tragic Life in Hollywood* (Jefferson, N.C.: McFarland, 2005), 104, 121–22.

32. "Milestones," *Time,* March 12, 1945; *Armenian Review* 2, no. 2 (1949).

9. Lost in the Stars

1. Spergel, *Reinventing Reality,* 185–86.

2. Larry Stempel, *Showtime: A History of the Broadway Musical Theater* (New York: Norton, 2010), 300.

3. Tim Carter, *Oklahoma! The Making of an American Musical* (New Haven, Conn.: Yale University Press, 2007), 42; Langner, *Magic Curtain,* 368, 369.

4. Langner, *Magic Curtain,* 370; Hugh Franklin, *Getting to Know Him: A Biography of Oscar Hammerstein II* (New York: Random House, 1977), 196–97; Agnes de Mille, *Dance to the Piper* (New York: Little Brown, 1952), 324.

5. Langner, *Magic Curtain,* 371; Franklin, *Getting to Know Him,* 194.

6. Meryle Secrest, *Somewhere for Me: A Biography of Richard Rodgers* (New York: Knopf, 2001), 253.

7. De Mille, *Dance to the Piper,* 323.

8. Ibid., 324, 327; Langner, *Magic Curtain,* 373.

9. Max Wilk, *OK! The Story of "Oklahoma!" A Celebration of America's Most Loved Musical* (New York: Applause, 2002), 156–57; De Mille, *Dance to the Piper,* 330; Rouben Mamoulian, "Recommended . . . a Divorce," *Theatre Arts,* June–July 1948.

10. Carter, *Oklahoma!* 151; Langner, *Magic Curtain,* 374, 375; William G. Hyland, *Richard Rodgers* (New Haven, Conn.: Yale University Press, 1998), 146.

11. "'Oklahoma!' New Musical Plays up Homespun U.S.A.," *PM,* March 31, 1943; Harriman, "Mr. Mamoulian."

12. Stanley Green, *The Rodgers and Hammerstein Story* (New York: John Day, 1963), 104–5.

13. Caryl Flinn, *Brass Diva: The Life and Legends of Ethel Merman* (Berkeley: University of California Press, 2007), 142–43; Oberstein, "The Broadway Directing Career of Rouben Mamoulian," 270–71.

14. Lys Symonette and Kim H. Kowalke, *Speak Loud (When You Speak Love): The Letters of Kurt Weill and Lotte Lenya* (Berkeley: University of California Press, 1996), 223; Rodgers, *Musical Stages,* 237, 238; Langner, *Magic Curtain,* 390.

15. Rodgers, *Musical Stages,* 238.

16. John K. Hutchens, "About a Man on a Tightrope," *New York Times,* May 6, 1945.

17. Langner, *Magic Curtain,* 391–92.

18. Rodgers, *Musical Stages,* 241; Ferenc Molnár, *Companion in Exile: Notes from an Autobiography* (New York: Gaer Associates, 1950), 214.

19. Cari Beauchamp and Mary Anita Loos, eds., *Anita Loos Rediscovered: Film Treatments and Fiction* (Berkeley: University of California Press, 2003), 273.

20. Langner, *Magic Curtain,* 393.

21. James K. Lyon, "The FBI as Literary Historian: The File of Bertolt Brecht," *Brecht Jahrbuch* 11 (1982): 225; James K. Lyon, *Bertolt Brecht in America* (Princeton, N.J.: Princeton University Press, 1980), 20; Rouben Mamoulian, letters to the Theatre Guild, April 6 and April 29, 1946, Theatre Guild Archives; Armina Marshall, memo to Theresa Helburn, January 12, 1948, Theatre Guild Archives.

22. Hugh Fordin, *The World of Entertainment! Hollywood's Brightest Musicals* (Garden City, N.Y.: Doubleday, 1975), 192.

23. Lena Horne and Richard Schickel, *Lena* (London: Andre Deutsche, 1966), 187.

24. Ibid., 188, 189–90.

25. Oberstein, "The Broadway Directing Career of Rouben Mamoulian," 202–4; Pearl Bailey, *The Raw Pearl* (New York: Harcourt, Brace & World, 1968), 65–66.

26. Oberstein, "The Broadway Directing Career of Rouben Mamoulian," 206; Bailey, *Raw Pearl,* 66.

27. John Chapman, *New York Daily News,* April 1, 1946; Lewis Nichols, *New York Times,* April 1, 1946; Kronenberg, quoted in Edward Jablonski, *Harold Arlen, Rhythm, Rainbows, and Blues* (Boston: Northeastern University Press, 1996), 204; Oberstein, "The Broadway Directing Career of Rouben Mamoulian," 211.

28. Rouben Mamoulian to Lawrence Langner, February 15, 1947, and Theresa Helburn to Rouben Mamoulian, February 4, 1948, Theatre Guild Archives.

29. Oberstein, "The Broadway Directing Career of Rouben Mamoulian," 319–20; Spergel, *Reinventing Reality,* 210.

30. Foster Hirsch, *Kurt Weill on Stage: From Berlin to Broadway* (New York: Knopf, 2002), 135; Symonette and Kowalke, *Speak Loud,* 204.

31. Kim H. Kowalke, "Weill, Modernism, and Culture: Offentlichkeit als Stil," *Modernism/Modernity* 2 (1995).

32. Symonette and Kowalke, *Speak Loud,* 435.

33. Hirsch, *Kurt Weill,* 259.

34. Ibid., 304.

35. Oberstein, "The Broadway Directing Career of Rouben Mamou-

lian," 211; Deborah Grace Winer, *On the Sunny Side of the Street: The Life and Lyrics of Dorothy Fields* (New York: Schirmer, 1997), 161–62.

36. Oberstein, "The Broadway Directing Career of Rouben Mamoulian," 211–13.

37. Ibid., 214; Wharton, *Life among the Playwrights,* 190.

38. Rouben Mamoulian, interview in *New York Herald Tribune,* July 3, 1950.

39. Hirsch, *Kurt Weill,* 312; Aram Goudouzian, *Sidney Poitier: Man, Actor, Icon* (Chapel Hill: University of North Carolina Press, 2004), 59–60.

40. Rouben Mamoulian, production notes for *Lost in the Stars,* Weill-Lenya Research Center, Kurt Weill Foundation for Music, New York.

41. Hirsch, *Kurt Weill,* 309, 312; Oberstein, "The Broadway Directing Career of Rouben Mamoulian," 218.

42. John Mason Brown, "Seeing Things Lost in the Stars," *Saturday Review,* November 26, 1949; Brooks Atkinson, "*Lost in the Stars,* the Musical Version of Alan Paton's *Cry, the Beloved Country,*" *New York Times,* October 31, 1949; Margaret Marshall, *Nation,* November 12, 1949.

43. Hirsch, *Kurt Weill,* 318.

44. Oberstein, "The Broadway Directing Career of Rouben Mamoulian," 225.

45. Spergel, *Reinventing Reality,* 214; Winer, *On the Sunny Side of the Street,* 165; William Hawkins, *World Telegram & Sun,* February 3, 1950.

10. Summer Holiday

1. Robert Porfirio, Alain Silver, and James Ursini, eds., *Film Noir Reader 3: Interviews with Filmmakers of the Classic Noir Period* (New York: Limelight, 2002), 92.

2. Foster Hirsch, *Otto Preminger: The Man Who Would Be King* (New York: Knopf, 2007), 101; Chris Fujiwara, *The World and Its Double: The Life and Work of Otto Preminger* (New York: Faber & Faber, 2008), 36–38.

3. Peter Bogdanovich, "The Making of *Laura* by Otto Preminger as Told to Peter Bogdanovich," *On Film* (1970).

4. Darryl F. Zanuck, memos to Otto Preminger and Rouben Mamoulian, March 20 and March 21, 1944, *Laura* file, 20th Century Fox Collection, University of California at Los Angeles.

5. Bogdanovich, "The Making of *Laura.*"

6. Ibid.; Louella Parsons, "Flickerings from Filmland," *Los Angeles Examiner,* May 15, 1944.

7. Joan Franklin and Robert Franklin, "Dana Andrews Oral History," 1958, Columbia University Oral History Collection.

8. Otto Preminger, *Preminger: An Autobiography* (New York: Doubleday, 1977), 90; Franklin, *Getting to Know Him*; Rudy Behlmer, *America's Favorite Movies* (New York: Ungar, 1982), 190–91.

9. Gregory J. M. Catsos, "Priceless: A Farewell Interview with Vincent Price," *Filmfax,* December 1993–January 1994.

10. Tierney, *Self Portrait,* 133–34.

11. Fordin, *The World of Entertainment!* 180.

12. Ibid., 187–88.

13. Ibid., 188.

14. John Fricke, *Judy: A Legendary Film Career* (Philadelphia: Running Press, 2010), 212; Fordin, *The World of Entertainment!* 189, 190.

15. Fordin, *The World of Entertainment!* 190.

16. Ibid., 191–92.

17. Ibid., 193.

18. The struggle for control between unions would only encourage the House Un-American Activities Committee in its investigation of Communist influence in the film industry. For an account of the labor unrest, see Otto Friedrich, *City of Nets: A Portrait of Hollywood in the 1940's* (New York: Harper & Row, 1986), 247–50, 277–83.

19. Doug McClelland, *Forties Film Talk: Oral Histories of Hollywood* (Jefferson, N.C.: McFarland, 1992), 385; Spergel, *Reinventing Reality,* 207.

20. Mamoulian, "Recommended . . . a Divorce."

21. Bosley Crowther, "'Summer Holiday,' the New Bill at State, Is Film Version of Eugene O'Neill Play," *New York Times,* June 12, 1948.

22. Gordon Kahn, *Hollywood on Trial: The Story of the 10 Who Were Indicted* (New York: Boni & Gaer, 1948), 27–28, 37.

23. Youngerman, *My Seventy Years at Paramount,* 90–91.

24. File 100-HQ-361511, National Archives Administration, Washington, D.C.

25. Kenneth L. Geist, *Pictures Will Talk: The Life and Films of Joseph L. Mankiewicz* (New York: Charles Scribner's Sons, 1978), 176.

26. Ibid., 179; "Mankiewicz Will Not Sign Oath," *Daily Variety,* October 11, 1950.

27. Quoted in Scott Eyman, *Empire of Dreams: The Epic Life of Cecil B. DeMille* (New York: Simon & Schuster, 2010), 408.

28. Youngerman, *My Seventy Years at Paramount,* 113; Anita Loos, *Cast of Thousands* (New York: Grosset & Dunlap, 1977), 227; "Speaking of Pictures . . . Fond Husband Pays a Flowered Tribute in Portraits Made of Petals and Leaves," *Life,* October 8, 1951.

29. *New York Herald,* July 3, 1950, quoted in Spergel, *Reinventing Reality.*

30. "Famous American Director to Work in England," *Times* (London), June 17, 1960.

31. James Howard, *Michael Powell* (London: BT Batsford, 1996), 68–69; David Lazar, *Michael Powell Interviews* (Jackson: University Press of Mississippi, 2003), 40, 59.

32. Laurence G. Avery, *Dramatist in America: Letters of Maxwell Anderson, 1912–1958* (Chapel Hill: University of North Carolina Press, 1977), 262; John McCabe, *Cagney* (New York: Knopf, 1997), 311.

33. Rouben Mamoulian Papers, Theatre Division, Library of Congress.

34. Steven Suskin, *Opening Nights on Broadway: A Critical Quotebook of the Golden Age of the Musical Theatre* (New York: Schirmer, 1990), 499–503; Brooks Atkinson, "'Oklahoma! Revived at City Center; Celebrating Rodgers and Hammerstein's Official Week," *New York Times,* September 1, 1953; President Dwight D. Eisenhower to the President of the Senate, Estimate No. 82, 83rd Cong., 2nd sess. (July 27, 1954).

35. Fordin, *The World of Entertainment!* 440–43.

36. Michael Freedland, *Fred Astaire* (London: W. H. Allen, 1976), 233; Fordin, *The World of Entertainment!* 444.

37. Fordin, *The World of Entertainment!* 445.

38. Peter J. Levinson, *Puttin' on the Ritz: Fred Astaire and the Fine Art of Panache* (New York: St. Martin's, 2009), 223.

39. Stephen D. Youngkin, *The Lost One: A Life of Peter Lorre* (Lexington: University Press of Kentucky, 2005), 390, 393.

40. Levinson, *Puttin' on the Ritz,* 216; Fordin, *The World of Entertainment!* 448; Freedland, *Fred Astaire,* 234.

41. Fordin, *The World of Entertainment!* 452; Levinson, *Puttin' on the Ritz,* 224; Bosley Crowther, "Silk Stockings," *New York Times,* July 19, 1957.

42. David Parkinson, *Rough Guide to Musicals* (London: Rough Guides, 2007), 156–57.

43. Arthur Max, *Goldwyn: A Biography of the Man behind the Myth* (New York: Norton, 1976), 343.

44. Alpert, *The Life and Times of Porgy and Bess,* 249.

45. Ibid., 254.

46. Samuel Goldwyn to N. Richard Nash, November 7, 1957, N. Richard Nash Papers, Wisconsin Center for Film and Theater Research; Nash to Leonard K. Strauss, January 14, 1958, Nash Papers; Nash to Goldwyn, January 7, 1958, Nash Papers; Nash to Goldwyn, February 7, 1958, Nash Papers.

47. Dorothy Dandridge and Earl Conrad, *Everything and Nothing: The Dorothy Dandridge Tragedy* (New York: Amistad, 1970) 188; Sammy Davis Jr., Jane Boyar, and Burt Boyar, *Sammy: An Autobiography* (New York: Farrar, Straus & Giroux, 2000), 330; Gary Fishgall, *Gonna Do Great Things: The Life of Sammy Davis, Jr.* (New York: Scribner, 2003), 128; Max, *Goldwyn,* 343–45; "'Porgy and Bess' Director Tells," *Jet,* January 23, 1958.

48. Dandridge and Conrad, *Everything and Nothing,* 189; "Goldwyn Studio Fire Razes $2,000,000 Set," *Los Angeles Times,* July 3, 1958.

49. Max, *Goldwyn,* 347–48; Samuel Goldwyn Archives, Samuel Goldwyn Foundation, Los Angeles.

50. Carol Easton, *The Search for Sam Goldwyn: A Biography* (New York: William Morrow, 1976), 277.

51. Rouben Mamoulian, Special Board Meeting transcript, July 29, 1958, Directors Guild of America Archives, Los Angeles.

52. Dandridge and Conrad, *Everything and Nothing,* 183, 189; Donald Boyle, *Dorothy Dandridge* (New York: Amistad, 1997), 410; statements issued by the Screen Directors Guild, n.d., Samuel Goldwyn Archives.

53. "'Porgy-Bess' Battle Blazing: Goldwyn Forces Counter Whipper Jab at Preminger with Bailey-Davis Support," *Hollywood Reporter,* August 7, 1958; "Racial Bias Thrown into 'Porgy' Fight, Stars Backing Preminger," *Daily Variety,* August 7, 1958; Dandridge and Conrad, *Everything and Nothing,* 199.

54. Irving Lazar, cable to George Sidney, Screen Directors Guild president, August 10, 1958, Directors Guild of America Archives.

55. Otto Preminger, transcript from Screen Directors Guild board meeting, February 2, 1959, Directors Guild of America Archives.

56. Loudon Wainwright, "The One-Man Gang Is in Action Again: At 76 Sam Goldwyn Conquers Crisis after Crisis to Produce 'Porgy and Bess,'" *Life,* February 16, 1959; Max, *Goldwyn,* 351.

57. Stephen Bourne, *Elisabeth Welch: Soft Lights and Sweet Music* (Lanham, Md.: Scarecrow, 2005), 72; Louie Robinson, "Dorothy Dandridge: Hollywood's Tragic Enigma," *Ebony,* March 1966.

58. Hargrave, "Interview with Rouben Mamoulian"; Sam Kashner and Nancy Schoenberger, *Furious Love: Elizabeth Taylor, Richard Burton, and the Marriage of the Century* (New York: Harper, 2010), 11; Geist, *Pictures Will Talk,* 308–9; Dick Sheppard, *Elizabeth: The Life and Career of Elizabeth Taylor* (Garden City, N.Y.: Doubleday, 1974), 251.

59. Geist, *Pictures Will Talk,* 309.

60. Sheppard, *Elizabeth,* 253.

61. Geist, *Pictures Will Talk,* 309–10.

62. Mamoulian, *Abigayil: The Story of the Cat at the Manger* (Greenwich, Conn.: New York Graphic Society, 1964).

63. Mamoulian, *Shakespeare's Hamlet: A New Version* (Indianapolis: Bobbs-Merrill, 1965); Rouben Mamoulian Collection, Library of Congress; Ron Pennington, "Curtain Calls," *Hollywood Reporter,* September 10, 1974.

64. Social Security Death Index.

65. Rohauer, *40th Anniversary Tribute.*

66. Joseph McBride, e-mail to the author, July 19, 2011; *Ararat* 32 (1991): 12.

67. *Variety,* October 4, 1966; A. H. Weiler, "Music Man Debut," *New York Times,* November 20, 1966.

68. "Dialogue on Film: Rouben Mamoulian," *American Film,* January 1983; Sarris, *Hollywood Voices,* 67; Museum of Modern Art press release, January 1986; "Rouben Mamoulian Addresses the DGA," special features, *Applause* DVD (Kino Video); Peter B. Flint, "Rouben Mamoulian, Broadway Director, Is Dead," *New York Times,* December 6, 1987.

69. Oberstein, "The Broadway Directing Career of Rouben Mamoulian," 176.

70. "Dialogue on Film: Rouben Mamoulian."

71. Dandridge and Conrad, *Everything and Nothing,* 167.

72. Emanuel Levy, *Vincente Minnelli: Hollywood's Dark Dreamer* (New York: St. Martin's, 2009), 56–57.

73. Guy Maddin, "Mamoo the Tropist! His Paramount Years," *Cinema Scope,* Spring 2004.

74. Gregory W. Mank, *Hollywood Cauldron: Thirteen Horror Films from the Genre's Golden Age* (Jefferson, N.C.: McFarland, 2001), 8.

Index

Screen Classics

Screen Classics is a series of critical biographies, film histories, and analytical studies focusing on neglected filmmakers and important screen artists and subjects, from the era of silent cinema to the golden age of Hollywood to the international generation of today. Books in the Screen Classics series are intended for scholars and general readers alike. The contributing authors are established figures in their respective fields. This series also serves the purpose of advancing scholarship on film personalities and themes with ties to Kentucky.

Series Editor

Patrick McGilligan

Books in the Series

Mae Murray: The Girl with the Bee-Stung Lips
Michael G. Ankerich

Hedy Lamarr: The Most Beautiful Woman in Film
Ruth Barton

Von Sternberg
John Baxter

The Marxist and the Movies: A Biography of Paul Jarrico
Larry Ceplair

Warren Oates: A Wild Life
Susan Compo

Jack Nicholson: The Early Years
Robert Crane and Christopher Fryer

Being Hal Ashby: Life of a Hollywood Rebel
Nick Dawson

My Life as a Mankiewicz: An Insider's Journey through Hollywood
Tom Mankiewicz and Robert Crane

Raoul Walsh: The True Adventures of Hollywood's Legendary Director
Marilyn Ann Moss

Some Like It Wilder: The Life and Controversial Films of Billy Wilder
Gene D. Phillips

Arthur Penn: American Director
Nat Segaloff

Claude Rains: An Actor's Voice
David J. Skal with Jessica Rains

Buzz: The Life and Art of Busby Berkeley
Jeffrey Spivak

Thomas Ince: Hollywood's Independent Pioneer
Brian Taves

Carl Theodor Dreyer and Ordet*:*
My Summer with the Danish Filmmaker
Jan Wahl